AFRICA
IS PEOPLE

AFRICA IS PEOPLE

Firsthand accounts from contemporary Africa

Edited by Barbara Nolen

discard

With an Introduction by
Dr. Mercer Cook,
Former U.S. Ambassador to
Niger, Gambia, and Senegal

Illustrated with photographs

NEW YORK: E. P. DUTTON & CO., INC.

FOURTH PRINTING APRIL 1969

ACKNOWLEDGMENTS

Permission to use the following material is gratefully acknowledged by Miss Nolen and the Publishers:

THE NIGHT OF THE LIONS From *The Dark Child* by Camara Laye. Copyright © 1954 by Camara Laye. Reprinted by permission of Farrar, Straus & Giroux, Inc.

OUR WONDROUS SOCIETY Reprinted from *My Africa* by Mbonu Ojike by permission of the John Day Company, Inc., publisher. Copyright © 1946 by The John Day Company, Inc.

LIFE AMONG THE KIKUYU From *Facing Mt. Kenya* by Jomo Kenyatta. Reprinted by permission of Random House, Inc. and Martin Secker & Warburg Limited.

I MARRY MY COUSIN DUMA From *Baba of Karo,* recorded by Mary F. Smith. Reprinted by permission of the Philosophical Library and Faber & Faber, Ltd.

FREETOWN BOY From *Kossoh Town Boy* by Robert W. Cole. Reprinted by permission of Cambridge University Press.

THE PAGAN WOMAN From *Drawn in Colour* by Noni Jabavu. Reprinted by permission of St. Martin's Press, Inc., and John Murray, Ltd.

WORLD LOST From *The Heart of the Hunter* by Laurens van der Post. Copyright © 1961 by Laurens van der Post. Reprinted by permission of William Morrow & Company, Inc., and The Hogarth Press, Ltd.

THE WAY OF THE ANCESTORS From *The Peoples of Africa* by Colin Turnbull. Copyright © 1962 by Colin M. Turnbull. Reprinted by permission of The World Publishing Company.

THE COMING OF THE PINK CHEEKS From *Kabongo* by Richard Baker. Reprinted by permission of A. S. Barnes & Company, Inc.

EXPRESS TO THE MOUNTAINS OF THE MOON Reprinted with permission from the September 1964 *Reader's Digest* and by permission of the author, David Reed. Copyright 1964 by The Reader's Digest Assn., Inc.

WATCH OUT FOR THE MASAI From *No Room in the Ark* by Alan Moorehead. Copyright © 1959 by Alan Moorehead. Reprinted by permission of Harper & Row, Publishers and Hamish Hamilton, Ltd.

LETTER FROM ETHIOPIA From *Peace Corps Volunteers Report: Volume I, Letters from East Africa.* Reprinted by permission of the United States Peace Corps.

THE PYGMY AND THE LEOPARD From *Madami* by Anne Eisner Putnam and Allan Keller. Copyright © 1954 by Putnam and Keller. Reprinted by permission of Prentice-Hall, Inc.

"TELL ME, JOSEPHINE" From *Tell Me, Josephine* by Barbara Hall. Copyright © 1964 by Barbara Hall. Reprinted by permission of Simon and Schuster, Inc., and André Deutsch, Ltd.

A HEAD GROWS PROPER From *New Song in a Strange Land* by Esther Warner. Reprinted by permission of Houghton Mifflin Company.

WHAT IS NEGRITUDE? From a speech delivered at Howard University, September 1966. Reprinted by permission of Léopold Senghor.

BEHIND THE MASK OF AFRICA From a speech delivered by André Malraux at the Dakar Festival, April 1966. Reprinted by permission of André Malraux.

IBO MUSIC From *Nigeria Magazine,* March 1964. Reprinted by permission of the author, W.W.C. Echezona.

LAND OF DARKNESS From *Portrait of Myself* by Margaret Bourke-White. Copyright © 1963 by Margaret Bourke-White. Reprinted by permission of Simon and Schuster, Inc.

JOY AND WOE IN JO'BURG From *Naught for your Comfort* by Trevor Huddleston. Copyright 1956 by Ernest Urban Trevor Huddleston. Reprinted by permission of Doubleday & Company, Inc.

WHO KILLED MR. DRUM? From *Dr. Schweitzer of Lambarene* by Norman Cousins. Copyright © 1960 by Norman Cousins. Reprinted by permission of Harper & Row, Publishers.

THE PROGRESS OF MAN IN AFRICA From *The Progress and Evolution of Man in Africa* by Louis S. B. Leakey. Reprinted by permission of Oxford University Press, Inc.

THE ROLE OF THE WRITER IN A NEW NATION From *Nigerian Libraries,* September 1964. Reprinted by permission of the author, Chinua Achebe.

THE CHILDREN'S CLINIC Reprinted with the permission of Charles Scribner's Sons from *African Encounter: A Doctor in Nigeria,* pages 21–25, by Robert Collis. Copyright © 1960, 1961 Robert Collis.

INTERVIEW IN ACCRA From *Holiday Magazine,* April 1959. Reprinted by permission of Curtis Brown, Ltd. First published in *Holiday Magazine.* Copyright © 1959 by The Curtis Publishing Company. Adapted.

MODERN ARTIST OF BENIN From *Nigeria Magazine,* March 1964. Reprinted by permission of the author, Ulli Beier.

TO SCHOOL WITH LOVE From *Africa Today,* September 1963. Reprinted by permission of *Africa Today* and Sheldon Weeks.

THE ROAD TO AMERICA From *I Will Try* by Legson Kayira. Copyright © 1965 by Legson Kayira. Reprinted by permission of Doubleday & Company, Inc.

EDUCATION FOR TOMORROW From *UNESCO in the Congo* by Garry Fullerton. Reprinted by permission of United Nations Educational, Scientific and Cultural Organization.

RURAL ANIMATION From *Africa: From Independence to Tomorrow* by David Hapgood. Copyright © 1965 by David Hapgood. Reprinted by permission of Atheneum Publishers.

"FOYERS FEMININS" From *The Third Annual Peace Corps Report.* Reprinted by permission of the United States Peace Corps.

ONE-PARTY GOVERNMENT From *Transition,* December 1961. Reprinted by permission of the author, Julius K. Nyerere.

THE PRIZE WINNER From *Chief Albert Lutuli of South Africa* by Mary Benson. Reprinted by permission of Oxford University Press, Inc.

DANGERS OF LEADERSHIP From *Africa: What Lies Ahead?* by Dunduzu K. Chisiza. Reprinted by permission of The African-American Institute.

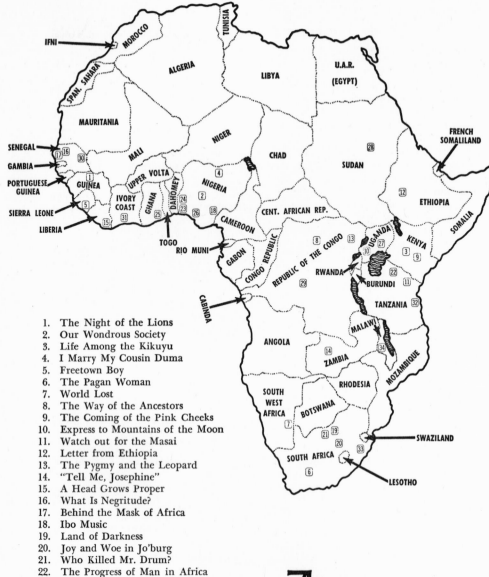

AFRICA

numbers indicate areas
represented
by selections

Editor's Note

The origins of this book, like the origins of early man, are clouded with a certain amount of obscurity, but there is no doubt that they lie in Africa. And they lie in contemporary Africa with all its traditions and hopes, its currents and cross-currents of family and tribal relationships, its tremendous vitality and eagerness to join the mainstream of twentieth century life.

The search for material to fulfill the purpose of this book has zigzagged back and forth from this country to Africa and back. It has ranged from private collections of treasured books about Africa and its people to large university collections of Africana; from small-town libraries to the Library of Congress; from sidewalk bookshops and government libraries in Africa itself to lectures and speeches freshly delivered even while the first pages of the book were being printed.

Always, the magic word "Africa" challenged the editor to find authors whose words have conviction and validity in human experience. The question was: would it be possible to bring within the covers of one book enough variety and enough universality so that the reader would feel that he had actually met a representative number of individual Africans? It should not matter whether the individual belonged to a tribal group in Nigeria or the Congo, whether he had grown up in the bush or in the city, or had been a wanderer across several countries in search of education or a job. Each author must speak for himself but at the same time his individual experience must be rooted in a wider frame of reference with others of his sex, his family, his tribe, his culture or his job, and his generation.

Using material by African authors was one of the basic ideas of the book. But the book is not limited to African authors since this restriction would rule out the valuable material about Africa by artists and anthropologists who have made Africa their home. It would also have ruled out the Bushmen and other non-literate folk who have not yet developed any indigenous writers of their own.

In its early stages, selections for this anthology included folktales and proverbs, poetry and fiction, as well as nonfiction. As collecting and sorting continued, because of the abundance of material the editor decided to limit this book to nonfiction, with priority given to autobiographical accounts by Africans themselves of the last fifty years. This period of great cultural change includes people like Chinua Achebe who said: "Our generation is fortunate because the old hadn't been completely disorganized when we were growing up."

At best, this book can be only an introduction to the wealth of material from contemporary Africa. If the selections fulfill their purpose, they will lead the reader on to the source books from which they are taken, and then on to further reading about Africa and perhaps to visit Africa and meet the people themselves. The list of books suggested for further reading may also serve as a further bridge to Africa.

No editor works in an ivory tower. The final word may be the editor's—indeed, it should be—but the end result is also a composite flowering of ideas, clues, concepts, and criticisms which are collected and incorporated from many sources.

If this editor had been limited to one library, the most valuable would certainly have been the Moorland Room at Howard University in Washington, D.C., where the Spingarn Collection of African authors saved hours of research. Equally important, the librarian of the Moorland Room, Mrs. Dorothy Porter, was especially helpful in sharing her own rich personal knowledge of African authors and types of materials. When the time came to assemble biographical information, this involved reaching out to editors and university faculties in Africa, and some foundations here and abroad. In this effort, the high standards and scholarly approach of Mrs. Porter and her willing staff were continually valuable.

I am indebted to Dr. Joseph Reason, librarian of Howard University, for his initial interest and encouragement and to the sympathetic and critical guidance of Dr. Mercer Cook who read the manuscript in its final stages and consented to write the Introduction.

I am also indebted to the staff of the Schomburg Collection of the New York Public Library; to the resources of the Library of Congress, especially the bibliography, *Africa South of the Sahara,* compiled by Helen F. Conover; to the librarians of neighboring Connecticut schools, particularly Hotchkiss and Kent, who searched their shelves for appropriate material; to the small public libraries of this area; and the generous loan services of the Connecticut State Department of Education.

Among the cultural organizations which were most helpful, I wish to thank especially the American Society of African Culture and their librarian, Miss Brooke Aronson; also Dr. Judith Gleason, special consultant of *African Forum,* for her helpful comments.

Thanks are due to the Washington Office of the United States Peace Corps, particularly Mr. Roger Landrum; to the Harmon Foundation for biographical information on contemporary African artists; to Dr. Luther Evans, formerly Director-General of UNESCO and to staff members of the United Nations and UNESCO, especially Miss Esther Grimes and Mrs. Dorothy Collings who said: "We cannot educate for world society without understanding."

Among colleagues who take a special interest in intercultural exchange of ideas and materials, Delia Goetz deserves special thanks; so does Sheldon Weeks of the Harvard Graduate Center for Studies in Education and Development; and other authors and editors who generously loaned their personal collections of African books and magazines.

Finally, I wish to acknowledge a debt of gratitude to my husband, David Fales Strong, who kept me company on the dusty roads of Africa and in the dusty shelves of libraries, sharing the joy of discovering exciting firsthand material and bringing to this choice his own keen feeling for historical balance and authenticity.

Barbara Nolen

Cornwall, Connecticut
November 1966

Contents

Part 1   The Way of the Ancestors

Part 2   Currents and Cross-Currents

Part 3   The Wind of Change

I fell in love at first sight with the title of Barbara Nolen's anthology. Almost unconsciously I compared it with certain other titles that had appeared during the past decade or so: *Devilman's Jungle; Incredible Africa; The African Giant; Africa, Angry Young Giant; Jeopardy and a Jeep: Africa Conquered by Two Women Professors; African Hunt; East Wind over Africa: Red China's African Offensive; Africa, World's Last Frontier;* and *Africa Is Adventure.*

Such titles reveal the great variety of possible approaches. At the same time they suggest that, despite our more enlightened attitudes toward what used to be called the Dark Continent, the popular image of Africa still revolves, to some extent, around the outlandish, the exotic, the adventurous, the sensational, or the monstrous.

Barbara Nolen's title places the emphasis where it belongs. Africa *is* people, more than two hundred millions, black, brown, and white, balkanized into some thirty-eight countries, many of which are economically unviable; separated by boundaries that are often artificial; faced by tribal, national, and global problems. How are they best to adjust to this mid-twentieth century which in ten years has brought independence to most of them? How do they adapt their leaders' lofty ideals of peace, prosperity, progress, and African unity to their personal lives in terms of better health, education, and jobs, or simply to the acquisition of a wife, a bicycle, or a transistor radio? Which traditional African values should they reject and which should they retain as their young people flock to the overcrowded cities and swell the ranks of the unemployed? How can they attain their human dignity and self-respect while millions of their brothers in South Africa are subjected to apartheid, pass laws, and intolerable working conditions? What we are grappling with here is basic, as the late Melville Herskovits, the distinguished American Africanist, recognized when he entitled his last volume *The Human Factor in Changing Africa.*

Turning from the title to the contents, we note that *Africa Is People* is primarily concerned with Black or Negro Africa, an area that spans the entire continent with the exception of Algeria, Morocco, Tunisia, Libya, and the United Arab Republic, which are largely Arab or Berber nations. Appropriately, almost half of Barbara Nolen's authors are themselves Negro Africans. In this group we find three heads of state, four of Black Africa's most gifted writers, a physician from Sierra Leone, a United States-trained Nigerian, a village chief, two schoolboys, a musicologist, a Malawi economist, and a much-married lady from Northern Nigeria.

The background and interests of the non-African contributors are equally varied. These include, among others, France's Minister of Cultural Affairs, a British anthropologist, an Austrian expatriate, an editor of a leading United States magazine, a priest, the author of *The White Nile* and *The Blue Nile,* and two Peace Corps volunteers. Between the two groups is a white South African, Laurens Van der Post, noted for such works as *The Dark Eye in Africa* and *The Heart of the Hunter.*

Even more important than the authors' identities are the interesting stories they have to tell. Each presents his African characters realistically, yet sympathetically, whether they be Congolese pygmies, hardworking Senegalese peasants, or the awesome, warlike Masai of Kenya. Realizing that Africa is people, the authors usually avoid the stereotypes that have done so much damage to interracial understanding. I have detected only one unfortunate cliché in this anthology. It occurs in Anne Putnam's chapter on "The Pygmy and the Leopard." When one character attributes a recent death to "the evil eye" and despairingly asks, "What is medicine against the evil eye?" Mrs. Putnam generalizes: "That was the voice of Africa, the real Africa." Of course superstition exists in Africa, as everywhere else, but it is by no means the sole or even the dominant note in the black man's register.

With this exception, the contributors, Anne Putnam included, are acutely sensitive to the myriad voices of the African: the religious, the joyous, the sorrowful, the hopeful, the militant, the political, the friendly. Several of the writers warn us against snap judgment, against the assumption "that everything that coincides with our beliefs, our practices, our approach to life is good; and that everything that smacks of his [the Ethiopian's] own culture of several thousand years of tradition is 'backward' and therefore bad." So writes our Peace Corps volunteer in Ethiopia and the same idea is developed by British anthropologist Dr. Leakey. A third contributor, Colin Turnbull, suggests that even the dread Leopard Society may serve a useful purpose, that of unifying the ethnic group. "And so it is with so many of the customs we consider as strange and barbaric. We have to try and see them in their proper surroundings, not to imagine them as being part of our own society. And if we do this, we find that even when customs seem most different from our own, they are usually working for exactly the same ends that we consider right and good: the maintenance of accepted morality, the preservation of individual rights, the safety of the tribe (or nation), in accordance with their belief in the will of the ancestors or God." Thus repeatedly cautioned against "thinking with your blood" (to quote Father Trevor Huddleston), the reader learns a most valuable lesson, one that far transcends the continent and peoples concerned.

The thirty-four selections in the anthology are presented under three headings: 1, The Way of the Ancestors, 2, Currents and Cross-Currents, and 3, The Wind of Change. It would be tempting but misleading to interpret these divisions in a strictly chronological sense. There is, for example, unavoidable overlapping between Parts I and II, while the innovations discussed in Part III have not yet become enough of a whirlwind to uproot the ancestral customs described in Part I, nor would the total disappearance of those customs be desirable. As Dr. Leakey puts it: "Long before the Europeans arrived in Africa, many Bantu tribes had already recognized the need for family planning. . . . Let me remind you too that before the coming of the white man, social organization in many African tribes was such that tragedies such as destitute widows and orphans, unloved lonely spinsters, unmarried mothers, and aged and uncared-for elderly people were unheard of and indeed could not occur, while prostitution was unknown."

Similarly, old Chief Kabongo complains in "The Coming of the Pink Cheeks": "The young men are learning new ways, the children make marks which they call writing, but they forget their own language and customs, they do not know the laws of their people and they do not pray to Ngai. They ride fast in motor cars, they work firesticks that kill, they make music from a box. But they have no land and they have lost laughter."

On the other hand, a younger African, the Nigerian novelist Chinua Achebe, urges a more objective view of the African past: "We cannot pretend that our past was one long technicolor idyl. We have to admit that like any other people's past ours had its bad as well as its good sides." And Ben Mady Cissé, who directs Senegal's interesting experiment in "Rural Animation," offers this ingenious argument in support of constructive innovation: "We must make it clear that change is true fidelity to our ancestors. Their way of life was in tune with their own environment. To be faithful to our ancestors means to adjust to our environment as they did to theirs, not simply to cling to old ways for no reason."

"Rural animation" is but one of the educational devices designed to improve the life of the African. The eagerness for education, which I have observed throughout West Africa, extends over the entire continent and is reflected in several selections in this anthology. Those who take their schooling for granted should read "To School with Love" or "The Road to America," in which a youngster walks from Nyasaland (now Malawi) to Khartoum (in Sudan), a distance of more than one thousand miles, in the hope of attending college in the United States. "Education for Tomorrow" describes UNESCO's program in the ex-Belgian Congo. An experiment in adult education for women in the Ivory Coast is discussed in "Foyers Féminins."

Occasionally a selection on a subject seemingly unrelated to education touches upon this vital key to progress. Thus, on the "Express to the Mountains of the Moon," David Reed meets a student from Makerere College and another young man who had worked in Kampala (Uganda) as an auto mechanic and was returning home "with enough savings to open what will be the first auto repair shop in his native village. Both typify the hope and ambitions of an Africa that is rapidly emerging into the modern world." By the same token, our Peace Corps volunteer in Ethiopia is confident that young Tafesse, who must walk seven miles each day to school, will become a successful, useful man. "If I could wish something for him, it would be that he could carry his parents' capacity for work, their humble generosity, their sincerity and their ability to glean pleasure from simple experiences and life itself, that he could carry these with him into his new role."

Art is another cultural activity that serves as a vital link between the old and the new Africa. "Saving us from despair," says Senegal's President Léopold Sédar Senghor, "this Negro art sustains us in our effort toward economic and social development, in our *determination to live*." Moreover, world recognition of the African's artistic contributions has provided a much-needed corrective for an inferiority complex caused by disparagement of the black man's ability to produce. Five of the selections—six if we include Senghor's comments on Negritude—discuss various aspects of the arts in Africa. With a population of some fifty-five millions and a rich artistic heritage, it is not surprising that Nigeria, the featured nation at Dakar's First World Festival of Negro Arts, has inspired three of the selections: "Ibo Music," "Modern Artist of Benin," and "The Role of the Writer in a New Nation." A fourth selection takes us to Liberia and depicts the reactions (and pidgin English) of a local domestic to the art of his American employer. The final selection in this category is a speech, "Behind the Mask of Africa," which André Malraux delivered at the Dakar Festival; in some respects it is a synthesis of the various types of African artistic expression.

Politics, which plays so important a role in emergent Africa and captures so many headlines, receives less attention in this anthology than education or art, but is not entirely neglected. One selection, Peter Abrahams' remarkable "Interview in Accra," records a meeting with an African leader who had recently led his country to independence. The other two political chapters are largely theoretical. President Julius Nyerere, of Tanzania, defends the one-party system, thereby providing a useful reminder that the African intends to follow his own road to democracy in the light of his own needs and traditions. Finally, writing on the "Dangers of Leadership," Dunduzu K. Chisiza, of Malawi, warns the new leaders that any attempt to conceal the absence of current "concrete achievements" by unduly eulogizing the glories of the African past would be tragically shortsighted.

Rhodesia and the Republic of South Africa, with their wealth, apartheid, and minority rule, are the settings for selections which range from letters to the editor of a local paper to an account of the ceremony at which Chief Albert Lutuli was awarded the Nobel Peace Prize for 1961. In between, there is a visit to the "Land of Darkness," the Johannesburg mines, by an American woman journalist; a murder mystery; and Father Trevor Huddleston's moving description of his work with underprivileged youngsters. Here again we catch intimate glimpses of the human side of Africa, even in an atmosphere highly charged with racial tension and inhumanity.

In sum, by its variety, readability, and sympathetic understanding, *Africa Is People* fulfills the promise of its title. As a brief introduction to a fascinating, complex subject, it should prove especially valuable to beginners, and it also contains much that we older African hands will find useful.

Mercer Cook

Washington, D.C.
1966

Part 1

THE WAY OF
THE ANCESTORS

"The white man talks of law where we talk of the way of our ancestors; he talks of what is right or wrong where we talk of what is good or bad."

—Chief Matungi in *The Lonely African*
by Colin Turnbull

The Night of the Lions

BY CAMARA LAYE

Camara Laye was born in 1924, the son of an African goldsmith of the Malinke people, who founded the great Mali empire in the thirteenth century. He grew up in a traditional society and his early education was in Mohammedan schools. Of great intellectual promise, he graduated from secondary school in Conakry, capital of French Guinea, and went on to Paris to study engineering. He expected to stay only one year. Instead, he stayed six years, working for a while in an automobile factory. During this time, he was often lonely and homesick for Africa.

To relieve his homesickness, Laye wrote his autobiography, *The Dark Child*. In this book he wrote poetically of his home, his family, and the ancient tribal ceremonies of his people. The following episode took place in Kouroussa where the family concession, or compound, surrounded by a reed fence, included the huts of his father and his mother and other members of the extended family circle.

First published in France, *The Dark Child* was so well received that Laye was recognized as one of the new African writers with literary merit. Equally important, the royalties from his book enabled him to return to Africa for a visit with his family, and to continue his writings. "The Night of the Lions" is one of the memorable chapters from *The Dark Child*.

Until recently, Camara Laye was a member of the National Research Institute in Conakry, capital of the new Republic of Guinea. He has also represented his country in diplomatic posts abroad.

I was growing up. The time had come for me to join the society of the uninitiated. This rather mysterious society—and at that age it was very mysterious to me, though not very secret—comprised all

the young boys, all the uncircumcised, of twelve, thirteen, and fourteen years of age, and it was run by our elders, whom we called the
big *Kondéns*. I joined it one evening before the feast of Ramadan.

As soon as the sun had gone down, the tom-tom had begun to beat.
Even though it was being played in a remote part of the concession,
its notes had roused me at once, had struck my breast, had struck
right at my heart, just as if Kodoké, our best player, had been playing for me alone. A little later I had heard the shrill voices of boys
accompanying the tom-tom with their cries and singing. Yes, the
time had come for me.

It was the first time I had spent the feast of Ramadan at Kouroussa. Until this year, my grandmother had always insisted on my
spending it with her at Tindican. All that morning and even more so
in the afternoon, I had been in a state of great agitation, with everyone busy preparing for the festival, bumping into and pushing each
other and asking me to help. Outside, the uproar was just as bad.
Kouroussa is the chief town of our region, and all the canton chiefs,
attended by their musicians, make it a custom to gather here for the
festival. From the gateway to the concession I had watched them pass
by, with their companies of praise-singers, balaphonists and guitar-
ists, drum and tom-tom players. Until now I had only been thinking
of the festival and of the sumptuous feast that awaited me, but now
there was something quite different in the wind.

The screaming crowd that surrounded Kodoké and his famous
tom-tom was getting nearer. Going from one concession to another,
the crowd would stop where there was a boy of an age to join the society and take him away. That is why it was so slow in coming, yet so
sure, so ineluctable. As sure, as ineluctable as the fate that awaited
me.

What fate? My meeting with Kondén Diara!

Now I was not aware of who Kondén Diara was. My mother had
often talked of him, and so at times had my uncles and whoever else
had authority over me. They had threatened me only too often with
Kondén Diara, that terrible bogeyman, that "lion that eats up little
boys." And here was Kondén Diara—but was he a man? Was he an
animal? Was he not rather half man, half animal? My friend Kouyaté believed he was more man than beast; here was Kondén Diara
leaving the dim world of hearsay, here he was taking on flesh
and blood, yes, and roused by Kodoké's tom-tom was prowling

around the town! This night was to be the night of Kondén Diara.

Now I could hear the beating of the tom-tom very plainly—Kodoké as much nearer—I could hear perfectly the chanting and the shouts that rose into the dark. I could make out almost as distinctly the rather hollow, crisp, well-marked beats of the *coros,* which are a kind of miniature canoe and are beaten with a bit of wood. I was standing at the entrance to the concession, waiting. I, too, was holding my coro, ready to play it with the stick clutched nervously in my hand. I was waiting, hidden by the shadow of the hut. I was waiting, filled with a dreadful anxiety, my eyes searching the blackness.

"Well?" asked my father.

He had crossed the workshop without my hearing him.

"Are you afraid?"

"A little," I replied.

He laid his hand on my shoulder.

"It's all right. Don't worry."

He drew me to him, and I could feel his warmth; it warmed me, too, and I began to feel less frightened; my heart did not beat so fast.

"You mustn't be afraid."

"No."

I knew that whatever my fear might be I must be brave. I wasn't to show fright or to run off and hide. Still less was I to resist or cry out when my elders carried me off.

"I too went through this test," said my father.

"What happens to you?" I asked.

"Nothing you need really be afraid of, nothing you cannot overcome by your own will power. Remember, you have to control your fear; you have to control yourself. Kondén Diara will not take you away. He will roar. But he won't do more than roar. You won't be frightened, now, will you?"

"I'll try not to be."

"Even if you are frightened, do not show it."

He went away, and I began waiting again, and the disturbing uproar came nearer and nearer. Suddenly I saw the crowd emerging from the dark and rushing towards me. Kodoké, his tom-tom slung over one shoulder, was marching at their head, followed by the drummers.

I ran back quickly into the yard and, standing in the middle of it, I awaited the awful invasion with as much courage as I could manage.

I did not have long to wait. The crowd was upon me. It was spreading tumultuously all around me, overwhelming me with shouts and cries and beating tom-toms, beating drums. It formed a circle, and I found myself in the center, alone, curiously isolated, still free and yet already captive. Inside the circle I recognized Kouyaté and others, many of them friends of mine who had been collected as the crowd moved on, collected as I was to be, as I already was; and it seemed to me they were none of them looking very happy—but was I any more happy than they? I began to beat my coro as they were doing. Perhaps I was beating it with less confidence than they.

At this point young girls and women joined the circle and began to dance; young men and adolescents, stepping out of the crowd, moved into the circle too and began to dance facing the women. The men sang, the women clapped their hands. Soon the only ones left to form the circle were the uncircumcised boys. They too began to sing —they were not allowed to dance—and as they sang, sang in unison, they forgot their anxiety. I too sang with them. When, having formed a circle again, the crowd left our concession, I went with it, almost willingly, beating my coro with great enthusiasm. Kouyaté was on my right.

Toward the middle of the night our tour of the town and the collection of uncircumcised boys were finished. We had arrived at the farthest outskirts of the concessions, and in front of us lay only the bush. Here the women and young girls left us. Then the grown men left. We were alone with the older boys, or should I say "delivered over" to them; for I remember the often rather disagreeable natures and rarely pleasant manners of those older ones.

The women and young girls now hurried back to their dwellings. Actually they can not have been any more at ease than we were. I know for a fact that not one of them would have ventured to leave town on this night. Already they found the town and the night sinister. I am certain that more than one who went back to her concession alone was to regret having joined the crowd. They took courage only after they had shut the gates of their concession and the doors of their huts. Meanwhile they hurried on and from time to time cast unquiet looks behind them. In a short while, when Kondén Diara would begin to roar, they would not be able to stop shaking with fright; they would all shake uncontrollably. Then they would run to make sure the doors were all properly barred. For them, as for us, though in a much less significant way, this night would be the night of Kondén Diara.

As soon as our elders had made sure that no intruder was present to disturb the mysteriousness of the ceremony, we left the town behind and entered the bush by a path which leads to a sacred place where each year the initiation takes place. The place is well known: it is situated under an enormous bombax tree, a hollow at the junction of the river Komoni and the river Niger. At normal times it is not forbidden to go there; but certainly it has not always been so, and some emanation from the past I never knew still seems to hover around the huge trunk of the bombax tree. I think that a night such as the one we were going through must certainly have resurrected a part of that past.

We were walking in silence, closely hemmed in by our elders. Perhaps they were afraid we might escape? It looked like it. I do not think, however, that the idea of escape had occurred to any of us. The night, and that particular night, seemed impenetrable. Who knew where Kondén Diara had his lair? Who knew where he was prowling? But was it not right here, near the hollow? Yes, it must be here. And if we had to face him—and certainly we had to face him— it would surely be better to do so in a crowd, in this jostling group that seemed to make us all one, and seemed like a last refuge from the peril that was approaching.

Yet for all our nearness to one another and for all the vigilance of our elders, our march—so silent after the recent uproar—through the wan moonlight, far from the town, frightened us. And we were filled with terror at the thought of the sacred place toward which we were going, and the hidden presence of Kondén Diara.

Were our elders marching so closely beside us only to keep watch over us? Perhaps. But it is likely that they too felt something of the terror which had seized us. They too found the night and the silence disturbing. And for them, as for us, marching close together was a means of allaying terror.

Just before we reached the hollow we saw flames leap from a huge wood fire previously hidden by bushes. Kouyaté squeezed my arm, and I knew he was referring to the fire. Yes, there was a fire. There too was Kondén Diara, the hidden presence of Kondén Diara. But there was also a reassuring presence in the depth of the night: a great fire! My spirits rose—at least they rose a little—and I squeezed Kouyaté's arm in return. I quickened my steps—we all quickened our steps—and the crimson radiance of the fire enveloped us. We had a harbor now, this kind of haven from the night: a huge blaze and, at our backs, the enormous trunk of the bombax tree. Oh! It was a precarious haven! But, however poor, it was infinitely better than the silence and the dark, the sullen silence of the dark. We assembled beneath the bombax tree. The ground beneath had been cleared of reeds and tall grasses.

Our elders suddenly shouted, "Kneel!"

We at once fell to our knees.

"Heads down!"

We lowered our heads.

"Lower than that!"

We bent our heads right to the ground, as if in prayer.

"Now hide your eyes!"

We didn't have to be told twice. We shut our eyes tight and pressed our hands over them. For would we not die of fright and horror if we should see, or so much as catch a glimpse of, the Kondén Diara? Our elders walked up and down, behind us and in front of us, to make sure that we had all obeyed their orders to the letter. Woe to him who would have the audacity to disobey! He would be cruelly whipped. It would be a whipping all the more cruel because he would have no hope of redress, for he would find no one to listen to his complaint, no one to transgress against custom. But who would have the audacity to disobey?

Now that we were on our knees with our foreheads to the ground and our hands pressed over our eyes, Kondén Diara's roaring suddenly burst out.

We were expecting to hear this hoarse roar—we were not expecting any other sound—but it took us by surprise and shattered us, froze our hearts with its unexpectedness. And it was not only a lion, it was not only Kondén Diara roaring; there were ten, twenty, perhaps thirty lions that took their lead from him, uttering their terrible roars and surrounding the hollow; ten or twenty lions separated from us by a few yards only and whom the great wood fire would perhaps not always keep at bay; lions of every size and every age—we could tell that by the way they roared—from the very oldest ones to the very youngest cubs. No, not one of us would dream of venturing to open an eye, not one! Not one of us would dare to lift his head from the ground; he would rather bury it in the earth. And I bent down as far as I could; we all bent down further; we bent our knees as much as we could; we kept our backs as low as possible. I made myself—we all made ourselves—as small as we could.

"You mustn't be afraid!" I said to myself. "You must master your fear! Your father had commanded you to!"

But how was I to master it? Even in the town, far away from this clearing, women and children trembled and hid themselves in their huts. They heard the growling of Kondén Diara, and many of them stopped their ears to keep it out. The braver arose—that night it took courage to leave one's bed—and went again and again to check the doors and see that they were shut tight. How was I to stave off fear when I was within range of the dread monster? If he pleased, Kondén Diara could leap the fire in one bound and sink his claws in my back!

I did not doubt the presence of the monster, not for a single instant. Who could assemble such a numerous herd, hold such a nocturnal revel, if not Kondén Diara?

"He alone," I said to myself, "he alone has such power over lions. . . . Keep away, Kondén Diara! Keep away! Go back into the bush!" But Kondén Diara went on with his revels, and sometimes it seemed to me that he roared right over my head, right into my own ears. "Keep away, I implore you, Kondén Diara!"

What was it my father had said? "Kondén Diara roars, but he won't do more than roar; he will not take you away. . . ." Yes, something like that. But was it true, really true?

There was also a rumor that Kondén Diara sometimes pounced with fearsome claws on someone or other and carried him far away, far, far into the depths of the bush; and then, days and days afterwards, months or even years later, quite by chance a huntsman might discover some whitened bones.

And do not people also die of fright? Ah! how I wished this roaring would stop! How I wished I was far away from this clearing, back in the concession, in the warm security of the hut! Would this roaring never cease?

"Go away, Kondén Diara! Go away! Stop roaring." Oh! those roars! I felt as if I could bear them no longer.

Whereupon, suddenly, they stopped! They stopped just as they had begun, so suddenly, in fact, that I felt only reluctant relief. Was it over? Really over? Was it not just a temporary interruption? No, I dared not feel relieved just yet. And then suddenly the voice of one of the older boys rang out: "Get up!"

I heaved a sigh of relief. This time it was really over. We looked at one another: I looked at Kouyaté and the others. If there were only a little more light. . . . But the light from the fire was sufficient: great drops of sweat were still beading our foreheads; yet the night was chill. Yes, we were afraid. We were not able to conceal our fear.

A new command rang out, and we sat down in front of the fire. Now our elders began our initiation. For the rest of the night they taught us the chants sung by the uncircumcised. We never moved. We learned the words and tunes as we heard them. We were attentive as if we had been at school, entirely attentive and docile.

When dawn came, our instruction was at an end. My legs and arms were numb. I worked my joints and rubbed my legs for a while, but my blood still flowed slowly. I was worn out, and I was cold. Looking around me, I could not understand why I had shaken with fear during the night: the first rays of dawn were falling so gently, so reassuringly, on the bombax tree, on the clearing. The sky looked so pure! Who would have believed that a few hours earlier a pack of lions led by Kondén Diara in person had been raging fiercely in the high grass and among the reeds, and that they had been separated from us only by a wood fire which had just now gone out as dawn came? No one. I would have doubted my own senses and set it all down as a nightmare if I had not noticed more than one of my companions casting an occasional fearful glance in the direction of the highest grass.

But what were those long white threads which hung from, or, rather, waved from the top of the bombax tree and which appeared to write on the sky the direction in which the town lay? I had not time to wonder very long at this: our elders were regrouping us; and because most of us were almost sleep-walking, the operation was carried out with difficulty, with shouts and with some rough treatment. Finally we started off back to the town, singing our new songs, and we sang them with unbelievably carefree abandon—as the steed that scents the approaching stable suddenly quickens his step, however weary he may be.

When we reached the first concessions, the presence of the long white threads struck me once more: all the principal huts had these threads on the very tops of their roofs.

"Do you see the white threads?" I asked Kouyaté.

"I can see them. They are always there after the ceremony in the clearing."

"Who puts them there?"

Kouyaté shrugged his shoulders.

"That's where they come from," I said, pointing to the distant bombax tree.

"Someone must have climbed up."

"Who could possibly climb a bombax tree?"

"I don't know."

"Could anyone possibly get his arms around such a huge trunk?" I said. "And even if he could, how could he hoist himself on bark all covered with all those thorns? You're talking nonsense. Can't you imagine what a job it would be just to reach the first branches?"

"Why do you expect me to know more about this than you do?" asked Kouyaté.

"Because this is the first time I have taken part in the ceremony, while you—"

I didn't finish my sentence. We had reached the main square of the town. I stared in amazement at the bombax trees in the market place. They too were ornamented with the same white threads. All but the humblest huts, indeed, and all the big trees were tied to one another by these white threads whose focal point was the enormous bombax tree in the clearing, the sacred place marked by the bombax tree.

"The swallows tie them on," said Kouyaté suddenly.

"Swallows? Are you crazy?" I said. "Swallows don't fly by night."

I questioned one of the older boys who was walking beside me.

"It is our great chief who does it," he said. "Our chief turns himself into a swallow during the night. He flies from tree to tree and from hut to hut, and all these threads are tied on in less time than it takes to tell."

"He flies from tree to tree like a swallow?"

"Yes. He's a real swallow and as swift. Everyone knows that."

"Isn't that what I told you?" asked Kouyaté.

I did not say another word. The night of Kondén Diara was a strange night, a terrible and miraculous night, a night that passed all understanding.

As on the previous evening, we went from one concession to another, preceded by tom-toms and drums, and our companions left us one after another as they reached their homes. Whenever we passed a concession where someone whose courage had failed him had refused to join us, a mocking chant rose from our ranks.

I arrived at our concession completely exhausted but very satisfied with myself: I had taken part in the ceremony of the lions! Even if I had not put up much of a show when Kondén Diara was roaring, that was my own affair; I could keep that to myself. I passed triumphantly over the threshold of our concession.

The festival of Ramadan was beginning. In the yard I saw my parents, who were dressed to go to the mosque.

"Here you are at last," said my mother.

"Here I am," I said proudly.

"What kind of time is this to come home?" she said, pressing me to her bosom. "The night is over, and you haven't had a bit of sleep."

"The ceremony did not finish until break of day," I said.

"I know, I know," she said. "All you men are mad."

"What about the lions?" asked my father. "What about Kondén Diara?"

"I heard them," I replied. "They were very close; they were as near to me as I am to you now. There was only the fire between us."

"It's crazy," said my mother. "Go to bed, you're dropping with sleep." She turned toward my father: "Now, where's the sense in all that?"

"Well, it's the custom," said my father.

"I don't like such customs," she said. "Young boys should not have to stay awake all night."

"Were you afraid?" asked my father.

Should I admit that I was very frightened?

"Of course he was afraid," said my mother.

"Only a little," said my father.

"Go to bed," ordered my mother. "If you don't get some sleep now, you'll fall asleep during the feast."

I went inside to lie down. Outside I heard my mother quarreling with my father. She thought it stupid to take unnecessary risks.

Later I got to know who Kondén Diara was, and I learned these things when the time had come for me to learn them. As long as we are not circumcised, as long as we have not attained that second life that is our true existence, we are told nothing, and we can find out nothing.

We begin to have a vague understanding of the ceremony of the lions after we have taken part in it many times. But even then, we are careful to share our knowledge only with those companions who have had the same experience. And the real secret lies hidden until the day when we are initiated into our life as men.

No, they were not real lions that roared in the clearing, for it was the older boys, simply the older boys. They created the roaring sound with small boards, thick at the center, sharp at the edges: the edges were all the sharper from having such a thick center. The board was ellipsoidal in shape and very small. There was a hole on one side that permitted it to be tied to a string. The older boys swung it around like a sling, and to increase the speed of the gyrations, they too turned with it. The board cut through the air and produced a sound like a lion's roar. The smallest boards imitated the roaring of the lion cubs; the biggest ones the roaring of full-grown lions.

It was childishly simple. What was not so childish was the effect produced at night on someone who did not expect it: the heart froze! If it had not been for the far greater fear of finding themselves lost in the bush, the terror it created would have made the boys run away. The bombax tree and the fire which had been kindled near it made a kind of haven which kept the uninitiated from running away.

From The Dark Child, *by Camara Laye, Farrar, Straus and Giroux, Inc., 1954.*

Our Wondrous Society

BY MBONU OJIKE

Mbonu Ojike, a Nigerian, was one of an increasing number of Africans who came to the United States seeking an education during the two decades before Independence. An articulate, eager student, Mr. Ojike was particularly interested in studying family customs and social life in the United States and comparing American ways with those at home in Africa. Beginning his studies at Lincoln University in 1938, he later received his B.A. degree from Ohio State and his M.A. from the University of Chicago. He was the first president of the African Students' Union in the United States.

For a time following his return to Nigeria, Mr. Ojike was editor of the *West African Pilot,* an influential Nationalist newspaper published in Lagos. He was associated with economic progress as Eastern Nigeria's first Minister of Works, planning the major roads of that region, and as Minister of Finance he initiated "Pay as you earn" taxation.

The title of his book, *My Africa,* published in 1946, is an indication of Mbonu Ojike's strong possessive feeling about his country and his continent. In the following selection, taken from his book, he tells about the importance of the "extended family," or clan. He considered himself a spokesman not only for Nigeria but for other African countries.

Since Mr. Ojike's death in 1956 many of the customs he wrote about have changed. His comments on leisure-time activities and sports are no longer explicitly true, but were true of the period about which he wrote. Mr. Ojike represented his generation with such fondness and perception that a new hospital now being planned for Nigeria will be named in his memory.

The Ojike Memorial Medical Center, to be located in the Orlu

Division of Eastern Nigeria where Ojike was born, will serve the nation as a whole and will specialize in tropical diseases and nutrition. The Center will engage in research and maintain a "flying doctor" service for remote areas. When this idea was first proposed in 1961, the Federal Minister of Aviation said: "This type of memorial will combine in one form all that Ojike lived and died for— humanity, patriotism, progress and service."

C lan is the bulwark of African society. It is so clearly organized that there is not a single African who does not know his own clan. Clans are the original units into which a nation was divided. Hence, each state bound together by one language consists of many clans or extended families. A large clan, like those within the Ibo and the Yoruba states, may number as many as half a million. Each clan is made up of towns; each town of villages; each village of families; and each family of individuals. In social life every activity follows these clans and their component divisions. In keeping with their economic ideal of cooperation and sharing together, Africans are thoroughly clannish. These organizations remain today the fabric of African society.

We are clannish in politics and clannish in religion. Social discipline and social structure follow a clearly distinguishable family structure. The African thinks in terms of his family, not individuals; of his village, not family; of his town, not village; of his nation, not clan; of his race, not nation; of mankind, not his race. This is rarely understood by those people whose social conscience runs in the opposite direction, considering the individual more than the larger groupings of nation, race, and mankind.

A family is not just husband, wife, and children. To us it is a number of households. Perhaps two thousand persons make a family. Often a family is so numerous and old that its members marry among themselves. When the family is small or relatively young, its members practice exogamy. By being young we mean that the elders therein can trace the genealogy of each person without a hitch. For before a lover can be betrothed to a girl, their genealogy must first be determined. If they are traceable into one household, they are pronounced brother and sister and cannot marry.

Our concept of family does not prevent the development of the individual, nor discourage personal initiative and self-reliance. What it does, in contrast to Western ways, is place the right of the family above that of man. That is why there are many social customs which bind an individual. The advantage of this system is that it makes for a more closely knit, stable, cooperative, secure, and happy society. Every citizen belongs to a specific family whose responsibility it is to help him in his "hour of trial." If he is sick or incapacitated, his family looks after him. Social security measures common in the West are, therefore, uncalled for—except as Western incursions into Africa have torn into our social fabric.

In the United States a Texan may migrate to Maine and there wed a girl and settle. Some years later, if he desires, he with his family may pack up again to live in California, perhaps for the rest of their lives. In this instance, the Texan does not, as it often happens, regard either Texas or Maine as his home. The obvious result on society is individualism and loose family links, which means that the whole society has to bear the burden of caring for its needy members. The United States must handle through social agencies what we treat in the family. While the American takes the trouble to say, "Mr. Jones is my nephew," to the African a nephew is just another brother. Not one of the hundreds of my village and town people have addressed me as "Mr."; they invariably write "Dear Brother."

Of course when one's affairs are at sixes and sevens, one likes to have many brothers, and all respond to one's needs. On the other hand, when one is prosperous, he is greeted by a retinue of brothers and sisters who easily trace their kinship to him and thereupon fall in line to partake of their brother's success.

In modern times this social conscience has been broadened into national consciousness. The African is as quick to organize as he is eager to learn. The impact of modernism has created cities and townships where members of different families and clans are learning to unite as Africans. Any number of social, athletic, religious, artistic, political, and literary unions have emerged throughout Africa. Some of these organizations, particularly labor unions, have pan-African and international affiliations.

It is a true sign of social awakening that the African is nationalistic beyond clannishness, internationalistic beyond nationalism.

I have never seen other people that take to leisure as Africans do. In the United States it appears that the upper-class man has more leisure than the common man, who is busy making a living. The idea of leisure, which includes rest and sleep, knows no class distinction in Africa. In fact, the common man enjoys more leisure than the upper-class man. This is uniform all over the villages. In cities the common man enjoys less leisure; he has to work harder, and leisure activities are not free as they are in village life. But our cities have not gone so far in this direction as those of the West. Most people are their own boss and are in a habit of working from eight to four, allowing for a brief midday siesta. In big cities such as Lagos, Accra, and Port Harcourt, few people work at night, while in villages there is hardly any night work. The evening, therefore, is a pleasurable moment.

While women are preparing dinner, their little ones are out playing and their men sit around in the parks or go hunting. The sun is down and the temperature cool. Few persons are patient enough to allow themselves to be still choked up with ties and collars. The popular evening fashion is the African flowing gown and slippers or sandals.

Our freedom of dress is proverbial. Some men put on light cotton or silk gowns and feel as though they were the President of the United States. Others, who are sportsmen, dress in white shorts and shirt and white canvas shoes and go with their ball-boys to tennis, golf, hockey, or cricket. Football may be played by younger men and schoolboys who, for the sake of economy, content themselves with brown khaki shorts, football jerseys, shoes or no shoes. Card games are also indulged in, and we play a very complicated form of drafts or checkers.

English or French chess is, indeed, simpler than the African game of drafts, called Azigo, played with a board of ten, twenty, or forty holes. In my community the forty-hole game is played.

This game is one of the most interesting pastimes in my community. It is an adult's game, and when it is in process no one talks. Both the competitors and the spectators remain mute, working with their eyes, heads, and hands. Sometimes a champion is tied up until his wife comes, overturns the board, and says, "Leave that nonsense thing and come for dinner."

During and following the dinner, that is about seven o'clock when it is all dark, all sorts of entertainment are going on in every community—city or village. Every evening someone or some group is putting on a dance or a musical, some birth or funeral ceremonial celebration is going on. And all is free—just think of that! It takes time, money, brains, and material to prepare such theatrical shows; yet they are presented to everyone, free. The only time in which an African artist gets paid is when anybody is so thrilled by the show as to "dash" the artist some money, or when the artist is deliberately hired for his talent. The African's is certainly a wondrous society, a leisure-loving community.

Wrestling is undoubtedly the most artful of our sports, requiring the greatest adroitness. Its code is entirely different from the American kind because its aim is different. We wrestle in order to train the youth in skill, strategy, alertness, and nimbleness. Accordingly, the methods are three. First, you may surprise the opponent with an attack by which he can be gathered and lifted above the ground. A fraction of an inch off the floor is enough. The judges declare you the winner. You let him fall. The assumption is that if you could lift him off the floor, you could put him on your shoulder and carry him home captive. Second, you may give him a clever push which forces him to lose his balance and fall. Third, you may manipulate him so deceptively that by a nimble and delicate twist, he turns his back while struggling to avoid a decisive fall. You have won, because turning one's back is retreat, and retreat, defeat. These techniques of wrestling take place so rapidly that little muscular ordeal is experienced by either party.

When I was at Ohio State University in 1941, I one day went to see how Americans wrestle. I did not intend to participate, because I was not a champion at home; but my professors and colleagues persuaded me to try. On a whim, I jumped into the ring to face an American about as heavy as I was. Bending on my knees, as is customary in Africa, I looked him in the eyes to read off his tactics. He showed a poker face. Suddenly he came slowly on, stretched his right hand and tipped my forehead. I was puzzled. I got up and looked most disturbedly to figure out what this meant. A poker face still! In reprisal, I stretched my left hand to tip his forehead; he gripped my wrist. I stretched the right; he seized both hands. What next? I asked myself. He twisted my hands this way and that way. It was awful! When I got rid of him I was panting and swearing never to wrestle any more in the United States.

Football is played in Nigeria, where it is called rugby. But it is not as exciting as in America. Basketball is more or less a feminine sport. It is thought to be a mild game, and therefore left to the fair sex. In a few more years it will attract boys and assume the intensity of fight and swiftness of feet it has attained in the United States. With the exception of ice skating and skiing, we play other games known in America. All of these enter into our leisure and game activities.

In descending order of popularity, the big games played in Africa are wrestling, football, tennis, and cricket. Track, boxing, swimming, and polo are rapidly gaining. West Africa has interstate football, tennis, and cricket leagues. Our Big Four are Nigeria, Gold Coast,* Sierra Leone, and Gambia, with the first two leading. Nigeria is overwhelmingly the largest in population and cannot, therefore, receive too many bouquets for its frequent victories. The ratio of the population of these four competing countries is roughly 660:80:4:½.

It is lamentable that our women are most of the time spectators. For since the purpose of sports and leisure is the development of the individual biologically, mentally, and spiritually, African women ought to become more participants than onlookers. The whole community should spend more of the evening in literary experiences such as studies and debates. Too much noise is caused by too much boogie-woogie sort of entertainment, which is, to be sure, a useful channel for excess energy. But in a world where everybody else has taken to literature, wings, and guns, the African must rapidly modify some of the ways he employs his leisure. If our wasted energy is reserved and turned into productive channels, we cannot but equal and even exceed Russian wonders in a continent so blessed as Africa.

From My Africa, *by Mbonu Ojike, The John Day Company Inc., 1946.*

* Now Ghana.

Life Among the Kikuyu

BY JOMO KENYATTA

Jomo Kenyatta, who became the first prime minister of independent Kenya in December 1963, was born in the last decade of the nineteenth century, the grandson of a Kikuyu witch doctor skilled in white magic. Kenyatta's life spans the period of tremendous change from Victorian colonialism to twentieth century independence. Nowhere was this change felt more sharply than in Kenya. Nowhere did its impact create more conflict than among the Kikuyu, the most numerous and enterprising of the original inhabitants of East Africa.

The first Europeans who encountered the Kikuyu varied greatly in their reactions. To some, the Kikuyu appeared friendly and industrious. To others, they were fierce and hostile. The crux of the mounting tension and dispute between the Kenya Africans and the British settlers during the colonial period was the problem of land alienation. Beginning with a grant of 100,000 acres in the Highlands to Lord Delamere in 1903, the exclusion of the Kikuyu from these ancestral lands became a "burning grievance" against the British government.

Kenyatta was the leader who organized resistance to the policy of exclusive European occupation of the Kenya Highlands. As early as 1929 he gave evidence to a Royal Commission and carried his pleas to England, where he successfully petitioned for schools to be founded and run by Africans.

In 1931 he went to England and stayed for fifteen years. He studied anthropology in London and was one of the first to emphasize the values of indigenous African culture in his study of tribal ways, *Facing Mount Kenya*, which was published in 1938. In the preface to this book, Kenyatta says: "I have tried my best to record facts as I know them, mainly through a lifetime of personal experience, and have kept under very considerable restraint the sense of political grievances which no progressive African can fail to experience."

In spite of his sense of restraint, Kenyatta was accused by the British government of instigating the Mau-Mau uprising and was sentenced to seven years in prison. He was released on the eve of Kenya's independence, when no other political leader had enough strength to command wide popular support. In the aftermath of colonialism, Kenyatta came to power from prison.

The chief occupations among the Kikuyu are agriculture and the rearing of livestock, such as cattle, sheep, and goats. Each family, i.e., a man, his wife or wives, and their children, constitutes an economic unit. This is controlled and strengthened by the system of division of labor according to sex. From the homestead to the fields and to the tending of the domestic animals, every sphere of activity is clearly and systematically defined. Each member of the family unit knows perfectly well what task he or she is required to perform, in their economic productivity and distribution of the family resources, so as to ensure the material prosperity of the group.

In house-building the heavy work of cutting timbers and putting up the framework falls to men. Carrying and cutting of the grass for thatching and plastering the wall with clay or cow dung is the work of women. Men build fences around the homestead or gardens and also cattle pens. They are the night watchmen to protect the crops against the wild animals.

The entire housework naturally falls within the sphere of women's activities. They cook, bring water from the rivers, wash utensils, and fetch firewood from the forests or bush. They also perform the task of carrying the loads on their backs. According to the tribal customs which govern the division of labor, no man would dare to indulge in any of these activities except in a case of emergency, or otherwise he would scandalize the women and it would be difficult for such a man to get any girl to marry him. Women are afraid of a man of this character, for they say that if he could perform women's work, what is the use of getting married, for how can a wife and husband be doing the same thing at the same time?

In cultivating the fields men clear the bush and cut big trees, and also break the virgin soil with digging sticks or hoes. Women come behind them and prepare the ground for sowing seeds. Planting is shared by both sexes. Men plant bananas, yams, sweet potato vines, sugar cane, tobacco, and also provide poles for propping up bananas and yams. Women plant maize, various kinds of beans, millet, and sweet potato vines.

Weeding is done collectively. Cutting drains or water furrows and pruning of banana plants, as well as making roads and bridges, is the work of men. Harvesting is done chiefly by the women. Tending of cattle, sheep, and goats, and also slaughtering and distributing the meat and preparing the skins, is entirely the men's duty. Dressmaking, pottery, and weaving of baskets is exclusively women's profession. Wood-carving, smith's work, bee-keeping, and hunting are men's occupations. Women take responsibility for grinding corn and millet, for making gruel, and pounding grains in wooden mortars. They also pound sugar cane for making beer.

Trading is done by both sexes. Carrying and selling grains at the markets is chiefly done by women, while taking sheep and goats or cattle to the markets and selling them is the job of men.

The land being the foundation rock on which the Kikuyu tribal economy stands, and the only effective mode of production that the people have, the result is that there is a great desire in the heart of every Kikuyu man to own a piece of land on which he can build his home, and from which he and his family can get the means of livelihood. A man or a woman who cannot say to his friends "Come and eat, drink, and enjoy the fruit of my labor" is not considered as a worthy member of the tribe.

A family group with land to cultivate is considered as a self-supporting economic unit. The group work harmoniously with a view to satisfying their immediate needs, and with the desire to accumulate wealth in the form of cattle, sheep, and goats. These are acquired through effective tillage of the land, except in a very few cases nowadays where some people are able to get money in some other ways than selling their products.

Marketing begins when crops are ripe and have not yet dried to be harvested. Various things are taken to markets, principally bananas, yams, a variety of beans, tree peas, maize, millet, potatoes and sugar cane. In these markets one finds all kinds of ornaments, articles of clothing, from skins of animals to the Lancashire cotton, different types of agricultural implements, running from digging-sticks to hoes made in Birmingham or in Japan. There are also sheep and goats, milk and butterfat, etc.

There are two ways of exchanging goods: one by barter and the other by money. The former is predominant, for the majority of the people still adhere to the old form of exchanging one article for another. For instance, if one man has beans and he wants yams, he goes to the man who has yams and is in need of beans and tells him, "I have my beans and I want your yams." Then they argue as to how many yams to a basket of beans. If they agree they exchange there and then; if not, each goes his own way, looking for someone else who will agree with him, for the exchange depends entirely on individual buyer and seller.

There are also fixed prices for certain goods dictated by the seasonal law of supply and demand. For instance, if a man wants a cultivating knife he goes to a smith who has fixed a general price for each of his articles according to their sizes. For example, a small knife is exchanged for a small basket of millet or two small baskets of beans. Again, if a woman wants an ornament she goes to a man or a woman who has them and there exchanges two heaps of sweet potatoes or one heap of yams for a bracelet or an earring.

In the markets things are bought and sold in small and big quantities by people who have too much of one thing and too little of the other. Take the case of a man who is about to stage a big ceremonial feast, and perhaps has not cultivated sufficient grain to enable him to display his generosity to his friends. He takes one of his sheep or goats to the market and exchanges it for three or four big baskets of millet or for any other commodity that he lacks. If a man has too many cows and fewer sheep and goats, he takes one of his cows, especially one that has no religious implications within the family group, and exchanges it for ten or more sheep and goats. Sometimes there are people who have been working for wages and have saved a few shillings after paying their poll or hut taxes. When one such returns to his home and wants to own a few of these valued animals, which are the recognized standard of wealth among the Kikuyu, he goes to the market and makes a good bargain with the people who have brought their sheep and goats to raise sufficient money for the government taxes. In these markets one can buy almost any conceivable thing that is available in the tribe. It is considered a sign of industry to be selling grain in the markets, for it proves that one has cultivated not only sufficient for the family but also a surplus for accumulation of wealth.

In many cases harvesting time is the busiest period for the majority of women, for the simple reason that they are the managing directors of the food supply in their respective family groups. Therefore it is considered right and proper for the women to handle the grain and store it according to the immediate and future needs of the family. The work of harvesting is divided almost equally between men and women. For while the women do the actual harvesting and carrying the harvest home, the men cut or root out maize or millet stalks, burn them, and spread the ashes in the field as a part of the manuring and to kill certain insects. Men also make new granaries or repair the old ones.

When the harvesting is completed, a woman's first thought is to store sufficient grain to last her family until the next harvest. After she has done so, and there is surplus grain left, she consults with her husband. Then, if there is something that the family needs, the surplus grain is sold immediately in the markets to satisfy the needs. If there are no immediate needs, the surplus grain is kept back and sold later when there is a scarcity of that particular grain in the markets.

The stored grain is dished out carefully by the wife, with the view neither to be wasteful nor starve the family. She prepares family menus with a variety of daily changes to balance the diets. For example, if she had prepared sweet potatoes and gruel for today's meal, tomorrow she will cook a mixture of beans, maize, greens, and perhaps bananas. Although food is changed almost daily, the wife takes great care not to exhaust the supply of one article of food. So when there is plenty of beans and maize, and less of bananas and sweet potatoes, she cooks more of what is abundant and less of what is scarce.

A wife who manages efficiently the economic affairs as well as other duties in her family group is highly respected, not only by her group but by the entire community.

To a Kikuyu the cattle in the first place are merely a display of wealth, for to be called rich a man must own a number of cattle. Because while every family has a number of sheep and goats, say, from one to hundreds, only a small minority owns cattle, and therefore to own a cow or two is the first sign of being a wealthy man.

Apart from being the display of wealth, cattle play a part in the economic life of the people. To start with, cow's milk is used for babies by those who can afford it. The milk is very little used in the Kikuyu diet except by those who own a number of cows. Hides are used for various purposes, for bedding, making sandals and straps for tying and carrying firewood and other loads. As a source of meat or butter supply, cattle play a very small part. Cows are never killed for food except at a time of famine, but bulls and oxen are now and again slaughtered for occasional meat feasts, and this is regarded as luxurious and practiced only by well-to-do persons.

Cows give the owner a prestige in the community, but are never killed for any particular sacrificial or religious ceremonies, except in very rare cases or when a bull or ox is substituted for a male goat or a ram. As economic assets cattle play a part in the marriage ceremony, where a cow or more is given as marriage insurance; but there, too, cattle are given as a substitute for sheep or goats, each cow being valued at ten sheep or goats and a bull or an ox at five sheep or goats.

In former days cattle had very little economic value to the owners apart from the fact that such owners were looked on as dignified, respected rich men. The milk was not sold, but used by the herdsmen and by visitors, especially warriors, who were the protectors of the villages against Masai or other raiders. The rich men, who naturally had more property to be protected, were responsible for feeding the warriors in the way of milk and providing oxen for meat feasts to keep the warriors in good healthy condition.

Sometimes the owner of cattle hardly had the pleasure of drinking his cow's milk, especially if they were far away from his homestead. In spite of this the owner of a large number of cattle was sentimentally satisfied by praise names conferred upon him by the community in their songs and dances. Nowadays some people, especially those who are near European towns, do sell their milk and derive a good income from it. This income could be improved by introducing a better breed instead of keeping a number of cows which give very little milk. From the economic point of view the present breed of cattle reared by the Kikuyu is very poor, and it would be a great advancement if the government could help the people to secure a few good bulls for breeding, and gradually replace the inferior types of cattle with better ones. This method would automatically improve the problem of congestion in grazing areas which faces the country at present, for people would learn the value of keeping a few cows, which would be useful economically, instead of keeping a large number of cattle for sentimental satisfaction.

In the Kikuyu country, before the introduction of the European monetary system, sheep and goats were regarded as the standard currency of the Kikuyu people. The price of almost everything was determined in terms of sheep and goats. This system still operates among the majority of the Kikuyu people, who have not yet grasped the idea of a monetary system and its value.

These domestic animals play an important role in the economic, religious, and social life of the Kikuyu. A man with a number of sheep and goats feels no less wealthy than a man with a large bank balance. The people look upon these animals as a good investment which gives them a yearly income, for if a man has two or three good sheep or female goats, within a year they increase to six or more, and people consider this a good profit. They would argue, saying that money is not a good investment, for one shilling does not bear another shilling, whereas a sheep or goat does. This, of course, is due to the ignorance of money speculation, and so they say it is better to buy a sheep or a goat instead of keeping shillings, which, if buried in the ground (the only form of saving money the majority of the people know), would rot and lose their value.

Sheep and goats, unlike cattle, are used for various religious sacrifices and purifications. They are the chief means of supplying the people with meat, while the skins are used as articles of clothing. Finally, without them a man cannot get a wife, for it is sheep and goats that are given as marriage insurance (*roracio*). If a man has cash money and he wants to get married he must, in the first place, buy cattle or sheep and goats, because the parents of the wife-to-be will not accept cash money as *roracio*. To them coins have very little meaning and have no religious or sentimental associations within the people's custom.

The real value of money is only realized when a man takes it and buys a cow or sheep and goats, or pays the government taxes; otherwise money as such has little function inside the Kikuyu country. With all the disadvantages connected with the rearing of sheep and goats, they are still regarded generally as the only means of expression of wealth. By disadvantages we mean that in some cases young men have been ruined by spending years earning money to buy these highly valued animals and sometimes sickness invades a homestead and kills every one of them in a few days. This means a loss of ten or thirty pounds, which, if it had been put in a savings bank, would have remained there and helped the young man to improve his standard of living. This is a question which is very difficult to settle, for some people would argue that the animals give better profit yearly, whereas shillings do not multiply quickly and do not give the same sentimental satisfaction. But let us hope that gradually people will be able to decide which one of the two systems is suitable for their advancement.

We have given a description of how the Kikuyu exchange goods among themselves in the market, and the types of articles sold and bought. Having done so, we will now enter into discussion of how the Kikuyu trade with their neighbors, i.e., the Masai and Wakamba. The articles of special value in trading with the Masai are spears, swords, tobacco, gourds, and red ocher. The Masai, who are not agriculturalists, and who regard the cultivation of soil as a crime against their gods, depend almost entirely on the Kikuyu for the supply of the three last-mentioned articles. Although the Masai have their own blacksmiths, the spears made by the Kikuyu were and still are regarded as the best.

There are intertribal markets where these goods are exchanged, but, apart from these markets, sometimes a group of men organize into a trading guild and take their goods into the heart of the Masai country. In former days this kind of trade was conducted in the homestead of a friend who acted as the guide and protector of his friends and their goods.

The Kikuyu, after collecting their trading goods, would send for their friend or friends in Masailand, asking them to meet the traders at the frontier and conduct them into the country. Thus goods were taken to villages and, after exchanging them for sheep, the Kikuyu would return escorted by their friends to the frontier to avoid any molestation by the hostile warriors who would only be too glad to have someone on whom to blood their spears. The same thing happened when the Masai wanted to enter into Kikuyuland for the purpose of trade.

As regards trade with the Wakamba, there are no special articles as in the case of the Masai. In fact the Wakamba being agriculturalists grow almost the same crops as the Kikuyu. The two tribes are racially and linguistically identical. It can be said that in the beginning of things the Kikuyu and Wakamba were brothers, but how and why they came to part is a matter requiring some investigation.

In former days there was very little hostility between the two tribes, and their trade depended on seasonal harvests. If there was a shortage of food in Kikuyuland and abundance in Wakamba country, the Kikuyu went and bought grain from the Wakamba, the exchange being sheep and goats or cows and sometimes ivory. The same thing happened in the case of the Wakamba. Apart from these contacts, there were frequent and friendly visits from both sides for trading or other purposes.

From Facing Mount Kenya, *by Jomo Kenyatta, Random House, 1962.*

I Marry My Cousin Duma

BY BABA OF KARO

RECORDED BY MARY F. SMITH

Baba of Karo lived in the early days of tribal wars and slave raids before the British came to the Zuria Province of Nigeria. Baba belonged to the Hausa tribe, the dominant ethnic group in Northern Nigeria, numbering over five and a half million. This region has been strongly influenced since medieval times by the Mohammedan countries to the north and east.

Baba's story is unusually full and well-documented for this period and region. The early missionaries, anthropologists, and explorers were usually restricted in their contacts with women. Mrs. Smith, who recorded Baba's story, was doing field work among the Hausa with her husband. She won the confidence of several women; of these Baba was one of the most articulate in explaining the details of her various marriages and the customs which governed a woman's relationships with the other members of her family.

In all, Baba was married four times: to her cousin who was a farmer; to a blacksmith; to another farmer who was also a prison warden—"a reasonable man"; and finally to Adama, a friend. She had no children of her own but adopted many, as was the custom. The following selection from *Baba of Karo* tells about her first marriage, to her cousin Duma.

When I was about fourteen years old, it was time for me to be married. I had grown up with our six "fathers," the sons of Ibrahim Dara and his younger brother Maidamishi, and when the time came they arranged my marriage within the family, a marriage of kinsfolk.

Duma's father Sidi and my father put their heads together. The

elder brother said to my father, "We will marry them to one another," and his younger brother replied, "Very well." They were always arranging marriages between kinsfolk in our family, everyone
married his kinswoman and took her to his compound. My mother
was dead at that time, and my father's sister Rabi was like my
mother, but she had been kidnapped.

My father sent for me and I went to him and curtsied. "Your kinsman desires you," he said; "I also desire him," I replied.

Dabo, the son of Sarkin Zarewa our town chief, loved me and I
wanted him, but my family would not agree to our marrying. They
did not like titles and title-holders; they were farmers, they liked
their daughters to marry farmers. That was why I could not marry
Sarkin Zarewa's son. There was also Malam Maigari who wished to
marry me. I promised him I would come to him later.

When my kinsman Duma came to visit me, I sent for my *kawa,* my
dear friend Yariya—her home wasn't far away, and she came to our
entrance-hut. I took out two mats and we gave them one and sat on
one ourselves. Duma came with his special friend, another man, and
I talked to his friend while Yariya talked to Duma; we were all
laughing and joking. Then his friend took out some money and
placed it on our mat. Then we arose and escorted them on their way
home, and when we returned home we rolled up the mats and went
into the compound. Yariya picked up the money and put it into a flat
basket, and I took my share, which was bigger than hers. When her
cross-cousin was courting her (she was daughter of the sister, he was
son of the brother) , she used to call me to go to her compound in the
same way, and I used to go. His name was Inusa. We all talked together, then Inusa's friend Yero came and put down the money in
front of me. When we had escorted them homewards, we came back
to Yariya's compound and I took up the money while she rolled up
the mats, then we went into her mother's hut and laid out the
money. Yariya gave me my share, a little, and kept her share, which
was the greater part. Then she escorted me home. We always showed
our mothers the gift, but the money was ours. If you like the man,
you say to his friend, "Yes I like him." Then they put down the
money and your kawa takes it. If you don't like him, you say, "Get
on with your work. You are too strong for us." They put down their
money, and your kawa says, "Take away your things, she does not desire you." Then you leave the money alone, you don't accept it. If

they come back the next day, you run away. But if you agree, they come every week to visit you and bring money; they keep on coming for a whole year.

When they were arranging my first marriage, my father talked to me and persuaded me to accept Duma; he wanted his kinsman to marry me. Since he wished it, I said, "Yes, very well." When Duma came to visit me we chatted and laughed a lot—we knew each other well; then I accepted his money because Father wanted me to do so. But because I didn't really love him I left him after a few years. Parents always hope their daughter will have children and settle down; if she doesn't have children she does not settle down—and some, even if they do have children, leave them and break up the marriage.

When it was time for me to be married the elders of our family met for the betrothal ceremony; a month later they "set the day"; and two months after that was the wedding feast. That is three months altogether. At the Salla feast before our marriage Duma came to visit me; he could come inside our compound—wasn't it also his father's house?—and he brought me money and kolanuts and perfume, and told me to go and buy cloth. I went to market and bought cloth. He came and we conversed together. I bought bowls and some flat baskets and a few plates. Then on the marriage day my father's family and my mother's family all came. They brought sacks of guineacorn, sacks of rice, baskets of salt, of onions and of locust-bean cakes, and oil. They decorated my new hut with all my things, they set out my plates and bowls and spread mats on the bed and the floor—both the mats the pagan tribes make and the ones from Bornu. Then they spread my blanket on the bed and set down the pillow.

If you are going to be taken to your hut today, there is drumming and drumming, and tomorrow your kinsfolk will bring you all sorts of lovely things. The men load their donkeys with sacks of corn and rice, and the women put on their best cloths and carry the plates and bowls. They bring it all to you and put your dowry in your hut.

Yesterday evening you were in your hut, you covered your head and wept—no more going to play with the young girls; you would hear their drumming, you would hear it but you wouldn't be able to go out and dance. You feel very angry. Then your mother comes and talks to you, "Be quiet, be calm, stop crying!" One of my aunts came (my mother was dead and Aunt Rabi was lost), she sent away the children, "Run away!" Then she talked to me and I was quiet. Then my husband's wife, my co-wife, came and took me to my new hut. She gave me some food and said to me, "Take out your spinning." We sat there spinning, and she coaxed me, and I felt better. Her name was Ture and when I married Duma she had a daughter Marka—that means steady rain, she was born in the rainy season—and a son called Ciwake, which means "eat-beans"; they were eating beans when he was born. She was a very good-tempered woman. Duma was tall and handsome and sensible; we lived together in peace with no quarreling or anything of that kind.

When I had been married for some time to my kinsman Duma, we heard news of my father's sister Rabi, who had been kidnapped. When her children and relatives heard the news—they heard from a traveler that she had been sold in Abuja—they pledged one of her twin slaves, they collected money, and they gave it to her eldest son to give to the *malams* so that they should make charms for him. He went to Abuja to fetch her, but on the way he wasted the money on women, and came home to say that he had not found her.

Then again they collected money, and they gave it to Nasamai, her second son. He sold a female slave to some rich people—the rich man made her a concubine in his house, he had had no children until she came, then she bore him eight. Nasamai took money to the malams, who did their work and said, "She is in the palace of the king of Abuja." Nasamai made ready and set out, the malams gave him charms to take both in his hand and in his mouth, *baduhu* for washing his eyes, *layan zana* so that he shouldn't be seen, charms to put in his mouth and charms to hold in his hand. He got them both for himself and his mother. When he got to Abuja—the malams had looked and said, "Go to the king's palace"—he went to the king's palace, he passed through the first entrance-hut; there were many courtyards and many entrance-huts, each with a lamp burning in it, the courtyards that kings' houses have. When he got inside he heard the king's chief wife calling, "Woman of the Hausa, bring me fire, bring me water, come and light the lamp." The slave answered, "Very well."

When he heard her voice (he knew where to look for her because of his charms), he went and touched her. She said, "What brings you here?" Then he put a charm in her mouth. The king's wife called,

"Bring the lamp!" She picked up only one cloth, Nasamai said, "Be silent!" He tied her on his back with a blanket, like a child—he was tall, she was very small. Swiftly he slipped out and carried her away. Only one man saw them; he went "A-hem!" and he said nothing; late that night he told the king, "I saw a man leave the palace today carrying a woman on his back."

When the king's chief wife called and there was no answer, then she began to look for her slave; she didn't see her. She went to the king and she said, "The Hausa woman is not here." Then the king called out his men and told them to search for her; there was a storm with pouring rain, at daybreak the men hunted for them on the road, but they could not find them. Nasamai took her to Gobirawa and there they ate; after three days they reached Zaria, and they sent a message to Zarewa to say Nasamai had found his mother.

We were delighted, we all gave her cloths, we gave her head scarves. As for Nasamai, everyone praised and blessed him, he was a determined man and everyone in the town rejoiced at him. Rabi had no husband, because he had escaped from the kidnappers and gone off somewhere and there was no news of him; so when she came home she married her kinsman Mamman—he and she were the children of two brothers. She had been exactly three years at Abuja; she did their grinding and spinning, they gave her food, she ate and was satisfied.

At that time I had been married for three years to my kinsman. His chief wife had two children when I married him, she was carrying one on her back and the other could walk. When father's sister Rabi (we called her "Baba's mother") was brought home from Abuja I was very happy. Everyone came to say "Blessings on your fortune, Baba's mother!" Everyone praised her resourceful son.

When she came home I no longer wanted to live in the hamlet; I preferred the town. It is nicer in a town, there are more people—Karo was four miles from Zarewa. My "parents" told me to go back to him, but I refused. Then my husband's "parents" came and said I must go back. When I still said I would not go, then all the elders, men and women, came to Aunt Rabi's compound and assembled in the entrance-hut. The old women sat with the men in the entrance-hut. Some of them said, "She must have patience and return"; others said, "Since she dislikes the marriage, it is better that they part."

Then they sent for me. I came in and they said, "You must put up with it, you must have patience; your husband is your kinsman, you must go on with your marriage."

I said, "No." Anja, Ayaske, Kunza—they were my grandmothers, wives of Ibrahim Dara, who liked me.

Duma was there, it was he who had said, "I want her to calm down and come home; send for her."

I came and knelt down, and he asked me, "What have I done to you? Be sensible and come back. You know I want you, stop being angry and come home."

I said, "No." He wanted me very much, but I didn't want him, I desired a son of the blacksmith, Maigari of the South Gate. When I was a girl he used to give me money on market-days; he wanted to marry me, but I refused so that my parents should not be angry with me and beat me. I had promised him I would come; I said "Be patient, I will not remain there."

When Aunt Rabi came home I knew she would help me. Before she was taken to Abuja, Maigari had begun to court me, then when she was not there they had married me to someone else. When she came back I felt good. I told her that I didn't like the marriage and she said, "Very well, go and break it up. You didn't want him," she said, "and they did that to you. Very well, go and get divorced, I am back." Aunt Rabi's daughter and I were born on the same day.

Aunt Rabi was there in the entrance-hut where they were discussing my marriage. She said to them, "She said she did not wish to marry Duma. Very well, you forced her. Now I have come back and she is not going to stay married to him."

Then my father said, "What business is it of mine? It has nothing to do with me." That was that.

Then to the chief's compound. All the fathers had come to Aunt Rabi's compound and she had told them off soundly. There were ten of them on Duma's side, we all went to Sarkin Zarewa's compound. But before that I had paid a visit to the chief's house; I went to see his head wife, I knew his wives. She said, "What brings you?" I said, "I have come to break off my marriage." She explained the matter to Sarki. When I went inside the compound to his own hut, I knelt down and greeted him.

"Allah preserve your life."

"Good. Woman of Karo, what brings you here?"

"I want to break off my marriage."

He said, "Indeed! Be patient and go back. What is his fault?"

I said, "He hasn't done anything, but I don't like the hamlet, I prefer the town."

Then he looked at me. Then he said, "Very well." We had known him ever since his father held the chieftainship, they were the Fulani of our town.

When he returned to the entrance of the compound, he sent his courtiers to Karo to call Duma's people. When they came, Duma said I was angry and he did not know the reason. Sarki questioned me. I said it was nobody's fault, I was just tired of village life. I did not mention the matter of Maigari. Sarki gave me a document and my marriage with Duma was over.

Duma and I remained friends, our kinship did not die. When I had been married to Maigari for two years, Duma's daughter, his head wife's child, came and spent twenty days with me. I gave her a small cloth and head-kerchief when she returned home. When she married I went and stayed for two nights in Duma's compound; Maigari did not prevent it, because of the kinship between us.

From Baba of Karo, *by Mary F. Smith, Faber and Faber, 1954.*

Freetown Boy

BY ROBERT WELLESLEY COLE

Robert W. Cole, born Robert Benjamin Wellesley Agah, in Freetown, capital of Sierra Leone, grew up to become a distinguished
surgeon, the first African to be awarded the Fellowship of the Royal
College of Surgeons.

His great-grandparents were of African origin by way of the West
Indies; they were liberated Africans who settled in the British colony
of Sierra Leone after the slave trade was abolished. At that time,
Freetown was safe harbor for many African "refugees,"—freed and
escaped slaves from Jamaica, Nova Scotia, the Cape Verde Islands,
and inland parts of Africa. Over a period of a hundred years these
refugees, originally speaking nearly a hundred different languages or
dialects, merged to become the elite of Sierra Leone, the educated
Krios or Creoles.

Dr. Cole's autobiography, *Kossoh Town Boy,* tells of his boyhood
and youth in the first quarter of the twentieth century as a member
of a typical Krio household, a cross-cultural mixture of Victorian
manners and traditional African customs.

O ur day started with family prayers. Our grandmother and aunts
usually joined us upstairs, and so did the foster brothers and
sisters. We sat around the room, and after the word of grace from
father, each read in turn a verse from the portion allotted for the day
in the Scripture Union card.

Almost unique among all the peoples of West Africa, practically
all Krios are literate. The poorest family would die rather than not
send its children to school even for a year, so that they could read. It
is considered a disgrace among them for a child to be illiterate.

This, together with such distinguishing features as dress, language, Christian religion, English or Anglicized names, the acceptance of monogamy, and even the type of their houses, all stemmed from the fact that the Krios of Sierra Leone started life as a settler community under Christian British influence.

Krio baby boys are circumcised when a week old. Baby girls have their ears pierced at the same age for earrings. The Krios, like their main ancestors the Yorubas of Nigeria, look to the East for their basic origin. But where the Yoruba ancestors thought of Yemen, Arabia, and Mecca, the Christian Krios think of the stories of the Old Testament.

Christianity was the central force of our home. But though a strict disciplinarian, father was not a bigot. Those foster children who were not Christians he left alone. They were not forced to attend family prayers nor to attend church. And when one after the other they asked to join us, and to go to church with us, he sent for their parents, and discussed the matter fully with them; and it was only after the latter had given their consent that he took steps to have them instructed in Christianity and prepared for baptism. I can remember one of them, who at the time would be in his late teens, being baptized at the same ceremony as one of my baby brothers.

All this fitted in with the family prayers at home every morning and evening. On Sundays we had singing of hymns and psalms at home as well. It was a great day when I too was able to read my share of the verses of scripture with the rest of the family. Later on I became the family organist and accompanied the singing of hymns and psalms on the family harmonium.

But it was playtime in the afternoon and evening that meant so much to me in those early days. I looked forward to three o'clock. Although I could not tell the time, I could sense when the hour approached, and would hover at the gate, peering out for my foster "cousins" to return home from school.

I can remember a long bench which stood against one wall of the house, in the yard. Around this we would sit or stand, and take part in all those pastimes which, all the world over, fill in the period between coming home from school and going to bed. Along another wall of the house were flowering shrubs.

Those afternoon play sessions in the yard must have done much to help me develop normally. As most of my brothers and sisters were not then born, but for this companionship of foster children I would for some years have been more or less a lonely child, a phenomenon which is rare in African society. As it was I grew up instead in the fold of young people.

Apart from this I also played with boys of my own age in our street. There was cricket, not to mention top spinning, hoop trundling, kite flying, and other activities.

When sent on an errand down the street I would debate whether to take my hoop or a top. If the hoop, I trundled it all the way by the simple method of hitting it with a short piece of stick in a straight line. This was the quickest method of getting to my destination.

On the other hand, the top was a more interesting if leisurely and erratic way of going on an errand. I would spin the top and lash it with the cotton thong tied to the end of a short piece of stick. On its flat surface I would make marks with chalk, and these would join into lovely patterns as the top spun. Thus I would progress sideways, with my jutting posterior describing little horizontal arcs like a waddling duck, as I lashed the top on its spinning course.

Eastertime was kite-flying season, and long before then we would get our colored tissue papers from the shops, and the special bamboo canes with which kites of different kinds were made. These varied from the simple skate design most commonly in use to the powerful giant *ognos* (Krio for "hog's snout"). This takes its name from the open triangular top segment of this hexagonal kite with its often double tail, altogether a ferocious-looking object.

As for cricket, we used the base of the street lamp post for stumps, or if we played in our yard we used an upturned pail or wicker basket. The bat was a curved blade shaped from the giant stem of the compound coconut leaf. As a result, the commonest stroke was the hook, and the usual method of dismissal was by the catch. This was no disgrace, as usually it was the result of a hefty swipe which might send the ball soaring to the roof of the house, from which it would bounce and roll down into the patient hands of a waiting fielder!

This ball was made from one of Mother's black stockings, the toe being rammed with soft cotton waste, tied hard at the neck, then turned inside out and tied tight again, the process repeated until the whole stocking had been taken up; then the edges were sewn to the surface. A well-hit ball has been known to stay lodged on the roof or in the branches of a tree. Then the game was abandoned as a draw.

Similarly, if a serious dispute arose among the players, each boy would walk off with his ball, bat, wicket, or whatever part of the gear belonged to him.

At home, among the young people, we all called each other "cousin." But among the servants they were all "brothers."

There were the four "hammock boys," who carried Father to and from work and on his various tours of inspection of waterworks installations in the peninsula. There was the "lunch boy" who called at eleven to fetch Father's hot lunch (this was called "breakfast") and take it to the office at the waterworks headquarters on Tower Hill, and brought the remains back in the afternoon. There was another "boy," somewhat younger, who did much of the heavy work and ran errands when the others had gone to school.

But over and above this there was the "head boy." I cannot clearly recall what were his precise duties. He was a major-domo, a butler, foreman, or chargehand, rolled into one. He was treated with respect, and he saw to it that the others reported for duty regularly and did their jobs well.

One day he came up and said to Papa, *"Masa, a de go kontri."* (Please, master, I have come to say good-bye. I am going back to my country.)

Papa wished him Godspeed and inquired when he would be returning. (*"Waka gud! Ustem yu de cam bak?"*)

But Sori, who had been with us so long that he was part of the family, had suddenly grown tired of life in the city. He wanted to go back to his people, marry, and farm his land. But he was not leaving his master in the lurch; instead, he said, *"Dis na mi broda!"* (I've brought you my brother), introducing another and somewhat younger man.

"But every time you bring a man for a job, you say he is your brother," countered my father, eyeing the newcomer carefully.

"Yes, master," Sori answered, speaking in Krio, which was the only language he knew apart from his own native Limba. "Yes, master, we are all brothers. Same country. Same chief. But this man, he is my real brother. Same mother." The new man took over the major-domoship, and when years afterward he too left he first brought a "brother" to take over his place.

Father abhorred smoking, and the servants would hide in all sorts of corners in the yard or in the garden to light their little short-stemmed white clay pipes. This they did by the simple method of tamping down the tobacco in the pipe bowl, tossing on top of it a piece of live coal from the fire, and making a run for it as far away as possible from the house and Father's sharp nostrils. Invariably if Father caught them he would confiscate the pipe.

My father was six feet one and a half inches tall, and slim. Rather ascetic looking, with lean features, high forehead, strong cuboid chin, and a trimmed mustache across the whole length of his upper lip. Often, having ridden on his hammock all day, he would prefer to walk on the way home. He took deceptively long strides, stooping slightly forward, marching ahead of the men, who, even with only the lightened hammock to carry, would have to run in order to keep up with him.

Certainly my brother Arthur and I had great difficulty in keeping up with him, years afterward when we were young men in our late teens.

"Come on, men, don't fall asleep," he would say to us as we marched manfully on, slightly irritated that we could not keep up with "the old man." Indeed there was another sore point with us concerning our father. We never grew taller than he! However much we measured our heights Arthur and I never exceeded six feet!

Although ours was a heterogenous household, yet it was in the fullest sense of the word a united family. We all loved our parents. Father's authority was ably backed by Mother's loyalty. Everyone knew his duty and did it.

When difficulties arose they were settled without ill feeling or a sense of injustice. Even when things were missing, somehow the culprit was always found, or confessed.

In serious cases of theft Father used a method of detection which I have not heard mentioned anywhere else. It was called the "Bible and key." We all sat in a circle, and father said a short prayer. Then a small Bible was opened at random, a door key was inserted into the open page, and the book was shut and bound with some cotton or other tape in such a way that the key was firmly clasped between its closed pages, leaving part of the stem and the oval handle of the key jutting out.

Then each person took turns with Father to support the bound

Bible and key, each inserting the tip of his middle finger under the edge of the handle of the key. The Bible was thus delicately balanced on the tips of the two fingers, that of Father and that of the person whose turn it was.

Father then spoke the following words: "By St. Peter and St. Paul and by the holy word of God, if it is A— who took this thing (naming the lost article), let this Bible turn around and fall down." These words he would repeat three times.

The curious thing was that nothing would happen with every other member in that circle. The Bible would remain delicately balanced on the two upturned fingertips, while the words were spoken solemnly, once, twice, three times. But when the culprit took his turn with Father, as soon as the words "Let this Bible turn around and fall down" were uttered, the Bible would twist out of their fingers and drop. It was picked up again, held in position, and the words repeated; again it would twist around and drop. It was uncanny. Try as one would nothing, no will power could prevent this happening when the culprit had his finger on that Bible and key.

Usually the culprit would confess after this exposure. Only once did the person continue to maintain his innocence. But many years afterward he wrote to Father and confessed.

From Kossoh Town Boy, *by Robert Wellesley Cole, Cambridge University Press, 1960.*

The Pagan Woman

Noni Jabavu says of herself: "I belong to two worlds with two loyalties: South Africa where I was born and England where I was educated." Miss Jabavu comes of a distinguished Xhosa family whose members have been educated for five generations. She has a rich cultural and educational heritage. Her father is the former Professor of Latin and Bantu Languages at Fort Hare University, established in 1916 for Africans in the Cape Province of South Africa. Her grandfather, John Tengo Jabavu, founded the first South African newspaper in the vernacular before the Boer War.

Educated in England, Noni Jabavu divides her time between London and the West Indies, with her husband, film director Michael Cadbury Crosfield. Her two books, *Drawn in Color* and *The Ochre People,* are both vivid personal accounts of her family and her reactions to life in her homeland during the last decade.

"The Pagan Woman" is the portrait of a country woman whom she met when she returned to the Cape Province for her brother's funeral. Tengo, her only brother, was shot and killed by gangsters while he was a medical student at the Witwatersrand University in Johannesburg.

At the funeral, or Concealment, of the murdered Tengo, distant relatives gathered to console the boy's father, the beloved "Professor." Respected throughout the whole province, he was loved by the educated Xhosa and also by the pagans, the "ochre" people who still keep their traditions and their family history alive through oral recitations.

We went to the station one morning to see off a party of relatives who were leaving us to return to their homes.

The morning sun, newly risen, shone with its broad African smile on the sweeping expanse of shallow hills dotted with thorn trees, the hilltops looking fresh and green in the clean new sunlight. In summer when pink and mauve and yellow flowers peep from between the boulders making tufts of color along the ridges, "the land looks beautiful like a young girl," as we say in Xhosa.

We watched the train approach, snaking its way along the sweeping contours, short green grass and trees and flowers, until it slid to a standstill, in our case high above us, so that we had to jerk our necks right back to speak to the travelers hanging out of the windows. Black and brown shining faces leaned out greeting everybody known and unknown on the ground below. And arms of raggedly dressed laborers going to work in the towns along the line handed out the luggage of passengers alighting from the third class, luggage consisting of thin suitcases or pillowcases filled with belongings and tied with string or rope.

From the second-class windows more neatly dressed people, teachers mostly, looked out. And Europeans hung out of their windows, necks craned towards our part of the train as always at country stations; at the bustling ones like Port Elizabeth or Jo'burg they do not bother, but at rural stations it is as though Europeans are fascinated and mesmerized by the spectacle of Africans with their great bursts of exclamations and laughter and greetings; they gaze with set, unsmiling faces as if this African jollity is hard to tolerate. They hang on our every word and gesture, red-faced, tight-lipped.

While we were handing our relatives their things, a pagan woman walked up and down along the "Non-Europeans Only" carriages, balancing a basket of cactus pears on her turbaned head. She was a "dressed" pagan, wearing an ankle-length cotton skirt that flared out in an immense fullness behind her not unlike the flared style of the red ochre-smeared pagan costume she would wear as a rule. There were many petticoats underneath this skirt, also full; and she wore an Edwardian style cotton blouse. I could tell she was pagan by the tiny bead circlets around each of her ankles.

The passengers began to clamor to buy prickly pears from her. "Give them here, *mama;* what money are they?"

"Tickey a dozen!" she shouted back, and an exchange hurriedly ensued amid cries and loud laments from her, for she was fearful of missing the tiny threepenny piece, the silver "tickey" thrown down

to her or passed from hand to hand. It was clearly a big thing for her
to part with the fruit that she picked so laboriously and prepared;
not only must she pick, dodging the long sharp-spiked cactus leaves,
but wipe each fruit clean of its own tiny, soft but devilish thorns arranged in harmless-looking furry tufts all over the peel. All that for a
tickey a dozen. If she charged more, nobody would buy.

My Jo'burg uncle pounced on her and started to bargain, struck
that moment by the idea of buying up the entire bucketful to give
these departing relatives as *umpako,* provision, for their long journey north.

The train was about to pull out now, so "Little Father" acceler-
ated his efforts to beat the price down. I wished he wouldn't and so
did all my cousins, but we knew that being a Johannesburg man he
felt it necessary to demonstrate city smartness to these pagans and
"country pumpkins," that being the punning English term town relatives call us in the Reserves, since country bumpkins grow and eat
many pumpkins!

She cried shrilly, "Make haste, brother, make haste. My money, I
want my money!" handing her bucket up to the window. Many
hands grabbed it to help her, helped my cousins empty it, then
passed it back to her anxious clutch. The station master waved his
green flag, the train whistled, its departure imminent, both making
her cry out in ringing tones, "Oh, my God, who will pay me?"—a
noble voice, stentorian and musical like an actress in an Elizabethan
play.

My uncle answered, "Hush, hush, sister-of-ours. Come with us. We
are of course going to pay you your *ndaliso,* one shilling and six-
pence."

"But who are you with your 'come with us?' I don't know you."
She appealed to strangers standing near by, at which those who had
finished waving farewells to their friends now turned to my uncle
and me and took it on themselves to reassure her. The matter became everyone's business.

"It's all right, *mama,* they belong here, these people. Go with this
man and this girl."

" 'Go'? Go where?" eyes flashing. How could she trust anyone with
this *ndaliso,* might she not find she had braved those spikes and
thorns for nothing?

"Where?" in despair, and was assured by a chorus.

"To Professor's, down there through the village!"

My Little Father started to walk. The train had pulled right out, the tail end of it about to round the first wide sweeping shallow contour of our Eastern Cape landscape. He strode out fingering his watch chain as if to show that even if he had no ready cash on him at that time in the morning, nevertheless a well-dressed city man like himself possessed a watch and chain and that meant resources somewhere.

The pagan woman fell in behind my uncle and me, a few respectful paces to one side, skirts rustling and swinging and tossing from heel to heel as she strode, holding herself so very erect, with the empty bucket on her head.

She said, "What people are you, brother?"

"Of here." I thought my uncle answered rather curtly, but said nothing. We walked on, his eyes roving round the green countryside, drinking in its girl-like beauty. We passed through the village of rondavels and square houses, the hunger a city man feels for the country, of which he was often telling us during this family gathering, clearly intensifying his pace as we walked.

Some homes looked bare because the owners did not care, but the more sensitive occupants of others had planted azaleas, clumps of the flamboyantly feathered red and yellow bird-of-paradise bush, bougainvillaea, geraniums. As far as the eye could see the landscape was a typically South African one, wide expanse of rolling shallow bare hills and in the distance a jagged blue frieze of mountainous edge.

The woman took up his reply. "O-h," she said, drawing it out in the undulating interrogative tone of speech. " 'Of here' then. Do you mean precisely, really, truly, in fact?"

"Ah, let me say rather, we are of-the-Professor. He is my elder brother."

"Ah!" At last the penny dropped. She had not really heard before when she had been told at the station how we belonged here and now exclaimed greatly and made sure of it by asking for repetition. My uncle gave it and added, "We are staying here. We came on the errand of this Concealment of my son."

"Aha, now I see! Oh my God, that was a terrible thing. What badness to happen to father Jabavu, his only son. My God, oh my God!" She paused, momentarily at a loss, but presently was able to continue. "Yet, we too had wanted to come, brother-of-mine, to that

Concealment, for those are people we know. But we are 'red' you see, pagans. This put us in a difficulty. All the same we prayed to God to bind you all, house-of-Jili. I pray for it the more now that I see you with my own eyes: " 'Let Him bind you, let Him make this heavy cloud pass from you.' "

"Thank you, thank you, sister," my classificatory uncle said, not slackening his step. The three of us were walking quite fast now. But I saw that he too was as moved by her outburst as I was, for he withdrew his sharp eyes from the landscape and fixed them in the middle distance, left his watch chain alone, and said with the formality which in our language covers up grief:

"That was nicely spoken, nicely spoken indeed, sister. The house-of-Jili thanks you for those words. Truly, such words bind us at such times. This so painful manner of passing of this son of mine, after all, then, demonstrates a wonderful thing to us all here at home: that the house-of-my-brother is loved even by pagans, even by such as you," which she at once confirmed with a tremendous reiteration: "But that is so indeed, young man, it is *so*, brother-of-mine!"

My uncle prepared himself to reply, in Xhosa fullness, thrusting his hands out in front of him now as he walked, as though to measure a rectangle.

"Now then, do you understand this thing?" he was saying, stretching his outheld arms out more to loosen his sleeves. "Is this something that you will understand when I explain it, friend-of-mine-who-is-much-prized? It is this: you pagan people should *come* to us Christian ones. You should come. You should have come to our son's Concealment, understand? You should not have felt yourselves in a difficulty. We are one people now here in South Africa. That other thing of old is no more, now, that idea that pagans who have not received the Word are different people from us converts who have received it. Oh, we are all one! You see that, you understand that thing?" His baritone voice rang, fairly filling the countryside as we went.

"Yes, brother," she said, her skirts swishing. "Yes, yes. You say so."

"*Eh-weh*, yes indeed I say it! Now then, you and yours should also come to us at church, often, just as you are; never mind coming only to pray for rain when the drought has got us by the short horns, when even then when you come, you spoil your presence by wearing borrowed dress—tut! Leave the dresses to the converts, I say! Dresses mean nothing. Come in your pagan habit, and *dress* in it, then! Embellish yourselves, my dear good person. Adorn yourselves, oh adorn, *dress*, embellish, make yourselves beautiful, *thrust* your ochre on! Pile your beads on, make everything about you speak of pride, sister, confidence, yes pride in yourselves. For you are beautiful! Nothing is ugly in God, not even pagan dress. Therefore wear it proudly and hold out your chests! And *then* come and pray too, along with us!"

I could see why this uncle was considered a speaker. He was a politician, had a magnetic personality. He was a celebrated organizer of men, gifted with a masterful voice.

There was a silence, broken only by the sound of our footsteps on the grass verge of the path.

At last the woman spoke. She was calm and at peace, no longer alarmed, flashing, crying out as she had done at the station when afraid about her tickey and her *ndaliso;* all that was put to one side and her mind was now occupied with higher things. She said, "After all, our pagan dress *was* our first dress, when we were a *nation!*"

"Aha!" triumphed my uncle. "You understand it, you see it."

"Indeed I see it, Jili," she said simply as we approached the house.

We went in by the back gate that you come to when you walk from the station. My uncle went indoors, through the passage by the kitchen, but calling out to her, "Stay here!" So she stood in the backyard where there were already standing groups of women, also wearing the kind of dress, the Edwardian style full skirts and mutton-sleeved blouses that she had borrowed.

Presently my uncle came back with *ndaliso* in his hand. And the pagan woman received it in the customary way, cupping both her hands and genuflecting a little. "You have helped me, brother," she said; a gracious way, I thought, of thanking for what was after all her due. "Let the Lord bind you all." And she made to move away.

My uncle held up the palm of his hand to her. "Don't go yet; stay, sister, stay. Let me call my elder brother. I mentioned your clan to him in asking him for the *ndaliso,* and at once he said he would speak with you. Say no more about your clan now, keep it for him!" He dashed indoors again, and after a while came out, this time walking slowly, accompanying my father who held a pencil and a small sheaf of plain white postcards covered with his handwritten notes.

My father never missed an opportunity to take down rare or unknown clan names, or of checking those he had already collected; he had been at this antiquarian hobby for more than thirty years.

Everyone fell back a little; a teenage boy, on his way past the group and going to the kraal at the far end of the back enclosure, leaped aside to pick up a battered orange box and brought it up to my father, who slowly lowered himself onto it and arranged his file of postcards in one hand and said, "Be good enough say, then, sister." It was too urgent a matter to be held up with preliminary greetings. They would follow afterwards, as everyone knew.

The pagan woman again started the recital of her clan names, and there were three more from where she had left off before.

My father took great pains. At the end he carefully folded up his files and squared them like a card player, slipped them into his waist-coat pocket, then addressed the entire group.

"You see then, all of you good ladies here today, these clan names and praise names are procured with extreme difficulty! for some do not *know* them." He talked solemnly of the passing into oblivion of our nationhood, our traditions, our background as a people, who had traveled from the far north, East Africa; about our Hamitic forefathers with their cattle, always searching for grasslands, and mingling their blood with Bantu and Hottentot and Bushman and who knows what other peoples as they went during those unknown centuries? For decades now he had been trying to gather up what he could of known genealogies and praise verses, which often threw light on the journey and adventures of their owners' group of forebears. In his travels up and down South Africa on educational and political missions, at public gatherings from agricultural shows, athletic sports displays, from concerts to religious gatherings like revival meetings, in chance encounters with strangers on trains and buses, he had carried on inquiries until at last he had published his findings in his book, *Imbumba yama Nyama*. And he told the attentive group:

"That book has galvanized many Xhosa readers into writing and sending me more names, more praise verses. And now, among the many things I am doing in my retirement from Fort Hare, I am working on a further edition and will incorporate the masses of fresh news I have received from people like *these!*" here lifting his hand and pointing to the pagan. Everyone looked at her as if for the first time, and older ladies showered congratulations on her. She gave a most engaging grin on finding herself the center of an uplifting little scene.

The pagan woman was all smiles now. She had quite lost herself and forgotten daily cares as the splendor of her lineage, her where-from, as we say, shone in glory before her and before my father—"A man who," as she put it to the company but indirectly addressing him, "was dazzling to her and hers because of his deeds, his fame, il-lustriousness, and blinding to behold now that he was in so dark a forest of grief."

She told him, smiling, "We are few left of that lineage, that house, oh, few indeed, father!" He discussed this decline and decimation with her at some length. Then changing his tone, my father teased her by punning on the praise name *Mafan'avele,* about how, decimated though they might be and almost vanished, yet there was that re-corded knack of her stock that it might reappear-for-no-apparent-reason, which naturally wound up the interview on a note that ev-eryone appreciated! And then he said, "Go then, *Ntlongontlongo,* and the Lord go with you."

She turned her radiant face away, in a smooth movement, that empty bucket poised on her head, and walked away, her skirts sweep-ing her heels.

From Drawn in Colour, *by Noni Jabavu, St. Martin's Press, Inc.,* *1962.*

BY LAURENS VAN DER POST

The world described here by Laurens van der Post is the world of the Bushmen, those few survivors of the First People of Africa. Once, the Bushmen roamed all over southern Africa. Their paintings may still be seen in scattered and remote caves. Now the few surviving tribes of these small, shy nomads have taken refuge in the desert of the Kalahari. They store their precious water in decorated ostrich egg shells and kill game when necessary with poisoned arrows.

The Bushmen live in a world where relationships between humans and the elements are intensely personal. With the Pygmies, they are the only survivors of the hunting and food-gathering neolithic culture. Their world is separated by more than miles from the twentieth century civilization with its skyscrapers and machines.

Laurens van der Post has made several journeys into the Kalahari in search of the vanishing Bushmen. In the following section from *The Heart of the Hunter,* he travels with a self-sufficient group: two Land Rovers and eight companions—a cook, a cameraman, guides and hunters, and their indispensible Bushman interpreter, Dabé.

We were still deep in the Kalahari moving slowly through a difficult tract of country into which the rains as yet had been unable to break. The farther we went in this way, the more we ourselves became affected by the desperation of the land. Though we carried enough food and water for our needs, the thirst, hunger, and fear of the earth became our own.

On the morning of the eighth day, the sun rose faster and angrier than usual. There seemed even to be no period of transition, short as it is in these latitudes at that time of year. At one minute it was dark and cool, the next blindingly light and hot. One of the remarkable features of life spent in these circumstances is that nature becomes an affair of personalities. Any scientific notions one might have held about it vanish quickly, until there is nothing of the abstract left in one's mind. Sun, moon, stars, wind, lightning, and rain all become great magnetic beings and one's relationship with them intensely personal. For instance, on this particular morning, dismayed by the onslaught of the day, I remember thinking of the sun as a powerful being driven mad by excess, leaping into the sky, beating his chest and shrieking "Look! Look! Look! Here I am."

As the day went on, the feeling of being locked up in a mad moment of the seasons increased. Within an hour it was so hot that the air began to run like melting glass. Long before noon the waves of heat were moving over the face of the desert so violently that everything upon it was blurred and broken up until the whole quicksilver scene looked as unsubstantial as a reflection of itself shattered in the surface of a gleaming pool by the impact of a stone.

The sky itself became a mirror filled with all sorts of incomplete bits of the scene thrown up at it by the heat from below. I saw the summit of a dune upside down in the sky stand upon the top of the real one whose base had been obliterated by the waves of heat. Fragments of trees, shrubs, and dry watercourses, which had suddenly lost their grip on the earth, were seen entangled with reflections of their partial selves in the polished sky. One reflection which held my attention for long because it appeared to have no connection with any of the shapes below and looked like some kind of Van Gogh train airborne on a heavenly journey, turned out to be the image of a deep, narrow cleft, still well below the horizon when we first saw its reflection thrown on the air.

By noon we were all searching for somewhere to rest our vehicles and ourselves. When a flag of green with silver stars and stripes showed up, I was prepared for it to be another illusion of the day, but nevertheless steered for it. Slowly stars and stripes diminished, the green increased, and finally there stood like a miracle before unbelievers a number of camel-thorn trees in leaf.

We stopped close by them. Someone jumped out of a vehicle and threw a handful of yellow dust in the air. The dust fell like lead without scattering and clearly there was no wind. Yet we turned our

Land Rovers in the direction from which the wind ought to come if there was ever to be any again, and drove them underneath the trees. We propped open their bonnets and unscrewed their radiator caps. Almost without having spoken to one another, we threw ourselves down in our first shade for days.

My companions were asleep at once, and how I envied them! I could do no more than rest my body. My eyes would not even stay shut: they kept on opening and searching the sky beyond those incredible leaves above me for a cloud. There was none except one slight white feather drifting down the blue like the emblem of the retreat of the storm of the evening before. Rain seemed farther off than ever. I lay there in this fashion for about half an hour, the high Kalahari noon hissing like a serpent in my ear. Then suddenly an urgent whisper broke through to me: "Moren! Master! Are you awake?"

It was Dabé, our old Bushman interpreter, who had grown very close to me. He had come as silently as only a Bushman can from the tree where characteristically he was resting alone. Not a single one of my companions, stretched out beside their vehicles and breathing heavily, was disturbed as he crept on his hands and knees to my side. There close to me, his lined and finely wrinkled face was puckered and creased against the violent light. His eyes barely showed, but the little that did was bright and alert.

"People! Out there, coming this way!" Straightening himself on his knees and waving a hand to the east, he spoke without waiting for my answer.

I got up immediately and walked with him into the open away from our sleeping companions. We stood in the sun and together looked and listened silently. I heard no sound except that of the day roaring like a furnace in my ears. "But I neither see nor hear any sign of them."

"You will. Just wait and listen, Moren!" He turned his head sideways and put a hand to his ear. We stood like that for some minutes more; then suddenly he grunted and said, "There they come! Surely you must hear them?"

I still did not hear anything except the day in my ears, but suddenly I saw the wings of a bird flicker in the distance and a dark little body alight on the top of the skeleton of a thorn tree. It stayed only a moment before taking off again and vanishing sideways behind a swell of heat. I thought the shape of a man briefly darkened the broken light underneath the tree like a figure walking in and out of a burning oven, but then it vanished behind some denser growths and I was no longer sure.

Dabé, however, had no doubts, exclaiming quickly, emotion deepening his voice, "You see! There they come, some more wild Bushmen!"

With that he walked towards the skeleton of thorn, calling out a formal greeting in his own tongue. Soon I and the rest of our party, now thoroughly awake, watched him bring a procession of little people towards us. They were a heartrending sight. Five grown-up men walked in front in single file. At first little more showed above the shimmer than the apricot gleam of their shoulders, the dark blur of their heads and the slender shafts of spears above them. Slowly their shapes became more solid and complete. We saw their bows held in one hand in front of them like some direction-finder of their determined spirit; then their legs, moving not with their normal resilience but at the slow, deliberate pace of men so exhausted that they appeared to be completing a nightmare ritual of their sleep. As they turned to avoid a clump of white thorn we noticed their spears were stuck into quivers crammed with arrows on their backs.

Between the men and the rest of their band there was a gap. They were close to us before the head and shoulders of the first six women and five children appeared out of the blaze in the east. The gap must have been greater because, when the first woman came into view, she had already broken into a pathetic attempt at running to catch up with the men. The others followed close on her heels with a strange stumbling lope, uttering the broken sounds of the hysteria of uncertainty between an old fear and a sudden new hope.

All of them were desperately thin, their cheeks hollow, lips black and cracked, and the dark brown eyes above the high cheekbones sunk deep into the shadows under their foreheads. The skin on their bodies was rough, and despite the heat of the day and their evident exertion utterly without sweat. They looked as if they had been burned in a terrible fire and the light in their eyes was hardly of the world any more. I have seen it only in the eyes of those close to death.

Yet such was their spirit that, as they stood before us at last on uncertain feet, they each raised a hand and politely gave us the traditional greeting of their race: "Good day. We saw you from afar and we are dying of hunger." I have known the greeting for many years, but only now did I seem to have a glimpse of the experience which had given it birth.

Their most immediate need, of course, was water. I was touched to notice that our three black servants had of their own accord already unloaded some jerrycans of water and were standing by to hand mugfuls of it to the Bushmen as fast as they arrived. They drank it in quantities that would have killed, I believe, any other people in the same condition.

Once their terrible thirst was quenched, they all sank down onto the sand in a kind of semicircle around us. The men sat with their heads bowed over arms clasped round their knees like long-distance runners recovering from the race of their lives. The women unslung the bundles tied in the shawls of duiker-skin on their backs and leaned on them as cushions. The children sat up tight against the thighs of their mothers, from time to time raising great oval eyes, shy with wonder, at us. The youngest woman of all took a small baby boy from her hip. His little body glowed like an apricot in the shade as she swung him to her breast. While he drank, the look on her face was so naked with tenderness that one felt an intruder watching her and looked away. It explained as no words could have done why the children were in better condition than the grown-ups.

They sat there thus, as if dazed with shock, not speaking for a while, though every now and then uttering wordless sounds to themselves. I was prepared for them to sit like that for hours, but they recovered with a speed which was impressive evidence of their quality. The first to do so was the woman who had come running after the men. She looked up suddenly to catch Jeremiah, our Barotse cook, who was filling a saucepan, spilling some drops of water on the sand. At once she was on her feet rebuking him in a low, clear, but stern voice for his waste. When he went to refill a can at the tap of one of the main tanks in the back of a Land Rover, she followed him, still protesting at his methods and clearly thinking he was unworthy of trust as a dispenser of water.

The sight of the clear water coming out of the tap, however, was magic to her and silenced her for a brief moment. Then in a voice ringing with wonder she called on the others to come and confirm the working of the miracle. Those with us jumped up and hastened to collect around her, an expression on their faces which made us feel we had never known before what water meant in the first spirit of men.

Suddenly the woman turned away from the bright flow at the tap and began examining the group of Bushmen as if counting heads. Dismay showed on her face and a cry of self-reproach broke from her. Running to her bundle of skin, she quickly untied it, took five ostrich egg shells from it, rushed back to the tap, and insisted on filling them with water immediately. That done, her hands shaking with haste, she plugged the openings in the shells with grass stoppers, ran back to her skin shawl, wrapped the shells carefully in it, and slung it round her shoulder. At an astonishingly firm pace she set out in the direction from which she had come, and soon vanished from sight.

We did not see her again until an hour and a half later, when she appeared leading a very old Bushman couple into our midst. They too were dreadfully thin; and yet, after having drunk only the water there was in five ostrich egg shells, they had been strong enough to come after us.

The old man was upright and very dignified. His behavior punctilious and formal, as if he bore all the responsibilities of a plenipotentiary of his race, appearing for the first time on a special mission among a foreign people. His old lady, dark and wrinkled with age like a passion fruit about to fall, had the sweetest of expressions on her face. She smiled at each of us tentatively like a young girl at her first ball.

Neither of them appeared fundamentally the worse for their experience. They needed no time even to catch their breath again after their long walk, but sat down at once to join with relish in eating the food we had distributed.

Meanwhile we had learned something of their story. They came from a plain called after a fabulous kind of sweet potato dug up there years ago. Their arms were not long enough to demonstrate the size of the potato to us. The plain was, as they put it in their tongue, "far, far, far away" to the east. It was lovely how the "far" came out of their mouths. At each "far" a musician's instinct made the voices themselves more elongated with distance, the pitch higher with remoteness, until the last "far" of the series vanished on a needle point of sound into the silence beyond the reach of the human scale. They left this "far, far, place" because the rains just would not come.

Their water was gone; the *tsamma*—melons which meanwhile sustained them and the game on which they live—were soon eaten up. The roots and tubers we compared to potatoes and turnips were more and more difficult to find and in any case not enough for survival.

The game had moved away first. Only snakes, lizards, scorpions, spiders, and some ants were left. Then one night lightning flashed over the horizon in the west. They knew at once what to do. Since they own nothing permanently which they cannot carry, they could act at once. The men just took up their bows, poisoned arrows, and spears and left the plain behind them; the women bundled up in skin shawls their water flasks of ostrich egg shells and their stamping blocks—the wooden pestles and mortars which are their most precious possessions and badge of womanhood. Grubbing sticks in hand, and for long hours with the youngest children on their hips, they followed their men. They made for the quarter in the west where the lightning flashed most. They had forgotten how many days they had walked towards the lightning, but they were "many, many, many."

The awful part was that, though the lightning went on flashing along the horizon every night, they seemed to get no nearer the rain. Their condition steadily deteriorated, the country became increasingly desolate, yet they had endured this sort of thing so often before that they took it entirely for granted. They seemed to think it hardly worth the effort of remembering and certainly not that of talking about it.

Yet despite the lack of detail and Dabé's difficulty in coping with their dialect, we gathered that on this cloudless day without the least hint of rain their desperation was nearing its climax. They had just left the old father and mother behind, not expecting ever to see them again, when they heard the sound of our Land Rovers.

We did not ask them what they would have done had they not met us, but the question provoked a lively discussion among my companions. The Bushmen had no food of any kind left. They had no water, and when I asked what they used instead of water they showed me some remains of a large root rather like an outsize turnip. They had six of these fragments in the slings carried by the women, and they were eighteen souls in all. By scraping the root with a wooden knife into their hands and squeezing the crushed material, they produced a bitter white juice which they said was better for thirst than water.

Water, the old father suddenly interjected, licking his lips at the memory of his last gallonful, was much too sweet.

I do not think we have ever made camp as fast or with so gay a spirit as we did then. It was as if a law without exceptions ordered these encounters with the Bushman in the Kalahari. Whether alone or in company, meeting him and giving him something no matter what or how little, even no more than a plug of tobacco, always made one feel fantastically happy.

We came across game quite early the next day and set about getting meat for the Bushmen as quickly as we could. The first buck we saw was a duiker. It had bolted on the first alarm and was already running full out when Wyndham spotted it. Normally he might not have shot, because it made an exceptionally difficult target. Once on the run a duiker never stops to look back.

Invariably it goes fast over bush and grass, its head down, showing little more than its back above the cover, all with a motion rather like that of a frightened porpoise diving in and out of the swell of the sea.

Today the shot was even more difficult than usual, for by the time Vyan had halted his vehicle and had his gun up, the back of the duiker was arching for the last time above a crest of the bush at the limit of our vision. Yet he brought it down with a deft instinctive shot, and the exclamation of wonder from the Bushman at my side was good to hear.

We went on for a while now without seeing more game or, what was far more discouraging, the spoor of any. When the noise of our vehicles finally woke a little steenbuck from his sleep and he rose out of the bed he makes more neatly and snugly perhaps than any other quadruped in Africa, I felt I had to shoot. Yet I hated doing it. For me the steenbuck has always been one of the loveliest and most lovable of African buck.

He stood as still and fine as an Etruscan statuette of himself. His delicate ears were pointed in my direction, his great purple eyes wide open, utterly without fear and shining only with the wonder of seeing so strange a sight at this remote back door of life.

Remembering the gaunt faces of the famished Bushmen, I shot quickly before he should get alarmed or the sight of his gentle being weaken me. I would not have thought it possible I could miss at so short a distance. Yet I did. My shot merely made the little buck shake

his delicate head vigorously to rid his ears of the tingle of the shock
of the explosion from my heavy gun. Otherwise he showed no trace
of alarm.

I took much more careful aim and shot a second time. Again I
missed. Still the little buck was unafraid. He just turned his head
slightly to snap at the wind raised by the bullet when it passed close
by his ears. So near was he to me that I saw his black patent leather
little nose pucker with the effort. I shot until the magazine of my
gun was empty and still he stood there unhurt, observing my Land
Rover keenly as if trying to discover what the extraordinary commo-
tion was about.

I believe he would have stood there indefinitely, taking in the
strangeness of the occasion, had I not entreated Vyan to shoot from
his vehicle much further away. Vyan succeeded merely in nicking
slightly the saffron petal of one of the steenbuck's ears. Only then did
the steenbuck whisk swiftly about, a look of reproach in his eyes. The
sun flashing briefly on the tips of his black polished toes, he vanished
with a nimble bound in the scrub.

I drove on very much aware that I had not lightened what promised just then to become the long task of getting enough food for the
Bushmen and, now that the steenbuck was safely gone, more put out
than I cared to admit by such poor marksmanship. Yet I was even
more disconcerted to find both Dabé and the new Bushman apparently highly delighted at the outcome of the affair. Indeed I expected
my companions to pull my leg about the incident for days to come.
Yet delight in someone so famished as our new companion so amazed
me that I interrupted something he was saying, a wide smile on his
fine-drawn face.

"What on earth has he said to please you so?" I asked the grinning
Dabé.

"Oh! He is just saying what we all know to be so," Dabé answered
in the indulgent manner of someone instructing an ignorant child.
"The steenbuck is protected with great magic and very difficult to
kill."

"What sort of magic?" I asked, remembering my association of the
buck with my childhood world of magic. "His own magic or the
magic of other people?"

"Oh. Just magic!" Dabé said in a superior voice, leaving unsatis-
fied the curiosity which always nagged me more than ever when the

curtain between the mind of the Bushman and our own lifted, only to flop back just as I thought I was to be allowed to see behind it. Yet my imagination had seized on the encounter more firmly than I knew. Throughout the long hot day, at all sorts of odd moments, my mind returned to the vision of that gentle little buck standing untroubled amid blast after blast from my gun.

Luckily for the Bushmen, Ben and Vyan were better and more dedicated marksmen than I. Soon afterwards we ran into more game and within two hours they had killed another duiker, two springbuck rams, and a lone old male ostrich. All that meat turned into biltong should last the Bushmen well into the country where the rains had broken. Stopping only to disembowel the game, we turned back, and traveling in the same tracks for the third time, found them so firm that we made our camp at the fall of night.

In our absence the camp had been transformed. Apart from the kitchen fires, another large fire was lit in the center and by its light we saw our companions and the Bushmen waiting together like old friends for our return. They started at once unloading the game, and went straight on to skinning and cutting up the animals with skill and dispatch. I watched them, absorbed in the grace of their movements. They worked with extraordinary reverence for the carcasses at their feet. There was no waste to mock the dead or start a conscience over the kill. The meat was neatly sorted out for specific uses and placed in separate piles on the skin of each animal.

All the time the women stood around and watched. They greeted the unloading of each arrival with an outburst of praise, the ostrich receiving the greatest of all, and kept up a wonderful murmur of thanksgiving which swelled at moments in their emotion to break on a firm phrase of a song of sheer deliverance. How cold, inhuman, and barbarous a civilized butcher's shop appeared in comparison!

The last red glow in the west died down behind the purple range of cloud, and it went utterly dark beyond our camp. Our own fire rose higher than ever, straining like a Gothic sphere towards the stars which were appearing in unusual numbers. Soon the stars were great and loud with light until the sky trembled like an electric bell, while every now and then from the horizon the lightning swept a long sort of lighthouse beam over us. At last the Bushmen stood up from their work with a deep sigh of satisfaction, scraped the blood from their arms with their knives and wiped their hands on stubbles of grass.

The women and children came silently forward to help them carry
away the meat piled on the skins. They vanished in the darkness beyond our fire, and only the sound of voices joined there in a common
purpose revealed that they had not gone for good. Then the voices
too faded out, and soon after the flames of their own fires began to
go up one by one. As always their fires were more circumspect than
our own. Ours was a cathedral of flame, theirs little more than slender candles burning in a night devout under stars.

The sight stirred me deeply. Never before had I had them all
around me for a whole night. Perhaps it was something unique and
could never happen again? The thought was too much for me. I told
my companions not to wait for me but to start the evening meal. I
got Dabé to accompany me and walked slowly towards the farthest of
the Bushman fires.

Out there between our camp and their shelters the desert was as
dark and still as I have ever known it. The only other living things
capable of uttering a sound were snakes, and no serpent would have
been so foolish as to hiss while about his business on a night so profound. There was no fitful air of summer even, no heat eddy of the
frightful day spinning about to rustle what was left of leaf and grass
on the scorched earth. But there was this intense electric murmur of
the stars at one's ears.

Then suddenly, ahead in a band of absolute black with no fire or
reflection of fire to pale it down, I thought I heard the sound of a
human voice. I stopped at once and listened carefully. The sound
came again more distant, like the voice of a woman crooning over a
cradle. I stood with my back to the horizon bright with portents of
lightning, waiting for my eyes to recover from the glare of our great
campfire. Slowly, against the water light of the stars lapping briskly
among the breakers of thorn and hardwood around us, emerged the
outline of a woman holding out a child in both her hands, high
above her head, and singing something with her own face lifted to
the sky. Her attitude and the reverence trembling in her voice moved
me so that the hair at the back of my neck stood on end.

"What's she doing?" I whispered to Dabé, who had halted without
a sound, like my own star shadow beside me.

"She's asking the stars up there," he whispered, like a man requested in the temple of his people to explain to a stranger a most
solemn moment of their ritual. "She's asking the stars to take the lit-

tle heart of her child and to give him something of the heart of a star in return."

"But why the stars?" I asked.

"Because, Moren," he said in a matter-of-fact tone, "the stars up there have heart in plenty and are great hunters. She is asking them to take from her little child his little heart and to give him the heart of a hunter."

The explanation moved me to a silence which Dabé mistook. Afraid, I suspect, that like most of the people he knew in his life of exile, I would scorn a Bushman's belief, he wanted reassurance immediately.

"But why don't you say something, Moren?" he asked, almost like an anxious child. "Surely you must know that the stars are great hunters? Can't you hear them? Do listen to what they are crying! Come on! Moren! You are not so deaf that you cannot hear them."

I have slept out under the stars in Africa for too many years not to know that they sound and resound in the sky. From the time I was born until I first went to school, I slept outside a house every night except when it was raining—and that was seldom. My first memories are of the incomparable starlight of the high veld of Southern Africa and the far sea-sound that goes with it.

I hastened to say, "Yes, Dabé, of course I hear them!" But then I was forced to add, "Only I do not know what they are saying. Do you know?"

Reassured, he stood for a moment head on one side, while the light of another flash from the horizon flew like a ghostmoth by us. Then, with the note of indulgence he could not resist using on me when he felt his authority not in doubt, he said, "They are very busy hunting tonight and all I hear are their hunting cries: 'Tssik!' and 'Tsá!' "

Had it not been for the darkness between us he would have seen, I am sure, the shock of amazement on my face. I had known those sounds all my life. Ever since I can remember, we ourselves had used them out hunting with our dogs. "Tssik!" repeated sharply thrice was the sound we used to alert our dogs when we were at the cover of bush, grass, cave, or donga in which we suspected our quarry to be hiding. Hearing it, the ears of our dogs would immediately prick up, their eyes shine with excitement, and their noses sniff the air diligently for scent. Another "Tssik" would send them to search the cover. "Tsá" was the final imperative note which released them from all restraint and launched them after our chosen quarry when it was flushed.

I had always wondered about the origin of these sounds. Neither of them had ever seemed European to me. I had asked the oldest of the old people of all races and colors. I asked one of the greatest of all African hunters, too. They could only say that, like me, they had been born into a world in which they were already in long-established use.

Stranger still, wherever I went in the world I found that, although hunters outside Africa did not know the sounds and therefore did not use them with their dogs, if I tried them out many of the dogs responded.

The revelation filled me with awe. I felt as if I had been allowed to witness the coming of the word in the darkness before time. I thought this was enough of magic in a day which in my encounter with the little steenbuck had begun with magic. My instinct was not to disturb the woman in so solemn an act of dedication. I thought of walking away into the desert; but the woman had already become aware of our presence. She lowered the child quickly, clasped it tightly to her bosom, and murmured in its ear some words burning with love, before placing it firmly in the classical Bushman position on her hip. Then she came deliberately towards us and, recognizing us, greeted us politely: "I am only a poor woman and I have had no time to prepare my place properly, but will you not come and sit by my fire?"

She said "my place" as though it were some stately country house, though it was just a patch of sand scrupulously cleared of grass and thorn and scooped out into a round shallow hollow. The skin on which she and her husband slept was already spread out in the bottom. Where their heads were to lie, branches of thick thorn were planted in the sand at an angle to keep from their faces the night air and the heavy dew that often falls so mysteriously in the desert. The man's bow and quiver full of poisoned arrows hung from one of the branches well out of the reach of young children; his spear was stuck in the sand beside them. The family's combined stock of ostrich eggshells, fifteen in all, now full of water, were arranged firmly upright in the sand piled crescentwise against the foot of the screen of branches. The woman's wooden mortar and pestle, or stamping block as we call it in Africa, stood nearby with her grubbing stick of

ironwood beside it. On some coals drawn to the side of the neat little
fire, strips of meat were laid to grill: with the subtle savor of wood
smoke they spread a most provocative smell on the still air. Small and
poorly appointed as her "place" was, it had been arranged to satisfy
some inner need of order.

Standing by her place with an endearing air of domestic pride, she
explained that her husband was away with the other men, spreading
the meat strips on the higher thorn bushes to dry in safety. She was
certain he would not be long, so again would we please sit by the fire.
She stooped to brush the clean sand with her hand, as a woman
might smooth a satin cushion for a guest in her drawing room. The
dark head of the star-dedicated child wobbled on her hip, but his eyes
remained tightly shut. However, we excused ourselves and moved on
to do a round of all the fires.

At each of the fires we saw the same level of shelter, the minimum
of material possessions, and the women with their children, centered
and at home beside their hearth. They received us with striking self-
possession. They appeared never at a loss for a word, expressing
themselves eloquently in soft voices and with many a vivid gesture.
Despite their terrible privations they welcomed us as if they had
riches and security for all. But as their men were still away working
somewhere in the outer darkness, we passed on until we found by the
last fire the old couple who had nearly had to be abandoned forever.

It was impossible to tell from the appearance or behavior of the
two that something well-nigh fatal had happened to them only the
morning before. The old lady was pounding some freshly grilled
meat to pulp in her stamping block, since neither her teeth nor her
husband's were good enough to chew venison whole. Like an over-
burdened housewife determined that nothing shall interrupt her
routine, she barely greeted us; but not so her husband. He was lying
on the sand on his side, his legs curled up and his body supported on
one elbow. Two little boys sat against him, each with an arm over his
legs. The moment they saw us, they all sat up straight and he gave us
an easy greeting. I asked who the two little boys were. He said, his
voice warm with pride, that they were his grandsons. "Their place"
was by the fire farthest from his own. They never failed, he added,
his hand on the head of the eldest, to come to him every night for
"some man's talk."

The old lady ceased pounding at the sound of my question and waited, pestle suspended over mortar, for his answer: when it was given, she resumed her work so eagerly that the wooden block resounded like a drum starting up a march.

Dabé and I sat down near them. The children looked up at me out of their slanted eyes, examining my face without fear, as I told him I too would be grateful for "some man's talk" with him.

For example, was it true that the stars were hunters? Did the little steenbuck really possess great magic, and if so, what sort of magic? His eyes brightened, and he said, "Yes. Oh, yes! Yes! It is true: the stars are hunters."

"All the stars?" I asked, my heart beating faster.

He paused for just a second, then it all came out at length. Yes! They were all hunters, great hunters, but some were greater than others. For instance there was that star there! He raised his thin old arm to point with a long finger at the brightest star in the Great Dipper. It just cleared the fringe of a camel-thorn tree and in the dry air was bright enough to lay a water-sheen on the topmost leaves. That star, he said, was a great hunter who hunted in faraway dangerous places in the shape of a lion. Could I not see how fierce its eye shone and hear the distant murmur of its roar? And there was one even greater! He pointed at Sirius, the star of the dog, at the head of the belted and nimble Orion.

Yes! You had only to look at it once, the old father said, to see what a great hunter it was. Could I not see how fat it was, how heavily it sat there in the midst of plenty in the sky? He paused and I hastened to ask, afraid that silence might cool the subject, "Is it the greatest of all the hunters up there?"

From the delight that shone in his eyes, I realized the pause had been a trap set to catch just that question. He shook his head vigorously. The greatest hunter was not there yet. It hunted in the darkest and most dangerous places of all, so far away that we could not see it yet. We could see it only in the early morning when it came nearer on its way home. There, there was a hunter for you!

The old father made a lively whistling sound of wonder at the greatness of the hunter. Yes, just before the dawn one could see him striding over the horizon, his eye bold and shining, an arrow ready in his bow. When he appeared, the night whisked around to make way for him, the red dust spurting at its black heels. He broke off and shook his gray old head as he once more uttered that sound of wonder, before asking as if the thought had just come to him: "But can't you hear for yourself the cries of the hunt going on up there?"

I assured him I could. He gave a grunt of satisfaction and leaned back on both his elbows with a look on his face as if to say, "Well, then! There is nothing more to be said about it."

I took the hint and changed the subject. I reminded him of my question about the steenbuck and its magic. He sat up and beat the sand with the side of his hand for emphasis. Of course the steenbuck had magic, great magic! Surely everyone knew that; even the children, like his grandsons there, knew it.

"But, old father," I insisted, "I do not know it. What sort of magic is it? What does it do?"

He answered readily enough. But the subject now was far more complicated than that of the stars as hunters. The assumptions on which his explanations were based had no parallel in our own thinking. Dabé, who always had his difficulties with the dialect not quite his own, struggled valiantly to find equivalents in either Sechuana or Afrikaans for me, but I suspect often failed.

I gathered that the magic of the steenbuck was that of the innocent, the gentle, and the beautiful combined in one. It was a creature—or a person, as he called it—too beautiful to be aware of imperfection, too innocent to know fear, too gentle to suspect violence. How it differed from the duiker! Had I not noticed that the heart of the duiker was full of suspicion and fear? At the first strange sound it assumed the worst and bounded away as fast as it could without a backward glance.

The steenbuck, however, when disturbed would stand quietly beside "its place" and look without fear out of its great eyes, its "little ears trembling and nicely pointed" to see what the wonderful noise could be about. The old father's eyes as he spoke seemed to become young and eager like the steenbuck's, his own Pan-like ear to point and tremble with innocent curiosity. The steenbuck, he said, would stand there all the time "looking so nicely and acting so prettily" that the person who had come hunting it would begin to feel "he must look nicely at the steenbuck and act prettily too."

The person who stood watching would suddenly find there was "a steenbuck person" behind him who "feeling he was looking nicely at the little buck, wanted him to act nicely and prettily too." When the person who had come to kill the steenbuck fitted the arrow to his bow and aimed to shoot, the steenbuck person behind him "pulled at his arm and made him miss." Yes, that was the magic of the steenbuck; it had a steenbuck person to protect it.

I should perhaps have left the matter there, but I could not resist an obvious question. Why if that were so, I asked, was the steenbuck ever killed? He looked at me almost in pity, as if I needed a reminder of the New Testament injunction that "it may be true that evil comes but woe to him by whom it comes."

Yes, he agreed in the end, steenbuck were killed despite their magic, just as the duiker was killed in spite of its speed and suspiciousness. Yet more steenbuck survived than were killed. Certainly in all his long years its numbers had never become less. How could so small and defenseless an animal have survived in a world full of powerful enemies without great magic? His old eyes here were suddenly childlike with mischief and he looked past me, as if he saw "a steenbuck person" standing beside me, to say he had been told I had tried hard that very morning to kill a little steenbuck and failed. Perhaps he had been misinformed, but if not . . .

That wonderful laugh of the Bushman broke from Dabé. The old lady, the children, the old man and I myself joined in: we made such a noise that the people from the nearby fires and the men at work in the dark all came running over to find out what the fun was about. By the time the joke was explained and they too had had their laugh, which invariably caused everyone else to laugh all over again, the chance for more "man's talk" with the old father had gone. I left them still giggling and went back to our camp.

Tired as I was after months of exceptional exertion without a single day of rest, my imagination was so stirred by the talk that I lay awake for hours and did not notice their passing. I thought of James Jeans telling me when I was a boy that every time a man lifted a finger he moved the stars. The important thing for me now was that the stars moved us as well and we all moved together. I felt a certain envy of the little apricot boy, and wished that I, too, had started life as godchild to a star.

From The Heart of the Hunter, *by Laurens van der Post, Morrow, 1961.*

The Way of the Ancestors

BY COLIN TURNBULL

Colin Turnbull is an authority on the peoples of Africa. Born and educated in England, he is now on the staff of the American Museum of Natural History. As an anthropologist, he spends more time in Africa than at his desk in New York. His most intensive studies concern the Pygmies in the Congo where he spent three years in the Ituri Forest. His research and writings about Pygmies may be found in *The Forest People* and also in *The Peoples of Africa* from which the following selection is taken. Of the Pygmies, he says: "It would be hard to find a more highly developed sense of respect, justice, and true morality."

In all his writings, Colin Turnbull stresses the values of African culture. In *The Lonely African* he examines the values and effects of tribalism on the African of today. One of the characters he portrays is Matungi, a wise and stern chief who says: "The white man talks of law where we talk of the way of our ancestors; he talks of what is right or wrong where we talk of what is good or bad. I have looked at their way and do not like it, and I do not believe it is good for our people."

Throughout their daily lives the traditional Africans are constantly remembering the past, remembering their ancestors. They are constantly performing little ritual acts. They do not always make a great fuss; it may amount to no more than throwing a few grains of food into the forest. Or it may be a great ceremony in which hundreds of members of the tribe take part, involving weeks of preparation. But all the time, every day, the ancestors are remembered in some way.

There are certain occasions, like birth, when it is particularly important to remember. This is taken pretty much as a matter of course, but there are always some special things that have to be done, offerings to be made to the family shrine, perhaps. And when the child is named, which may not be for some time, it is an even more important occasion, and he may be given the name of some elderly or dead relative, so that a name never dies with the body. The next important occasion during the life of the individual occurs when he or she is ready to take on adult responsibilities. This is the time for initiation of one kind or another. It prepares you further for this life, but it also prepares you for the next, and makes you pleasing to the ancestors. This is often the biggest and most important of all tribal ceremonies.

Then comes marriage, and married life is full of small daily observances as the couple go about their work. For them the final act is, of course, death and burial. Burial may be accomplished with little formality, as among the hunters or Masai pastoralists. Among the cultivators, it is generally attended by much more elaborate ritual, and in the case of the complex tribes with chiefs or kings at their head, the burial of the nobility can be extremely costly, calling for a long period of mourning during which the bereaved family sometimes has to feed all the mourners, making great sacrifices.

On all these occasions the family takes part, the number of relatives included depending on the particular context. There are times, then, when the family unites, when members who are otherwise separated may meet and renew old friendships. Probably death brings more of the family together than any other event, and the death of a chief or king involves the entire family—that is to say the tribe or nation. So once again we see the African sense of family loyalty emerging, here on occasions of what might be called crisis. For in a sense even marriage is a crisis, for it involves either the boy's or girl's leaving his or her parents and joining another group as a stranger; it means that they have committed their families just as they are bound as individuals; it means that each is now to be put to the real test.

At times of lesser crisis the family need not be called upon to take part, but the people may use what we loosely refer to as magic. It is difficult for us to understand because much of the magic that is performed is obviously, to us, without any effect. When a man lets some moss fall from his fingers, held above his head, and blows on it so that it blows away from him, we know that this will not cause the rain clouds to pass over him, as he hopes they will. Maybe he knows it too though, and it may be no more than calling the attention of the ancestors, the spirits, or of God himself, to his plight. Many so-called magical acts are really acts of faith and correspond more to the western notion of prayer than anything else.

Then there are moments when the individual feels powerless and asks for help from the ritual specialist, that much-misunderstood person we generally call the witch doctor. He would be better known simply as the doctor, because he has much the same kind of profession. Often he knows medically effective treatments, some of them even more powerful than modern drugs, such as antidotes to snake bite, and antiseptics used on open wounds. When he does not know a remedy, however, he pretends that he does. We all know that if a sick person believes that he is going to get well, part of the battle is already won. And so it may be that the belief in the doctor, even if his medicines and incantations are of no medical use, will help toward recovery.

But the doctor is more than just the healer of bodies. He is also often the healer of wounded pride, of hostility, of enmity. Because of the importance of his position and the fact that he is so greatly respected, he usually knows everything that is going on in the community. So when someone falls ill, he may give his verdict that the illness has been caused by someone else causing the sick person harm by witchcraft. This is a serious accusation, and everyone will want to know who the witch is.

The belief is that witchcraft is a substance which is usually found in the stomach. The witch may not even know that he has it, and it makes him do things he would not do otherwise. He can not be absolutely blamed for what it makes him do, but if he finds he has it, he has either got to get rid of it in some way, or render it ineffective.

The doctor will find out who the witch is by divination. Throwing bones or using a rubbing board are some of his methods. The bones fall in a certain pattern which he interprets much like reading tea leaves in a cup. The rubbing board is rubbed with a finger or a lump of wood while the doctor asks it questions. When his finger sticks, he has the answer Yes. He will ask all sorts of questions, and because of his knowledge of all the local gossip, and by watching his patient very carefully, he will eventually name someone who perhaps had some personal grievance against the sick man. That person is formally accused of being a witch, and of course he will deny it. All he has to do is to take medicine that will render the witchcraft substance harmless, if he has it, and then everyone is happy. He is not punished in any way, though he may have to pay a small fine of some chickens, and perhaps drink beer with his enemy, or provide a feast to show publicly that there has been a reconciliation.

You may ask how this helps, what good it does. It may not help the sick man get well, although it may give him confidence. It is done primarily because in this way the enmity between the two people is made public—everyone knows about it. This means that they will not dare to harm each other in any way, because then they will be accused immediately, and this time they will, if found guilty, be subject to much more serious punishment. In this way the doctor helps greatly to keep the peace and the law in his community.

Sorcery is something quite different, and is everywhere regarded as evil. It is believed that certain people who have this witchcraft substance in their stomachs come to know about it and deliberately use it to further their own ends. Or else they may sell their power to others. Nobody will ever admit to being a sorcerer, for by definition a sorcerer is an enemy of society, while a doctor is its protector. Even so, the belief that such people exist is not a meaningless fantasy.

Suppose a violent quarrel breaks out between two members of a tribe, and in a fight the one accidentally kills the other. We would say that he was guilty of manslaughter or murder and punish him accordingly. But in Africa the traditional legal system works differently. An African tribunal would investigate the cause of the quarrel, and might find that in fact the man who died was a real troublemaker and had provoked the fight. Someone has to be made responsible for the death, otherwise a feud would result between the two families, each killing each other in retaliation; yet to accuse the survivor of murder would be an obvious injustice.

He can not, however, be excused by saying he was made to kill by witchcraft substance in his stomach, because generally witchcraft substance works at night when the witch is asleep and does not know about it. This man killed in daylight, in the middle of a fight. So then the doctor says that the cause was sorcery. As nobody ever admits to being a sorcerer, there is nobody to punish; but the man actually responsible for the death is excused. The doctor "proves" his case by divination, or by consulting some oracle and getting the appropriate answer. He will give his judgment, not saying that the dead man deserved to die, but that some sorcerer, unknown, caused his death through the hand of the man who fought him. He will say that the power of the sorcerer is great, and that it must be defeated by an even more powerful sacrifice.

In this way he threatens everyone concerned, hinting that if they do not do what he says, then more killings will occur. He tells them to kill a goat and prepare a feast for the ancestors. He supervises the ritual side of the feast, but an essential part is that the two families —that of the dead man and that of his slayer—are made to sit down together and share the same food. This is a sign that peace is restored between them, that there will be no feud. The honor of the dead man's family is maintained; the man responsible for the death is not held responsible, but will probably have to pay the cost of the feast in order to "clean the blood from his hands."

To the African the letter of the law is not so important as the spirit of the law. The spirit of the law involves a sense of family obligation, either at the level of the individual family or that of the tribe. The doctor, or witch doctor, is one of the people best fitted to interpret the law in this spirit, and the beliefs in magic, witchcraft, and sorcery enable him to do so with extreme justice and wisdom. Without these institutions he would be powerless, and there would be no law.

There are other things which sound even stranger to our ears, and which might appear even more "savage." Yet again if we look at them in their whole context, they seem quite different, and understandable. Let's take just one, perhaps the most frightening of all —the Leopard Man Society. There are various forms of this spread widely across West and Central Africa, differing greatly from each other. Perhaps the best known, and the most misunderstood, is the Anyota society of the BaBali people, in the east-central Congo. The common idea about the society was that its members simply dressed up as leopards and went off, usually at the command of the chief, to kill his enemies. They were thought of as common murderers and cannibals. But in fact they were something quite different and were highly respected.

In times of crisis, the great need in tribal life is for the tribe to be firmly united. If the tribe weakens and divides amongst itself, then neighboring tribes may combine and attack. One of the most dangerous times of all occurs when a chief or king dies. Amongst the BaBali people the chief may have several wives, and the sons of any of them may succeed him. There is a great deal of rivalry between the wives, each one naturally wanting her son to become the new chief. Because of family feeling, the tribe will divide its loyalties, each group supporting its own family member. Something has to be done to bring the people together, rapidly and effectively. The Anyota society exists for this purpose.

Its members are chosen when they have proven themselves, as youths, to be strong and fit, and above all to be respectful of the ways of the ancestors. They are bound by the most powerful oaths. At times of crisis, when the problem is acute and can not readily be solved in any other way, the members of the Anyota take action. They dress like leopards, painting the body with spots, covering it with a leopard skin or spotted cloth, wearing a leopard mask. As they do this they gradually identify themselves with this, their chosen symbol, the leopard. They fix metal claws to their hands, razor sharp, and they become leopards.

The leopard is the symbol of death, for it brings death silently, swiftly, and without discrimination. The leopard strikes young and old, good and bad; its behavior can never be predicted. It is as sure as it is mysterious, and it also possesses many of the qualities admired by the Africans. It has the beauty and grace of a dancer, the physical strength and courage of a hunter and fighter. But above all it is the bringer of death. The ancestors have passed beyond death, and it is impossible to join them without dying. They may be invoked to give aid, but the way of the Anyota is more direct.

A man becomes a leopard. He loses all his personal identity; he moves and thinks like the bringer of death. He stands at the threshold of death and of the afterlife. Through this identification he is able to contact the ancestors in the world beyond death, and receive their instructions. Acting on their instructions, with their blessing, he lives for a short while as a leopard; he lies in wait and he kills. He does not choose his victim because he belongs to this family or that, because now he thinks like a leopard, not a man. So he hides in a tree, down by the river, just where the leopards would, and he chooses his victims just as a leopard would. This means that he generally kills women and children, for a leopard will not attack a group of armed men, or any large group of people. But he will kill a single woman or child coming down to get water. And having killed, just like the leopard, tearing the jugular vein with his claws, the leopard-man eats—just like the leopard. A small portion of the body is eaten; the rest is left. After this he becomes a man again, and he does not know what he has done.

The villagers find the body, and they know what has happened, for although one such killing may be thought to be by a real leopard, a whole series will not. And although the Anyota leave leopard footprints with a special wooden club they use, they can not always hide their human tracks. Usually after a couple of killings the people know for certain that the Anyota is taking action. They know that for as long as the crisis continues, for as long as they continue to disagree amongst themselves, the ancestors will command the Anyota to kill and eat. The killing is horrible enough, particularly as no one knows who is going to be killed next. But even worse for these people is the thought that their own people are eating human flesh, for this is as repugnant to them as it is to us. It is precisely because the whole thing is so terrible that the society does its job. The disagreement is quickly resolved, and once the tribe is united again, the ancestors are pacified, and the Anyota is forgotten. But the threat is always there, and it serves as a constant warning.

In a way, the tribe has committed a crime against the ancestors by disagreeing amongst itself. It is a crime that could bring disaster, even death, to innocent members, particularly if they are invaded by a hostile tribe. So there has to be punishment, and the situation has to be resolved. This is their way of doing it. Everyone shares the responsibility equally, the tribe being considered at this level as one family, so the punishment may fall anywhere with equal justice. And with only one or two deaths, perhaps the whole tribe is saved. Viewed in this light, as a means of preserving the tribe from even greater evil, it is better understood.

And so it is with so many of the customs we consider as strange and barbaric. We have to try and see them in their proper surroundings, not to imagine them as being part of our own society. And if we do this, we find that even when customs seem most different from our

own, they are usually working for exactly the same ends that we consider right and good: the maintenance of accepted morality, the
preservation of individual rights, the safety of the tribe (or nation),
in accordance with their belief in the will of the ancestors or God.

From The Peoples of Africa, *by Colin Turnbull, World Publishing,*
1962.

Part 2

CURRENTS AND CROSS-CURRENTS

"Strong family relationships, a spirit of kindness and forgiveness, love of music, dance and rhythm, a willingness to live and let live, such are the currents and cross-currents of emotions which help to determine the shape of things in Africa."

—D. K. Chisiza in "The Outlook for Contemporary Africa"
in *Journal of Modern African Studies,* March 1963

The Coming of the Pink Cheeks

BY CHIEF KABONGO

AS TOLD TO RICHARD ST. BARBÉ BAKER

Kabongo was a chief of the Kikuyus in Kenya. His life spanned a
period of eighty years—the happy days of his youth and the trou-
bled, anxious years after the coming of the white man. Among the
Europeans who came to Kenya was a forest officer, Richard St. Barbé
Baker, the only white man ever initiated into the Kikuyu Council of
Elders. He wrote a book, *Kabongo,* in which he set down in the
Chief's own words the story of the changes that took place in his life-
time.

There were two prophecies among the Kikuyu concerning the
white men. One was the prophecy of a medicine man who dreamt
that strangers would come, with sticks that made fire and an iron
snake no arrows could kill. He warned the Kikuyu against these
strangers.

Another medicine man, a rain-bringer, had a different prophecy.
He dreamt that the god of their people, Ngai, spoke to him, saying:
"A people from over the seas will come, a people with pink cheeks
and pink ears. When they come, listen well to their words, for they
are a wise people and will bring you good."

So it happened that when the "Pink Cheeks" came to East Africa,
Kabongo's tribe welcomed them. One man leased land to them for
planting until such time as his grandsons were grown. Others sent
their sons to the white man's schools. Still others went to work for
them in their big *shambas,* or farms, further north.

For some years my eldest son had been going to a school kept by
some Pink Cheeks only two hours' journey away. These were not
the White Fathers, to whom my brother had gone, but were quite

different. They wore clothes like the Pink Cheeks who farmed, and many of them were women. They had a medicine house where there were many ill people; there were good medicine–men and good things were done and sick people were made well. Every day my son would go before the sun was high and would come back before the sun set. Then he would eat and fall asleep, too tired to sit around the fire and be told the stories and history of our people or hear of the work that had been done or learn the customs and ways of our people and their laws and conduct.

It was in these days that a Pink Cheek man came one day to our Council. He came from far, from where many of these people lived in houses made of stone and where they held their own Council.

He sat in our midst and he told us of the king of the Pink Cheeks, who was a great king and lived in a land over the seas.

"This great king is now your king," he said. "And this land is all his land, though he has said you may live on it as you are his people and he is as your father and you are as his sons."

This was strange news. For this land was ours. We had bought our land with cattle in the presence of the Elders and had taken the oath and it was our own. We had no king, we elected our Councils and they made our laws. A strange king could not be our king and our land was our own. We had had no battle, no one had fought us to take away our land as, in the past, had sometimes been. This land we had had from our fathers and our fathers' fathers, who had bought it. How then could it belong to this king?

With patience, our leading Elder tried to tell this to the Pink Cheek and he listened. But at the end he said, "This we know. But in spite of this, what I have told you is a fact. You have now a king—a good and great king who loves his people and you are among his people. In the town called Nairobi is a council or government that acts for the king. And his laws are your laws."

For many moons this thing was much talked of by us. Then, when no more Pink Cheeks came and things went on as they had always been, we spoke no more.

Sometimes we heard of strange happenings, or even saw them our-selves, but for the most part life was still as it had always been. The Iron Snake, which I had never seen, had come and had carried men on it, not of our people; then a big path was made through the coun-try half a day from our land. It was wide enough for three elephants to walk abreast. And stones were laid on it and beaten flat, so that grain could have been threshed there.

As the years passed and more and more strange things happened, it seemed to me that this path or road was a symbol of all changes. It was along this road now that came news from other parts; and along it came the new box-on-wheels that made men travel many days' journey in one day and that brought things for the market that the women wanted to have, clothes or beads to wear and pots for cooking. Along this road the young men went when they left to work with the Pink Cheeks and along it too they went when that day came that they traveled to fight in the war over the sea that the Pink Cheeks made against each other.

It was along this road that many did not come back and some came with no legs, or who could not see. Two of my sons went and only one came back, and he brought only one hand and many strange new ideas and tales. Along that road, too, went the trees that men cut down when they made more and more farms. Without trees to give shade the ground was hot and dry and food grew not well.

By the time that my father, Kimani, died and his spirit joined those of our ancestors, our own land was poor too. For even though many of our family had gone away to work for the Pink Cheeks, our numbers had increased and there was now no room for the land to rest and it was tired. The food it grew was poor and there was not enough grown on it for all to eat. Those of our family who worked for the Pink Cheeks sent us food and coins that we could buy food with, for else we could not live.

Little by little, too, the rains fell less. When I was a boy I remember the rains came in plenty twice every year, the little rains and the big rains and on the hottest days there would be heavy dews, for the trees kept the land cool.

Now it was different; now the little rains had gone and the big rains had become little rains. The big rivers had become little ones and dried up in the hottest time and I saw this was not good.

Now that my father, Kimani, was dead, I had been chosen Muramati of our mbari. I was also now a Ceremonial Elder, a member of the Sacrificial Council.

It seemed to me that Ngai was tired of us. He sent so little rain. We must ask him to look upon us again and must sacrifice a ewe to please him.

I spoke of this one evening and the Elders said it was good to make sacrifice, for the time of rain had long passed. So the day was fixed and I was chosen to be the leader at this ceremony.

Little Kabongo, my eldest grandson, who bore my name according to our custom, sat with us; he spoke then as do the young age group today before their elders, but which when we were young we did not.

"That is good," he said. "For three weeks the Pastor at the Mission School has prayed for rain."

"Which will send rain, do you think, the God of the Pink Cheeks or Ngai?" asked a small boy.

"Neither," announced a young man, son of one of my brothers who was a schoolteacher. "I have read in books that it is the trees that make the rains come. Now the trees are cut down there is no rain. In the Sacred Grove on the hills there is rain."

The small boy was listening, full of wonder.

"And who makes the trees grow? Surely that is God," said my grandson. "For the Pastor says that God made everything, that God is greater than Ngai."

Such discussions among the young were frequent and to hear them made me sad. For this new learning seemed to pull this way and that way so that no one knew what was right.

But all this talk did not make more food nor bring us rain.

As there was now so little land and we were so many, the boys as they became men would go away, some to work on farms for the Pink Cheeks, some to a new kind of school-farm for men where they learned the new customs and also some curious ways; for these grown men were made to play games like little boys, running after balls which they threw. This they did instead of good work.

Munene, one of my younger brothers, had been one of these. He had been away a long time and when he came back he wore clothes like a Pink Cheek and he came with one of them, in a box-on-wheels, which is called motor-car, along the new road.

The Pink Cheek called a Council together and when all, both Elders and the young men, were assembled and sat round, he spoke. He spoke of Munene; he told us of his learning and of his knowledge of the customs of the Pink Cheeks and of his cleverness at organizing.

"Because of this," he said, "and because he is a wise man, the Government, the Council of Muthungu that meets in Nairobi, have honored him and, in honoring him, are honoring you all."

He paused and looked around at us. Beside him Munene stood smiling.

"He has been appointed Chief of this district and he will be your mouth and our mouth. He will tell us the things that you want to say and he will tell you the things that we want to say to you. He has learned our language and our laws and he will help you to understand and keep them."

We Elders looked at each other. Was this the end of everything that we had known and worked for? What magic had this son of my father made that he who was not yet an Elder should be made leader over us all who were so much older and wiser in the ways of our people? It was as if a thunderbolt had fallen among us.

The Pink Cheek went on.

"Your new Chief will collect the tax on huts, and choose the places for the new schools that you will build everywhere, so that your children may be taught to read and write. He will raise the money for that from you all. I have spoken."

When the Pink Cheek had gone there was much talk. We asked Munene to tell us how this had come about and why he was set above the Elders in this way.

"It is because they do not understand our laws and Councils," he told us. "Because I speak their language and because when I went away in their wars I had many medals."

The medals we knew about, for we had seen them. Many had them.

We spoke then of the tax on huts. It was heavy, for some men had many huts. Those men who had gone to work on the farms of the Pink Cheeks sent us money, but this we needed to buy food. More men, therefore, must go.

Munene gave us some good advice. He told us that men were wanted in Nairobi to build the new houses made of stone, both for the Pink Cheeks to live in and where they sat to make business and trading. Our men could go there and earn coins and then they could come back when they had plenty.

This was good, for in this way we would pay our tax and no man would be taken by the Pink Cheeks for not paying. So our young men went away down the new road, we were left to grow what food we could, and all was as usual.

It was while these men were still away to make money for our hut

tax that ten of our people came back from the farms where they
worked. They were not needed, they said, there was no work for
them there. With many others, they had been sent back without
money and without food, because there were bad people who trou-
bled the land.

This was the beginning. Along the new road had come big boxes-
on-wheels that they called lorries, in which they had carted logs from
the forest. Now these came filled with people. Many had no homes,
for their land had gone to the Pink Cheeks. Some had no homes because their land had gone to be mined for gold. We could not let
them starve, so we took them on our land.

It was the end of the dry season and there was little food left in the
storehouses. Our mbari had now grown big and all these newcomers
on our land must eat too. Altogether there were twelve hundred people on the two hundred acres of land my grandfather's father had
bought. There was not enough room to grow all the food.

In the dry season many goats and cattle had died for want of water.
The harvest had been thin and there was little left, and there was no
money to buy food; the last had gone for our hut tax. I heard the
crying of children and I saw the women weaken in their work. The
old men would sit near their huts, too feeble to walk.

Wangari, whose once-strong breasts hung like empty bags and
whose eyes were deep in her head, came to me where I sat by my
hut.

"Kabongo, son of Kimani," she said, sitting close, "we women are
tired; there is no food and the children are hungry; the young men
have no stomachs and the old men are withering as dry leaves. You
yourself are weak or before this you would have taken counsel with
the Elders. Speak now, for our people wait to hear your word."

I was roused. What she said was true. This was no time to sit and
wait. We must hold Council.

The Council met again under the Mugomo tree. There were few,
for the new laws of the Pink Cheeks had forbidden big meetings. I
looked round at my friends and was sad. Their faces were anxious
and their skin was loose on their bones. Even Muonji who always
used to joke had no smile. For each one had been hungry for many
days and each one told the same story. Everyone there was a shortage of food, for there was no land and all the time people were being
sent back from distant parts. There was uneasiness and some of our

tribesmen were troubling our people too much because they wanted to drive the Pink Cheeks from our country. This the Elders told in Council and were uneasy, for we wanted no war with the Pink Cheeks; we only wanted land to grow food.

"We must ask the Council of the Pink Cheeks to lend us some of the land we had lent to them," said one who came from a place where there was land held by the Government for future farms and not yet in use.

All agreed that this would be good and for Munene, who as Chief was our spokesman, we made a message to give to the Governor. What we told to Munene he made marks with and, when we had finished, he spoke it to us again and it was good.

Munene took our message and he took also a gift of honey and eggs and went away down the long road and left us to wait.

We waited many days, with hope. It was a whole moon before Munene came back. He came to us slowly and sadly and we knew from his way that the news was bad.

"They will not give the land," he said. "They say they have no more land for us."

And he told us many things that were not good; he told us of rebellions of some of our people, bad men who took our laws and ceremonies and degraded them; of the Pink Cheek warriors and of some he called Police who did unjust things to our people, who took good men and loyal to the Queen away from their work, and after much useless talk, sent them too to live on this land where there is no food.

So I am sitting before my hut and I wait. For soon the time will come for me to creep away into the forest to die. Day by day my people grow thinner and weaker and the children are hungry; and who am I, an old man, to eat the food that would come to them?

As I sit I ponder often on the ancient prophecy of Mogo wa Kebiro. Has the Pink Cheek brought good to my people? Are the new ways he has shown us better than our own ways?

Something has taken away the meaning of our lives; it has taken the full days, the good work in the sunshine, the dancing and the song; it has taken away laughter and the joy of living; the kinship and the love within a family; above all it has taken from us the wise way of our living in which our lives from birth to death were dedicated to Ngai, supreme of all, and which, with our system of age groups and our Councils, insured for all our people a life of responsibility and goodness. Something has taken away our belief in our Ngai and in the goodness of men. And there is not enough land on which to feed.

These good things of the days when we were happy and strong have been taken and now we have many laws and many clothes and men dispute among themselves and have no love. There is discontent and argument and violence and hate, and a vying with each other for power and men seem to care more for disputes about ideas than for the fullness of life where all work and live for all.

The young men are learning new ways, the children make marks which they call writing, but they forget their own language and customs, they know not the laws of their people and they do not pray to Ngai. They ride fast in motor-cars, they work fire-sticks that kill, they make music from a box. But they have no land and no food and they have lost laughter.

From Kabongo *by Richard St. Barbé Baker, A.S. Barnes, 1955.*

Express to the Mountains of the Moon

BY DAVID REED

One of the most interesting railroad trips in the world is on the narrow-gauge railroad that links Mombasa, Kenya's port on the Indian Ocean, to the Mountains of the Moon, the source of the River Nile. Back and forth for a thousand miles this unique train shuttles, carrying merchants and missionaries, farmers and laborers. Its freight cars are loaded, both ways: tools and manufactured goods for African use; coffee, copper, and animal products for the markets of the world.

There are not many railroads in Africa, but where they exist, they provide an opportunity for the traveler to get acquainted with a cross-section of the country and its people. The views, also, are spectacular and rewarding, whether one is traveling from the mountains to the sea or from the sea to the mountains. David Reed, a journalist who has been on assignment in Africa over a period of years, made the trip of which he writes here in 1964 after both Kenya and Uganda were independent.

Each evening, at a few minutes after six o'clock, a crowd gathers in the railway station in the old Arab city of Mombasa, on the coast of Kenya. Africans and Indians mill around in massive confusion, while here and there one sees an Englishman trying his best to remain aloof from the uproar. A warning bell sounds, and everyone scrambles aboard the waiting train. Then, promptly at 6:30, one of the world's most fabulous railway journeys begins. Destination: the Mountains of the Moon.

To the railroad's British managers, the train is simply "One Up"

—Train No. 1, upbound. But few rail journeys are as spectacular as this two-and-a-half-day trip. Along its winding route all the pageantry of East Africa, one of the world's most fascinating yet least-known regions, unfolds.

Soon after the *gari la moshi*—the vehicle of smoke—leaves Mombasa, whistle tooting, the palm trees and lush vegetation give way to the savage *nyika,* or East African bush. This wilderness of stunted thorn trees and brush is largely responsible for East Africa's long isolation. Although the Portuguese occupied Mombasa for two centuries and American and British merchants were trading in nearby Zanzibar in the early nineteenth century, no white man ever ventured into the interior.

Somewhere in the hinterland, however, lay the birthplace of the Nile, the mighty river that brings life to Egypt's millions. In a treatise written in the middle of the second century, the Greek geographer Ptolemy traced the Nile to the *Lunae Montes,* or Mountains of the Moon. Yet no European had ever been able to confirm that these mountains existed. Guarded by deserts, swamps, and hostile tribesmen, they remained through the centuries a tantalizing legend.

An earlier generation of Africans bolted in panic at the approach of a train. They called it the "iron snake." Today's generation has taken to the *gari la moshi* with a relish. Indeed, it was the railroad, more than anything else, that created modern East Africa. Over its ribbons of steel, colonial officials and missionaries rode into the interior to impose peace on warring tribes. In later years, the railroad brought doctors, who ended the great epidemics of the past, and teachers, who imparted modern knowledge.

Today the route is operated by the three East African governments and serves as the economic artery of a frontier region almost as large as Western Europe. Upbound freights bring the materials and tools to build cities and factories; downbound freights carry coffee, cotton, tea, timber, wheat, sisal, frozen meats, hides and skins, copper and soda ash, for distribution to markets all over the world.

It's an interesting assortment of passengers aboard the coach I'm in tonight. One is a well-dressed African government official, polite and friendly. Another is a British engineer on his way to open a new power station. There is an Indian merchant who talks about his business in Nairobi with the nervous excitement customary among his people. And then there is an elderly American missionary who has spent a lifetime in Africa and who says he will count himself lucky if he can die here at his work.

Third-class coaches are packed with Africans carrying enormous mounds of baggage and produce. Railway officials have struggled for years, in vain, to convince Africans that they should check their possessions in the baggage car, but they refuse to let any of them out of their sight. The railroad charges three cents (U.S.) for each chicken brought aboard, but draws the line at goats, much to the outrage of some of the passengers.

Railroading in Africa, one soon learns, is a far cry from that in other lands. Because of the narrow gauge (one meter) and sharp curves, trains are never able to go faster than 45 miles an hour and, more frequently, crawl. If a passenger misses a train, he can always take a taxi to the next station, with perfect assurance that he will have time to spare before the train arrives.

Kenya's elephants are a delight to visitors, but often a headache to train crews, for trains have been derailed after collisions with these monsters. From time to time a rhinoceros takes a dislike to a passing train and charges head on into it. Giraffes sometimes get their necks entangled in the railroad's telegraph wires and, struggling to get free, pull them down. Some African tribes have a great passion for copper wire, and whole sections of line occasionally disappear, to reappear later as bracelets and bangles jingling merrily on the bodies of happy tribesmen.

There are other difficulties. An Indian stationmaster once telegraphed to Nairobi: "Four lions with consorts aggressively on platform and have taken full charge my official functions."

By dawn, the *nyika* has been replaced by the open grasslands of the sun-drenched Athi Plains. Now, off to the south, purple-tinted Kilimanjaro, highest mountain in Africa, comes into view. Few sights are so awesome. While most mountains lie in closely packed ranges, Kilimanjaro stands alone on the plains, rising to 19,340 feet above sea level.

At 8 A.M., after the train has crossed 330 miles of wilderness, the

skyline of Nairobi appears. Once a sleepy colonial outpost, Nairobi
has been transformed in recent years into one of the prettiest capitals
in Africa, with a population of a third of a million. Baby skyscrapers
have sprung up along boulevards splashed with brilliant tropical
flowers. New hotels have been built to accommodate the ever-
growing number of safari hunters and tourists from all over the
world. Here are elegant restaurants and nightclubs, expensive shops,
a television station and drive-in movie theaters.

Elsewhere in Africa, Europeans suffer greatly from heat and humidity and from malaria and other tropical diseases. Not in mile-
high Nairobi. Here the climate is one of perpetual spring. At night,
people even sleep under two blankets, though the equator is just
eighty-seven miles away.

Not far out of Nairobi, One Up enters the perpetually green
Kikuyu Reserve, home of one of Africa's most advanced peoples.
Here the countryside is crisscrossed with steep ridges; icy streams,
many of them stocked with rainbow trout, cascade into the valleys.
The Kikuyu are exceptionally industrious, and virtually every inch
of the red earth is intensively cultivated with terraced fields of maize,
bananas, coffee, tea.

Ten years ago, this lovely land was drenched in blood. Masses of
Kikuyu took the Mau Mau oath to drive the whites from Kenya. For
four years they tied down large numbers of British troops in savage
guerrilla warfare. Although the Mau Mau lost the battle, they succeeded in speeding up the timetable of Kenya's independence. And
Jomo Kenyatta, the Kikuyu leader imprisoned for allegedly organizing the Mau Mau, has become the first prime minister of an independent Kenya.

After climbing through dark forests of black wattle trees, the train
emerges, at an altitude of 7,600 feet, on the edge of the breathtaking
forty-mile-wide Rift Valley. The Rift is one of the wonders of the
world. An enormous trench in the earth's surface, it has its beginning
in southern Turkey and extends thousands of miles southward,
through the Red Sea, then across the highlands of eastern Africa,
ending finally in Malawi (formerly Nyasaland). The scenery in the
valley is so spectacular that it makes your senses swirl: high, wind-
swept plains, purple mountains, plunging cataracts. On the valley
floor are soda lakes, containing water so bitter it cannot be drunk.

Because of the altitude and the proximity to the equator, the sunshine is so brilliant that colors seem to jump out at you.

As the train descends the escarpment, trees are replaced by acacia thorns and open grassland. At 2:30 P.M., One Up rolls into Nakuru situated in the shadow of an extinct volcano. Nakuru is the center of what used to be known as the White Highlands. On its streets one sees a surprising number of Europeans, bronzed from years of farming in Africa. Soon after the railway reached Lake Victoria in 1901, the British government invited white settlers to take up farming along the line so as to make the railway a paying proposition. For decades, Englishmen and others streamed into the highlands, where they built manor houses and lovely gardens, plowed fields to the horizon, introduced new crops and built up herds of sleek cattle and fat sheep.

In the early years, the settlers had dreams of an independent Kenya in which they would rule the Africans. When independence finally came, it was the other way around.

Leaving Nakuru, One Up climbs laboriously through forests up the other escarpment of the Rift. Shortly before sundown, it crosses the equator and reaches its highest point—9,136 feet. Nights here are bitter-cold, and frost sometimes appears. Looking out the windows, one sees Africans in tattered British army greatcoats, warming themselves around fires. Crossing the Uasin Gishu plateau, the train skirts massive Mount Elgon, a 14,178-foot extinct volcano, then descends gradually into Uganda.

After the thundering crescendos of Kenya's spectacular scenery, Uganda comes as a delicate relief. Situated on a plateau at an altitude of around 4,000 feet, much of the country is covered with gently rolling, emerald-colored hills. Rainfall is heavy, the days are warm and humid, and the country is prospering.

At 9 A.M. the train rolls into Kampala, capital of Uganda. A picturesque city of 47,000, Kampala is also the capital of Buganda, one of four native kingdoms within Uganda. The people, called the Baganda, are among the most fascinating in Africa. Long before the first European explorers arrived, they had developed a highly advanced society of their own. At a time when other Africans lived in crude huts and went about almost naked, the Baganda built imposing houses of finely woven mats and clothed themselves in elegant, toga-like garments made from softened bark. Today the Baganda are prospering in raising coffee and cotton, and many even employ laborers from other tribes for tilling their estates.

Kampala is the end of One Up's 824-mile run. Ongoing passengers must wait for an evening train, 53 Up, which leaves Kampala for the Mountains of the Moon three times a week.

Only a few people are aboard 53 Up. One is a young student at Makerere College, in Kampala, on his way to visit his parents in an outlying village. Another young man, having worked in Kampala as an auto mechanic, is on his way home with enough savings to open what will be the first auto-repair shop in his native village. Both typify the hopes and ambitions of an Africa that is rapidly emerging into the modern world.

Next morning, rounding a curve, the train emerges onto the edge of the escarpment of the western branch of the Rift Valley. A thousand feet below, Lakes George and Edward sparkle in the morning sun. Then, off in the distance, an enormous range of snow-crowned mountains appears. These are the legendary Mountains of the Moon, or Ruwenzori, as they are also known, whose melting snows course first through Lakes George and Edward. Eventually they join the Victoria Nile, which tumbles from Lake Victoria Nyanza, the world's second-largest freshwater lake, to form the White Nile, the great flood that surges out of the deserts of the Sudan on its way to Egypt.

The Mountains of the Moon are among the most elusive and seldom-seen peaks in the world. Most days they are hidden in mist and clouds. Explorer-journalist Henry Stanley camped near them for weeks in 1888 before he finally got a glimpse of their snowy summits, thus becoming the first European to confirm that Ptolemy's mountains did, indeed, exist. Even today, only a few venturesome climbers and naturalists ever brave the dense forests and raging snowstorms on the ghostly peaks.

Slowly the train descends the escarpment. It crosses a causeway through a papyrus swamp, then comes to a railhead at Kasese. Up in the mountains, blizzards howl and avalanches thunder down precipitous slopes, but in Kasese the sun burns fiercely in a cloudless sky.

The passengers alight amid exuberant whoops from waiting Africans and Indians. Wild struggles erupt as porters battle for the shilling tip to be had from carrying the white men's burdens. The locomotive lets out a last gasp of steam. Having traveled 1,032 miles from Mombasa, up across the roof of Africa and down the other side, the *gari la moshi* has come to the end of what is, indeed, one of the most remarkable train rides in the world.

"Express to the Mountains of the Moon," by David Reed, Reader's Digest, *September, 1964.*

Watch Out for the Masai

Alan Moorehead is best known as the author of *The White Nile* and
The Blue Nile. In these two books he re-created the bloody history
that followed the arrival of explorers, traders, and colonists along
the rivers and through the forests of what was then called the Dark
Continent. Mr. Moorehead first became interested in Africa as an
Australian journalist covering the campaigns of World War II in the
Mediterranean and North Africa. After the war, he traveled
throughout the continent and studied its history.

In *No Room in the Ark*, from which the following article is taken,
Mr. Moorehead writes about the problem of vanishing wildlife as he
found it in Central and East Africa in the decade prior to independence. Poachers were wantonly slaughtering elephant, zebra, wilde-
beeste giraffe, and crocodile. Many methods were used: poisoned arrows, traps, nets, and pits. Public opinion often favored the poachers
who felt that their tribal rights were at stake. Among the tribes concerned are the Masai, the nomadic herders of East Africa.

You ou hear about the Masai almost from the first moment you arrive
in East Africa. One is either for them or against them, and an endless controversy rages over the tribe. The Masai number about 55,000
in all, and they are by some way the most interesting and certainly
the most spectacular people in all black Africa. As a tribe they have
done the thing that practically no other Africans have succeeded
in doing: they have rejected the twentieth century and the white
man's world and have, instead, remained loyal to their ancient tribal
customs.

It's quite a startling thing when you first meet a Masai warrior. He is not like an African at all. He stands six feet tall, a slim hipless figure with a rust-colored cloak hanging over one shoulder and a broad-bladed spear in his hand. His face is thin with very high cheekbones, his eyes are two narrow mongolian slits, and no man on this earth, not even a Red Indian chieftain, can look at you with so much arrogance and fierce pride.

To Thomson and the other pioneers who first penetrated into their tribal areas the Masai were a holy terror. If the warriors were not fighting one another or raiding the neighboring tribes—and they usually were—they took a delight in falling upon these white intruders, and if they felt like it they murdered them. Since those days the Masai have become a good deal less aggressive with strangers, but in almost all other respects they have remained the same.

They never wash. At certain times they streak their faces with colored grease and dirt, and braid their hair so as to give it the appearance of a mop. The lobes of their ears are pierced and stretched fantastically with heavy ornaments. They drink deeply of the local beer and some of their tribal ceremonies are said to be barbaric. Yet none of this in any way disturbs the Masai's absolute conviction that he is an aristocrat, a member of a superior race. He disdains all forms of trade and ordinary labor—even his weapons are made for him by inferior tribes—and he is too a mighty man in slow portentous rhetorical argument, just as he is in lion killing, and every young man is supposed to kill at least one lion alone and only with his spear.

The women don't count for much in the social organization of the tribe. But from birth the men are fixed in a rigid and patrician system. In turn they enter each of the three main tribal groups: the adolescents, the warriors, and the elders. Each of these groups appoints a leader who has a hand in the inner councils of the tribe, and in addition to these, dominating the race but not actually leading it, are the libans, the medicine-men who are in touch with the mystical divine being who lives, some believe, on the topmost snowy crest of Kilimanjaro.

The Masai is a nomad and he lives by grazing cattle. Cattle are his wealth, his social standing, and his food. Having milked his cows he punctures a vein in their necks so that he can draw off a quantity of blood to be added to the milk, and this, together with maize, is his staple diet. To insure that there is an adequate supply of this exotic nourishment the Masai drive great herds of cattle across the open plains of Kenya and Tanganyika,* and they are constantly adding to their stock.

In recent years the herds in some parts have increased beyond all calculation; where once a family might have got along on thirty beasts they now possess three hundred. As cattle they may be poor specimens and diseased as well, but this does not matter. They take the place of currency; it is their numbers that count in all matters of bartering, including the bartering for a bride. And so, inevitably, the Masai are forced to spread further and further afield in search of water and fresh grazing in order to keep their swollen herds alive. This is where the conflict comes in between the tribe and the people who want to preserve what is left of the wild game, since clearly there is not enough grazing and water to go around; eventually either the wild animals or the Masai herds will have to go.

The problem is not really a local one since the Masai spread over such a large area of East Africa, but it so happens that the Serengeti Park is involved, and the Serengeti has been a name to conjure with in East Africa in recent years.

I had heard a good deal about this place in Nairobi and elsewhere when I first arrived in Kenya. The Serengeti, I was told, supported the last great concentration of wild animals left alive in the world. Here and only here in all Africa could one find such masses of big game as Thomson had seen in 1882. It is a large park covering roughly 6,000 square miles just inside the northern borders of Tanganyika, and it reaches all the way from the shores of Lake Victoria to the Ngorongoro Crater, which is almost within sight of Kilimanjaro. The importance of this particular stretch of country is that the animals use it as a migration route; as soon as the wet season ends they move eastwards from Lake Victoria in tens of thousands, breeding and pasturing as they go along, and then when the rains begin again they turn back towards the lake. To see these hordes in motion is one of the most arresting sights in Africa.

And now the Masai had entered the scene; some five thousand tribesmen were living in the park, and they had with them about a hundred thousand head of cattle and perhaps double that number of small domestic beasts like sheep and goats. The soil over a great area of the park was not deep, water was scarce, and clearly the wild game

*Now Tanzania.

was fighting a losing battle for survival. At first the Tanganyika government's only reaction to the problem had been to resign itself to a compromise; it proposed to preserve two areas at either end of the park for the wild game and hand over all the central part, more than half the entire park, to the Masai.

At once there was an outcry from the wildlife societies and by the time I reached Kenya a public and bitter controversy had arisen. Quite clearly a fundamental issue was involved: it was the ancient conflict between those who believe that man has inviolable rights on earth—that all other forms of life are bound to succumb to his increasing needs—and those who quite simply disagree. And the issue was still further confused by the fact that the Masai, perhaps because of their very toughness and intransigence, are rather admired by white men in Africa in the same way as, too late, the Red Indian came to be admired in North America.

Then, however, the picture improved. In 1957 the Government of Tanganyika appointed a Committee of Inquiry to advise on the future of the Serengeti National Park. A number of eminent ecologists were called in to give their opinion; as a result, the Park has been enlarged in the western and central Serengeti area and is—to quote the Fauna Preservation Society—"designed to insure for the future the living space and migration routes of the famous herds of wild ungulates (hoofed animals) and their attendant predators . . . a precious part of the world's inheritance." The Ngorongoro Crater has been excised from the Park and included in a Special Conservation Unit, and there is apparently some reason to hope, at least in the opinion of the experts, that the Masai and the wildlife will manage to coexist in peace.

From No Room in the Ark, *by Alan Moorehead, Harper & Row, 1957.*

Letter from Ethiopia

by A PEACE CORPS VOLUNTEER

Letters from Peace Corps Volunteers around the world reveal something of the writer and something of the people in the country to which the volunteer is assigned. The letter which follows was written by a PCV who had been in Ethiopia six months, long enough to realize the truth of a statement he had read during his training period for an overseas assignment:

"Potentially, the most tremendous social force of the 1960's will be the people who know they no longer have to be hungry and poor, who want education and freedom, who want bicycles, refrigerators, movies and radio, who want to see the city, who want what science and technology have made possible in the West, and who want it now . . ."

During the early sixties, Ethiopia asked for and received a large delegation of Peace Corps Volunteers, enough to double the number of secondary school teachers in the country. It was part of a massive build-up of education in an area where English is the language of instruction in the upper grades.

The following letter illustrates that the job of a Peace Corps Volunteer is as much "learning" as "teaching."

I wish to undertake a task in this letter that is not an easy one. I wish to introduce to you, in as accurate and unbiased a light as possible, the life of the average Ethiopian. It being an agricultural, predominantly rural, nation, I can portray the "average" Ethiopian only by selecting the farmer. My average picture will be slightly tinted off-color by the fact that I intend to portray the farmer of Wallega

Province—who differs slightly in custom, manner, dress, and language from his neighbors in their respective environmental frames, hung in different parts of this vast natural gallery. My portrait may be brighter than a true average would allow, since this area is generally more prosperous than others. But with all its shortcomings, this endeavor will be an honest attempt to introduce you briefly to the Ethiopian farmer—with all of his generosities and shortcomings, as I have come to know him. My greatest fallacy in writing this, and yours in reading it, will be to assume that everything that coincides with our beliefs, our practices, our approach to life, is GOOD; and that everything that smacks of his own culture and of several thousand years of tradition is "backward" and therefore BAD! Forgive us both!

At the risk of boring you, I want to recall and reprint my description of Ato (roughly equivalent to Mr.) Gemechu Feyisa, an inhabitant of these parts to whom I earlier introduced you.

Standing as a pathside observer on the Ethiopian scene, I noted the approach of a familiar figure. As this figure drew nearer, I observed that he was "slender and of average height. He carried a tall, stout stick for support and for custom. He was attired in white. Tight, white leggings extended to just above his ankles. From these protruded a pair of toughened feet—feet that have never graced the inside of a pair of shoes. His torso was clad in a loose, blouselike shirt of white. Around his shoulders was wound (like gauze around a finger) his shama. The shama consists of several yards of colorfully and beautifully bordered cloth that finishes off his costume and lands handsomely in loose folds and drapes about his body. His handsome chocolate face protruded as an island from this sea of white and his sparkling teeth flashed in an almost perpetual grin."

As he approached, his step was light, his demeanor pleasant. As he passed, his smile was punctuated by two staccato *t* sounds, as the traditional greeting *"TenayisTillin"* ("Let him who is the giver of health give you an abundant helping") passed his lips and rippled the afternoon air in my direction.

"TenayisTillin, indemin allu?" I returned his greeting and asked after his well-being. (Had I been an old friend, our greetings to each other would have encompassed a full five minutes! We would not have been satisfied to ask after each other's health, but would have ranged to an asking after wives, children, all livestock—oxen, donkeys, even chickens—and then would have finally returned to check

out each other's general condition once more. We would then have passed on without the necessity of conducting any kind of conversation. But who needs conversation with a greeting like that!) As he and his answer passed, I allowed my eyes, ears, and mind to fall in step behind him, and this is what they saw, heard, and thought.

Ato Gemechu was returning from the market place where the price of talk among old friends is cheap, and plenty of conversations are bartered and exchanged. If, by chance, he bought or sold something, then this simply insured the success of an already fine day. The "market" as an institution would not die merely for the lack of things to market. The Ethiopian market is the street corner, the Kiwanis Club, the beauty parlor, and all of the discussion, jabber, and gossip institutions of our society rolled into one. Even their language labels the market place *Beckejamma*—"gathering place."

The path slowly wound its way in every direction. The straight line does not exist in Ethiopia, or is regarded as a foreign innovation where it does. Fences, fields, the path that could be straightened to save miles—all are laid down more by chance or expediency than by forethought. If Gemechu ever looked out over a long stretch of his path, he must surely see that it is unnecessarily crooked. But his eyes are more likely fixed on the trail near at hand, for more reasons than one. First, he must exercise some care in where he sets his bare feet. But more important is the fact that he is not a tomorrow dweller, his gaze and curiosity do not penetrate beyond the next hill, around the next corner. He is not a stargazer—his language has no names for the constellations. His life is cemented in his own little environment, he lives each day only as it comes along, dwelling neither in the past nor the future, and the playground for his eyes is near at hand, not in the distance.

Beside a small forest of stately eucalyptus trees stands his home. Surrounding it are small patches of corn and cane. Scattered coffee bushes advertise their productivity with red berries. The breezes trace wave patterns in his fields of teff grain. The earth around his hut is flat and concrete hard—packed by countless steps, and baked by as many suns. A giant, wooden mortar, or grinding vessel, stands as a sentinel just outside the door. A grim residue around its rim hints that Gemechu's wife has spent several hours today lifting and slamming the great pestle homeward into the leaves and herbs which, once ground, will make her husband's beer. A swarm of bees rattle the air and terrain in one of the eucalyptus trees. The hot afternoon sun has plastered a ragged, skinny dog into a small shady spot, and rendered him too lazy to combat the flies. A bare-bottomed child sits on the bare earth and chortles gleefully as its daddy walks into the compound.

Gemechu—puffing slightly from the last hill, with his shama trailing in the breeze behind him like clouds of white steam—is reminiscent of a locomotive as he enters his round house. Home for Gemechu and his family is a circular plot of earth about eighteen feet in diameter. The windowless walls are eucalyptus logs that have been quartered Abe Lincoln fashion and stuck as uprights into the ground. Some of his neighbors may have plastered the chinks with mud. At Gemechu's, however, the myriad cracks serve as tiny entrances for his smaller visitors—occasional vermin and the endless stream of Africa's homeless insects in search of housing.

The roof is thatch on a cane frame. (When clusters of these huts and their thatched roofs are found together—some more peaked than others, some with flowers growing out of the thatch at a rakish angle —they remind one of women with their new hats in church on Easter morning.)

A fire roosts unconcernedly in the middle of the floor and ears of corn roast at its perimeter, giving off a pleasant aroma as their only protest. Rains render a hole in the roof impractical, so smoke from the fire collects as a dancing, eddying fog under the roof and escapes whenever possible—through the chinks, out the door, into the inhabitants' lungs.

Gemechu props his walking stick near the door, goes first to inspect the fire and the cooking pot, and then greets his wife. (Same order of events as the average American Dagwood follows.) Yes, he has sold the two chickens. One fold of his shama is realigned to reveal a neat string of small bundles hung on a cord. Today he has brought home peppers and other condiments to strengthen and escort his "Watt" to the stomach.

His wife has spent her day gathering or chopping wood for the fire, grinding those leaves for the "Talla" beer, roasting some coffee beans that the sun has dried, fixing her daughter's hair into a myriad of tiny braids, feeling her back bent as she carries water in a staggeringly heavy jog along a crooked path from the spring a half mile away, gathering corn for the evening's roasting, and finally finely chopping the bits of chicken and hot peppers and vegetables and hot peppers and spices and hot peppers that go into the "Watt" sauce, the mainstay of their diet. Yesterday was "Injerra"—baking day— and she kept an immense fire of coals and a small earthen oven busy turning out the spongy, quarter-inch-thick and two-foot-diameter bread.

When 8:00 or 8:30 comes, when the sun is comfortably set and when meal time arrives, the family sits on benches and stools around the fire and eats from earthen plates. The Watt, once served on the plate awaits its fate. A piece of Injerra is torn off from the whole and serves as the only utensil. As carefully as a detective picks up a sus-pect weapon with his handkerchief, Gemechu secures a mouthful of Watt in the piece of Injerra and delivers it. At feasts and celebrations it is the custom to feed others and be fed by others. (I have some-times found it difficult to be festive—I am more likely restive—when the skin is coming off my mouth in flaming pieces. . . but I man-age.)

Hives are hung in trees to discourage attack by the bees' greatest enemy, the ant.

The average home has a life span of six years. Houses have high priority on the termite menu. (Leave a hammer on the ground over-night, and you will have only the metal head left as a token remem-brance by breakfast time.)

Meat does not make an appearance at every meal—far from it, in fact. Slaughtering is generally reserved for holiday or festivals, but fortunately the calendar is relatively saturated. Raw meat is often preferred to cooked, though as the meat ages after slaughtering, it is added to the Watt. For Ethiopia's Coptic Christian (comprising the majority of the population for centuries), every Wednesday and Fri-day are fasting days when no meat is taken. The two months prior to Easter are also a fasting period when Gemechu's diet sees no meat or animal by-products.

Coffee follows the meal and is served carefully, almost ritualisti-cally. I am sure that the formula is three parts coffee to one part water. (Whenever I have made coffee to be served to our Ethiopian friends, I have always perked the coffee once, then dumped out the grounds, added four more scoops of coffee and perked again. Some-day I plan to get mad when, as our guests leave, they thank me for the tea!

The happy and playful whimper of a dog greeting its master heralds the arrival of Gemechu's oldest son. Tafesse greets his parents and sets his school books aside. (Ethiopian mothers never have to worry about their sons tossing their school books into the nearest corner—in the round house there aren't any.) Tafesse's full name is Tafesse Gemechu (literally: Tafesse, son of Gemechu). Sons and daughters always take their given name plus their father's first name. If Tafesse has a son someday and names him Berhanu, he will be Berhanu Tafesse.

Neither parent is angered by the late, post-supper arrival of this son. They are proud of him, for he is a student at the government school. That his future is bright is enough to let them face old age with ease. Today was the day of the athletic competition and the games and events had made him tired even before he began to walk the seven miles that separated his home from the school. But the sound of the hyenas on the prowl in the darkening forest had quickened his pace. And now, as he relishes his supper (the first food he has tasted since breakfast—because his family does not have enough money that he may purchase his lunch in the town), he finds new energy with which to relate his prowess in the competition. His talk is directed to his younger brothers and sisters, but he is hoping, of course, that his parents are hearing too.

There is a noticeable difference here between father and son. The son wears pants of a foreign cut. They are belted at the waist. He is reaching the climax of his tale to the younger ones around him, and as his chest swells with pride and vigor for his storytelling, a shirt that was once white is visible beneath a khaki waistcoat. These clothes are a mark of his separation—or at least transition—from the old to the new. They were bought for him by two proud parents when he passed the examinations at the end of the eighth grade and, thereby, earned the right to continue his education in the government school. He has worn this same suit every day since. Its exterior shows some diligent patchwork, and Gemechu is hopeful that he can replace the suit for his son before he enters his senior year.

When the supper is finished and the tales are told, Tafesse will add more wood to the dying fire and light his oil lamp to provide study light. The family is settling onto cane beds. There is little left in a day on the African highlands once the sun has set, the supper is finished, and the fire itself is continually trying to sleep. Tafesse must follow soon, for the morning mists that spread themselves over the hills will signal the start of his long trek back to school.

Tafesse is the one really caught in the middle—pulled by the weight of custom, and attracted by the pull of new forces and new ideas emanating from the twentieth century to which he has been awakened. If I could wish something for him, it would be that he could carry his parents' capacity for work, their humble generosity, their sincerity and their ability to glean pleasure from simple experiences and life itself—that he could carry these with him into his new role.

I know Tafesse, and I know that he is destined for a successful life. He will complete his studies here, will perhaps earn the privilege of studying abroad, but the years ahead will find him serving his country in one useful capacity or another.

Tomorrow Gemechu will fall into step behind his oxen guiding his wooden plow along the crooked rows. Next year he may have a new, steel plow that will turn the sod and permit him to plow and plant more. He has been promised some new seeds by the extension agents to replace his old, worn-out strains. These promise him greater yields and perhaps enough margin for profit. If this is true, he will have a little money to spend for himself and his family.

On some future day Gemechu will whistle his oxen to a halt and will rest wearily on his plow. Love and pride will lift his eyes to the hazy distance, to some faraway city where a son of his lives separated from his father and family by more than the miles. For between them will be several centuries of human progress and knowledge.

It is a new experience for Gemechu to have his thoughts range beyond today, for his eyes to scan the horizon and beyond. But he stands a little taller in the process. And as his eyes gaze back across the intervening pastures, perhaps he will notice that that path is crooked—and straighten it out tomorrow.

From Peace Corps Volunteers Report: Volume I, *Letters from East Africa, 1963.*

The Pygmy and the Leopard

BY ANNE PUTNAM

"Madami" is the name that the Pygmies of the Ituri Forest gave to Anne Putnam, a young American artist who spent eight years in the Congo with her husband. Patrick Putnam, an anthropologist, was a public health officer for the Belgian government during the 1940's. As a sideline the Putnams ran a small hotel for traders and scientists, a first-aid station, and a small zoo for wild animals.

Their station, called Putnam's Camp, was in the middle of the Ituri Forest on the banks of a tributary of the Congo, almost in the geographical center of Africa. Their closest neighbors and constant companions were the Pygmies who lived in villages in the surrounding rain forest and supplied Putnam's Camp with meat. The relationship of which Mrs. Putnam speaks in the following selection from *Madami* started as a matter of business and developed into real affection.

It was well after daybreak when I heard the shouting. Then there were footsteps on the veranda and a voice saying, "Madami, Madami, a woman is here who fought with a leopard."

Outside I found a great crush of little people—Pygmies of both sexes—who had dumped a crude stretcher fashioned of a blanket and liana vines on the porch floor. I didn't want to look at the pathetic figure of the woman lying on the litter but I couldn't avoid it.

She lay a quarter over on her side, eyes open in fright, her little hands pressed against her belly where the leopard's claws had torn at her intestines. The blanket was sodden with her blood. In all the press of people she was the only quiet one.

"Ageronga," I said to one of the boys, "get Pat. Tell him to hurry."

My husband came running with a first-aid kit. The Pygmies scattered like quail when a dog runs through a field, then halted in the yard at the veranda's edge, as Pat bent over the wounded woman.

Pat worked over the woman without moving her, there in the brittle morning light, trying to patch the hideously torn body and quench the flow of blood. He knew a lot about medicine, but he was no doctor. A surgeon, working in a modern operating room, would have found it impossible to put things right. The best Pat could do was to clean the wound, sprinkle sulfa powder through it liberally, and see what happened.

He picked her up as if she were only a little child, carried her tenderly inside, and put her down on a bed. I could hear him cursing in a low, determined voice, cursing because he had no blood plasma and no apparatus for a blood transfusion. He rigged up a bottle and a tube and started giving her intravenous saline injections. He lifted her head, cradled it in his arm, and made her drink water. He wanted to replace in her body some of the liquids lost by the massive bleeding. Within twenty minutes he had done everything he knew to do to save her. So he covered her with a blanket and stepped out upon the veranda.

"Who is this woman?" he asked the Pygmies.

It was Faizi who answered, the little bearded gnome who was one of a handful of elders who ruled the Pygmy village.

"She is Ukana, wife of Sikona," he said.

"How did the leopard get her?"

"She was cooking manioc for the morning meal," said the Pygmy. "Sikona was with her by the fire. Needing something in the house, she went inside. Sikona went on mending his hunting net.

"Suddenly there was the spotted one. It bounded out of the forest, cleared Sikona with one jump, and went through the doorway inside. Ukana screamed when the cat seized her and kept on screaming until Sikona ran inside. I don't know whether it was the woman's great noise or Sikona's appearance with a spear that did it, but the leopard dropped her and raced back outside. There were all the others around, but it paid them no attention. It was gone before anyone could throw a spear."

All this Faizi told, speaking in Kingwanna. His face was screwed up as if in pain, trying to get the words out. It was as if they all had sharp corners or were too large. His native dialect was KiBira, and the kitchen Swahili or Kingwanna, which is what enables a white man to get by in the Congo, didn't come easily to him. Once or twice in his excitement he dropped back into KiBira, and we had to guess at his meaning.

Pat went back inside to look after the woman.

Faizi turned to me, his eyes looking strange because of the puckering of the flesh around them. I had known him for four years now and admired him as I have admired few persons in all my life.

"Madami," he said, "will she die?"

"Who can say?" I answered. "The white man's medicine is powerful but Ukana is badly wounded."

Faizi turned and walked away, his tiny chocolate-colored body sagging as if woefully tired. Some of the other little people went with him. Some stayed on. Almost unconsciously I became aware of drums and the sound of sticks being beaten against pans and pails. Back in the Pygmy village they were making a hideous racket, hoping to drive the leopard farther away if he were still lurking in the nearby woods.

That was all I needed. My throat went dry. My knees felt as if they had turned to pulp or jelly. After four years in the heart of the Congo I was still a white woman, prey to all the fears any woman at home would have known.

"Anne Putnam," I whispered to myself, "you are a fool. What made you come to Africa?"

Fortunately I had no opportunity to indulge in prolonged self-pity. I heard the woman calling for a drink and went to brew some tea.

Pat came into the kitchen and said the Pygmy was still bleeding internally.

"There isn't a man within thirty miles who could help her," he said.

"You don't have to make excuses," I said. "Even the best surgeons lose some cases."

When the tea was ready I poured it, let it cool, and took it in to Ukana. I noticed how tiny and light she was as I held her up enough to put the cup to her lips. She drank thirstily. There were tears in her eyes,

"I am sorry to cause Madami trouble," she whispered. "I would not have had it this way for anything."

Her courage and quiet dignity made me ashamed of having been afraid. Few civilized women would have remembered to mind their manners if a leopard had clawed them.

Once when I looked in at the Pygmy woman she muttered, "Why would anyone want to put the evil eye on me? I have harmed no one."

That was the true Pygmy speaking. To Ukana it was not a natural accident. It couldn't be. No, this was the work of someone with the evil eye.

We kept up the saline infusions. We placed hot bricks under the woman's covers because she seemed so cold. Later we doubled the covers, but still she shook and shivered as though the Congo's ever-constant tropical temperature had suddenly dropped below zero.

The hours went by without our noticing them. Time is one thing to a dying person, something else again to those who watch. Ukana knew it was slipping away too quickly.

Through every window in the house peered two or three Pygmies, their faces strangely immobile and solemn. Beyond them the trees of the forest showed pink and russet in the light of the afternoon sun. Through the trees came the sound of drums as other Pygmies went about the business of scaring off the man-eating leopard.

Once when I dashed over to the hospital for new supplies I noticed some of the boys tagging along, each one armed with a spear or bow and arrows. Terror was in their eyes. No one had ordered them to accompany me. I thought how scared they were, yet how selflessly they went about protecting me.

Evening found little change in the injured woman. It became more and more apparent that the leopard's victim was paralyzed from the shoulders down. Pat said he thought the weight of the cat had broken her spine. He changed the bandages and gave her morphine to deaden the growing pain. She spoke hardly at all, but the way her eyes followed his movements left no doubt that she was in agony and that she knew her only hope rested in his hands.

A few more Pygmies drifted away to their village; but most remained—some inside the house, some outside. They squatted on their haunches, watching our every move, obviously convinced that their suffering relative or friend needed them close at hand.

At two o'clock in the morning Pat gave Ukana another shot of morphine.

"There's nothing more I can do," he said. "We might as well turn in."

In the morning she was still alive, her eyes like chips of mica set in her reddish-brown, melted-chocolate colored face. Pat looked at her wounds, dressed them, and went about sending word to the neighboring chiefs to have pitfalls dug and traps set to catch the leopard.

It was as if he had taken a pen and signed her death certificate. I realized he knew there was nothing more he could do for this victim and wished to prevent another attack. If I had had any doubts before, this ended them. The woman was going to die.

Just then two visitors drove up. They were white men, part of an expedition that had been touring the area near us for snakes and other reptiles. They had spent several days with us before and wanted lodgings for the night. I walked with them away from the house and was explaining why I couldn't ask them into the parlor, when loud wailing broke out in the front of the building.

It was a great caterwauling, a rising and falling of sound, that beat on my ears as the sea rushes against the rocks, only to fall back to gain new strength. It penetrated my pores, and my heart felt as if ice water were pouring through it.

We entered the room where Death was and looked at Ukana, lying still and small on the great bed. Her relatives clustered about, looking for all the world like little Negro children, except that the men had beards and the women's breasts were fully developed.

I recognized Sale, already a grandfather six times over; Herafu, the quiet philosopher; and faithful, fearless Faizi, most respected of the elders in the Pygmy village. I could hardly stand it to look at them. The dead woman must have been particularly well-beloved to judge by the sorrow in their eyes.

Herafu tugged at the hairs of his scrawny beard.

"Madami," he said, speaking with the peculiar bass voice of the little people, "this is a bitter day for us. Ukana was a good woman and much too young to die. It would be more difficult to bear, however, if you blamed yourself, or if Bwana did so. After all, this is the work of the Bolozi—the evil eye—and what is medicine against the evil eye?"

That was the voice of Africa—the real Africa.

I turned to the little people, wanting very much to tell them how deeply I sensed their loss. My mastery of Kingwanna would have been equal to the task, I'm sure, but my throat was dry and no words came. I sat down and blubbered like a baby as the Pygmies covered their dead with mourning cloths and bore her away to their village, their wailing rising and falling ever more faintly as they passed out of sight among the giant trees.

All that day and the next there was the sound of sawing and hammering as a trap was built near the hospital to catch the man-eater. Pat supervised everything. In his twenty years in the Congo he had picked up many strange arts.

Chiefs of neighboring villages were busy building their own traps. Some dug deadfalls in the game trails, covered them over with branches, and dragged the carcasses of dead animals around to lure the big cat and hide the smell of man. Others built cage traps, like ours at the hospital. The one we erected was a huge cage of logs, lashed together with ropes and liana vines. It had two sections, each separate from the other. In one a poor old goat was imprisoned as a lure. The other section had a trap door with a trick arrangement that would cause it to fall shut if the leopard went inside seeking a way to get at the goat.

The men built it with great care because a leopard is a powerful animal. Pound for pound, it is probably the most destructive of all predatory beasts. Its muscles are steellike sinews. Although the largest male will seldom weigh more than one hundred sixty pounds, it is so powerful that it will drag an antelope or sondu twenty feet up into a tree after it has killed it rather than have genets finish it off. Its claws can slash through anything but the stoutest vines or ropes.

In the middle of all the excitement I went out into the garden to work. I told myself it was because the weeds were getting ahead of the beans and peppers, but it was because I had to do something to keep from busting wide open. Two boys with bows and arrows did sentry duty. Lord knows they would have been small protection, but there's comfort in numbers and I felt better to have them on guard.

By twilight the tension had mounted until I could stay outdoors no longer. The boys were getting jittery anyway as the shadows lengthened. We all went into the compound feeling as though thousands of leopard eyes were following our every footstep.

In the Congo, twilight does not bring peace and quiet. It ushers in a great outburst of discordant sounds in the jungle. There is a concert of insect noises that rivals a Chinese orchestra tuning up. There are katydids and crickets and a hundred other bugs that seem to want to "go on the air" just at sundown. Then there are owls and storks and other birds as well as different animals that snort and sneeze and cry and wail and cough as they start their nightly search for food. In its own way it's as noisy as New York at night.

When full darkness came, however, the symphony was over. A hush fell upon the land. From the banks of the Epulu River in front of the hotel to the far reaches of the forest there was almost complete silence. Occasionally an animal large enough to dare betray his presence roared defiance at his enemies. Smaller denizens of the rain forest kept silent in fear.

That night nothing happened. The next day the goat was alive and well and the other half of the cage empty. The little people in their village started the funeral dance for Ukana immediately after daybreak. All through the long daylight hours the drums boomed as the little people chanted of their sorrow.

After lunch a band of Pygmies dashed in with news of the big cat.

They said they had been on their way to the village of the Ba-Nadigbi, the dead woman's people, when one of the party noticed a movement in a tall slough of marsh grass. Then they all saw the animal's head. Although they had spears and bows and arrows, they knew their danger in the corn-high grass, so they legged it for home as fast as they could make it.

All hope that the leopard had been scared away had to be abandoned. Pat took his gun down from the rack and had his ammunition brought out of a closet. He hadn't hunted anything but germs for five years or more and the Congo's high humidity had ruined everything. The gun was rusty, the shells swollen, and the powder damp.

Pat blew his top, ranting and raving at a climate that, given time enough, can rot iron and steel like old leather. Then realizing he was making an ass of himself and not doing any harm to the leopard, he had the drums beaten, rounded up some boys, and went off to build a new trap near the village of the BaNadigbi.

"I hate to risk all these prime goats as bait," he said before he left, "but it will be a good investment if we catch the cat. I can't just sit back and wait for another attack."

Toward evening Pat and his party returned. It made me feel a lit-

tle braver. When we went to bed I could hear the goat in the trap by
the hospital bleating fearfully. We couldn't tell whether he scented
the leopard or whether he was just lonely out there by himself in the
velvet darkness.

For a week nothing happened. The Pygmies regained their normal
jollity, went net-hunting again, and saw no leopard spoor. I weeded
the garden without the luxury of sentries. Pat kept the traps baited,
however, and the native chiefs did the same.

The excitement had about died down when we went to bed early
one night to read some books and magazines that had just come in
from Stanleyville. I was deep in a mystery story when I heard a sound
from outside. It seemed to be somewhere up on the roof. Pat whispered "leopard" in my ear. My heart started thumping and I felt as if
I were paralyzed. Then I remembered that I hadn't fastened the
doors or drawn the wooden shutters at the windows.

Pat, who had emphysema and could barely use his legs, crawled off
the bed to get something to use for a weapon. I could only lie there,
trembling in silence. Suddenly something dropped lightly into the
room. Mademoiselle, my basenji dog, started howling and I thought
I was going to die right there in the bed. Finally I forced myself to
look. There in the faint light cast by the hurricane lantern was our
cat, sitting on the table, washing herself and preening as if she always
entered the bedroom through the smoke vent in the roof.

Two days later Alili brought us our morning coffee, his eyes wide
with terror.

"The evil one caught one of Bwana's goats last night," he said,
spilling coffee on the covers and on my arm.

A search party followed the goat's bloody trail and found where
the leopard had feasted. The big jungle cat had eaten only the head
and neck, so we salvaged the balance. For dinner that night we had
tender goat for a change from our customary fare of forest antelope.
It was delicious. The leopard had disregarded the tough old goat in
the trap and had picked out one of the youngest, tenderest goats in
the herd.

The next night the leopard struck again, this time making off with
an older animal. Pat kept the animals in a stockade which had been
raised until it was twelve feet high after the attack on Ukana. I mar-
veled at the strength of the beast. It had jumped over the barrier,

seized and killed the goat, and scaled the fence, carrying the full-grown goat as if it were a rabbit.

Pat was furious.

He had the boys dig a deadfall just a few feet away from the stockade in the direction in which the cat had taken its victims. That night he was so sure the animal would return he went to the hospital to wait, leaving me alone in the house except for a couple of boys.

I went to bed, scared silly, but trying to be brave. One of the boys slept in the kitchen, another in the living room. Neither one would risk it on the veranda. I tried to quiet my nerves by reading *The Romance of Leonardo da Vinci* but could hardly turn the pages for trembling. All I could hear above the pounding of my heart was the sound of the goat crying in the big cage. I knew how he felt. With an animal's greatly developed power of smell, he could probably scent the jungle cat waiting for his chance, out in the forest.

When I fell asleep, thinking how safe and peaceful even medieval Florence and Pisa must have been compared with the Congo, it was to toss and turn in terror. My dreams were full of leopards.

I was awakened by the guards' shouting. It was as dark as Satan's evil.

"They've got the leopard," shouted Alili. "E-e-e-y-a-h, they've got the leopard."

He urged me to go over to the trap and see it.

"You go," I said. "I don't want to see it."

What if he got loose, I thought. I was all for sticking it out where I was, but Pat sent word for me to come. Reluctantly I dressed and walked over to where the boys were milling around the cage.

Even in death the animal was terrifying. It was a male. He lay crumpled in one corner of the cage with a bloody hole in his side. The latent sense of power that still clung to him somehow made me think of a wrecked locomotive I had once seen, hissing and panting in a gully beside the tracks. He was a good eight feet from the tip of his tail to his great whiskers.

"It's the man-eater," Ageronga said. "Forest leopards are always darker than those on the savannahs. Bolozi leopards are darkest of all."

The cage was secured so other animals could not molest the dead leopard's body and everyone went back to bed.

In the morning Alili informed me that he had found the leopard's tracks all around the house, even under my windows, which had nothing on them but small wooden bars.

"He came to inspect the goats in the stockade," said Alili, "but he would have preferred another kind of meat. Maybe the basenji dog changed his mind."

I went outside and looked at the great footprints in the soft dirt of the flowerbeds beside the wall. Then I looked at the windows with their flimsy wooden slats—and fainted dead away.

From Madami, *by Anne Eisner Putnam, Prentice-Hall, Inc., 1954.*

"Tell Me, Josephine"

EDITED BY BARBARA HALL

Beginning in 1960, a column of personal advice headed "Tell Me, Josephine" appeared in the *Central African Mail,* a weekly newspaper published in Northern Rhodesia, now Zambia. No one knew the identity of the columnist whose answers were so friendly, sympathetic, often wise, and sometimes witty. As a matter of fact, Josephine did not exist as an individual. The column was written by a panel of several Africans, young and old, modern and traditional. An African clergyman and sociologist served for a while on the panel, also a young newspaper man and two young educated women.

"Josephine" won many admirers for her sympathetic and practical answers to the problems of young people.

In England and the United States more women than men write to newspaper columnists for advice. In Africa it is just the opposite; most of those who seek advice are men. Possibly this is because more men than women have learned to write, or perhaps because the women of Africa today are less emancipated than the men.

Barbara Hall, who collected samples of Josephine's correspondence for publication, says: "Most of Josephine's letters come from people in the towns, but some are from far away in the bush—written by candlelight in mud-and-wattle huts. The language is sometimes bizarre, but at the same time very moving and graphic. Often the letters have a Biblical turn of phrase, because many Africans have been taught English in mission schools."

BRIDE-PRICE

The many tribes of Northern Rhodesia are almost all agreed upon two things about a prospective marriage: you must first get the consent of the relatives of the woman of your choice, and you must then make a payment to them. This bride-price is called lobola.

But a money payment alone does not satisfy some tribes. For them, payment must be partly in cattle. So if the suitor comes from a tribe which does not own cattle, he is really in difficulty. He has to find the cattle elsewhere.

If he comes from any of the vast areas infested by the fatal tsetse fly, there will be no herds available for hundreds of miles. If he is a townsman, working in the copper mines or as a clerk in some administrative center, he may have to get leave from work and travel far into the bush in search of a cattle farmer able and willing to sell him the required beasts. Then he has to get them to his girl's village. Otherwise, he must try to persuade the girl's parents to accept cash.

The amount demanded varies from £5 * to more than £100, according to the value set on the girl. An educated one rates high. But the money must be paid either at once or in installments, or the wife may be whisked away at any time, back to her father and perhaps to a new suitor with ready cash.

Some tribes demand the main payment at the wedding, some after the birth of the first child, others after the second. (A wife who does not produce a child promptly is a poor bargain.) If the husband has not managed to collect the money by then, he loses wife and children—for many tribes are matriarchal and the children are the property of the wife's family.

Should the couple quarrel and divorce, the father again may lose all the children, and the same thing happens if his wife should die. Her relatives take the children away. If the man belongs to a patriarchal tribe, and the marriage breaks up, then they really have a wrangle about the fate of the children.

Getting consent of the girl's relatives has it snags—as "letters to Josephine" show. Sometimes she has belligerent brothers; and if the man happens to belong to a different tribe, he is certain to face suspicion and hostility from older relatives.

* At the time this was written, the pound (£) was worth about $2.80 in U.S. currency.

His own family, as well, insists on having a say in the matter. Frequently father or uncle claims the right to pick out a bride for him. In the old days they went unchallenged, but now young men are more independent and may resent having a strange girl thrust on them. If they do not respect the wishes of their elders, however, they feel guilty about it.

These, then, are just a few of the pitfalls in the path of an African Romeo.

"Tell me, Josephine"

I love a girl till Kingdom Come. But she is Chewa by tribe and I am Tumbuka. The Chewa folk use cattle for paying lobola but in my tribe we do not own cattle for this thing. Easier for me to deliver wild buffaloes from the forest! It is a stupid thing they ask of me.

But at the thought of losing her, tears come to my eyes.

Answer

Few girls are worth a dowry of buffaloes. Why not save your money and go to buy cattle from the tribes that keep them? It is wise to respect tribal custom, if possible.

"Tell me, Josephine"

We intend marriage, but my Martha's parents demand two head of cattle as lobola, plus £5. I have not got these things. I have only a good lot of money, since I am a miner and cattle cannot be bought in the town. But the parents refuse to listen, they say they do not want money only.

Answer

Ask your District Commissioner where cattle can be bought. If he does not know, tell the parents that their child must remain unmarried unless they take money, since cattle cannot be bought at the mines. Most parents want their daughters to marry and a miner has a good job.

"Tell me, Josephine"

I am from Barotseland and the girl of my choice is not. I wrote a letter to my parents, trying to explain all the love in my heart but they say I must leave the girl alone.

They say, "We have found a girl for you to marry—just send your picture and the money for lobola."

I was in town soon after birth, educated in town, and have never visited my tribal home, so know nothing of it. Can I have my girl without my parents' consent, or must I obey and send money and picture for a girl "cash with order"?

Answer

Since you are paying the lobola I think you have the right to choose the wife. It is one matter to follow tribal custom if you live in the village and your parents help with lobola. But these ways do not always suit people who live in town.

Stand firm—marry the girl of your choice. Why let old customs spoil your life? Apologize to your parents and send them gifts.

SAUCEPAN RADIO

Around 1949, the Director of Information in Lusaka, Mr. Harry Franklin, was stepping up broadcasts on the African service. One snag was that few would-be listeners could afford a radio set.

A saucepan factory gave Mr. Franklin and his advisers an idea for providing cheap hard-wearing containers for the sets.

A battery manufacturer helped, and soon after, the first "saucepan radios" were shipped from Britain to Lusaka. They had a dry battery and simple short-wave receiver and sold for £6/5s. A blue-glazed iron saucepan, nine inches across, was used, with the handle removed. It stood on its side and the front had a gauze-covered opening, a knob for switching on and volume control, with a cardboard dial below.

The set was painted blue since the various tribes had superstitions against almost every other color. The sets were an enormous success and spread all over Africa.

"Tell me, Josephine"

Wedding bells were promised with a girl of fifteen, but when her parents were asked to send marriage messages, they said "no."

They say she has an elder sister unmarried and it is against custom for the young one to be married first. My girl refuses to ask the older one to marry as this would disturb her studies.

Another thing—I have given my girl a lot of presents and a saucepan radio.

Answer

What is your hurry? Fifteen is young for a wife. Let her go on with her studies too for a while. Arrange for her to take a domestic science course, perhaps, so that she will learn to feed you well. She will think of you as she looks at your presents and listens to the radio. Then when the course ends, her sister may have married.

"Tell me, Josephine"

I recently married Miss Right, and have no objection to continue matrimony till death us do part, but one problem hurts us. This is our £35 radio.

Being of different tribe from my wife, I do not know what to do every afternoon at four when the studio broadcasts in vernaculars. She calls for one tongue, I for another. What shall we do? Must we remain without a radio?

Answer

One day she listens to the radio while you read the newspaper. Next day you listen while she reads the newspaper.

TRIBAL GENEROSITY

"Tell me, Josephine"

I am well known, with a big family to feed. My house is by the bus stop, and every day I receive visitors from the home village. It is my duty to give my tribesfolk food and money for their journey needs. But my family suffer from hunger and I go without the decent clothes my position calls for. Though I have a good job, I am kept poor by home people.

I do not dislike them, but what can I do to be saved from them?

Answer

Word has got around of your generosity and willingness to put tribal custom before your own family's needs.

You must be less generous. When you are paid, go straight to buy the clothes you need most urgently. Lock up your house sometimes when the bus is due, and take your family to visit friends.

When visitors come, say they are welcome to stay overnight if in exchange for your accommodation they will share out a little of the food they have brought for the journey. Explain that having so many visitors has made you a poor man, and your children hungry.

If things still do not improve, try to move to a house further from the bus stop.

BICYCLES ARE IMPORTANT

Perhaps the most useful and highly prized family possession in Rhodesia is the bicycle. Here, it is not used to speed one man alone over the long stretches between villages and townships; it may be required to carry the whole family—father pedaling, mother on the crossbar with baby strapped to her back, and another child on the carrier behind.

Light sports models are not popular. What everyone prefers is a strong heavy job, capable of carrying the family, a load of firewood, or a 100-pound bag of meal.

Young men cycling the hundreds of miles from town to town in search of work carry all their worldly possessions, usually in a fiber suitcase and a blanket roll. The more clothes-conscious will hook a clothes hanger in the back of their collars, and cycle with uncreased shirt or jacket streaming out behind.

Charcoal burners bring their sacks out from deep in the woods by bicycle, trudging alongside with the charred wood balanced from handlebars to saddle.

"Tell me, Josephine"

I plan to buy a bicycle for leisure use, and when I am at work I will let my wife ride on it for shopping. She says her lady-skirts are too tight to get her on a man's bicycle so I must buy one made for a lady.

I tell her she will be sitting sideways on the crossbar when we go out together, and our son on the back barrier. If there is no crossbar, she must stay home when I take leisure trips.

She still firmly argues that this bicycle will be no good to her. Yet if I buy her kind, my friends will laugh and call me woman. How can our dilemma be solved?

Answer

Buy your wife a new wide skirt for bicycling.

WHEN THE LIGHTS GO OUT

"Tell me, Josephine"

At nights after work I study for my GCE by correspondence. I have a single room and pay to have electricity. Our block is the only one at present with the lights. We do not have a light each, there is a hole in one wall and the bulb is set here, shining on me one side and my neighbor next door too.

We cannot turn the lights on and off; they are set to come on at sunset and go off at nine o'clock. I cannot study late. My neighbors do not care to study so do not complain. They sleep at nine. They say I have no case for complaining to the authorities. I argue against this. What do you say?

Answer

Since your neighbors are all content with the arrangement and want to sleep at nine, I doubt if the management would keep the light on just for you.

You are only paying for the time that the light is on. I think it worth your while to buy a kerosene lamp to use when you study late. Put it on the table, not high up, so that the light will not disturb the man next door.

From Tell Me, Josephine, *edited by Barbara Hall, Simon and Schuster, 1964.*

A Head Grows Proper

BY ESTHER WARNER

Esther Warner was the wife of a botanist who went to Liberia during the Second World War to work on research problems for the Firestone Rubber Company.

After several years in Liberia, Mrs. Warner returned to the United States and wrote a book called *New Song in a Strange Land.* In "A Head Grows Proper," a chapter from this book, she describes one of her typical experiences as a sculptor in which her sympathy and understanding evoke similar response from the Mandingo, Bassau, and Vai tribes with whom she came in contact. Her story is flavored with the quaint pidgin English of the area.

At the end of her book Mrs. Warner says: "I only know that the wealth of the country is not in the things that white men, since the days of the Portuguese sailing ships, have gone there to find—gold, ivory, pepper, slaves and rubber. The real wealth is in the intrinsic fineness and the amazing culture of the native tribesmen."

From the day I discovered that the wood in the woodbox was solid mahogany, I longed to try it under my chisel. Except for a few experimental chips, I had to wait until a carpenter could be found to make a work bench, and until a palaver-house studio could be built.

The work bench started with the live tree, standing in the bush. Willie Sawyer and his brother Moses took a day to explore for something they called "black gum," which makes good planks. They took me to the tree when they had found it, hacking a path through the dense undergrowth with a cutlass. Saw grass cut through the sleeves of my shirt and laced my arms with narrow gashes. The leather of my shoes was cut through by the razor edges. The double-pronged barbs of the climbing palms caught into my flesh and held me helpless as a fish until I released myself. Yet Willie and Moses walked ahead of me barefooted and without clothing except for brief loin aprons, and they were unscathed.

"It be a way of walking, Ma," Willie told me. "When Ma walks, she go ahead with force the whole time. So walk all your people. It be the United States way. The grass catch you, and hurt you the whole length of the leaf. We-part can't fight the leaf so; we let the leaf bend we, we no bend the leaf."

When we reached the tree, the salty perspiration that was streaming from my every pore smarted in the fretwork of gashes that covered my body. I sat down wearily on a log while Willie talked to the great tree in Bush Bassau.

"What's the one you are talking, Willie?"

"I make a begging to the tree, Missy. I tell the tree I sorry too much to put ax to the tree, Missy. I tell the tree that Missy need him. I say the Missy got good heart for everything that live, and she can have good ways for the wood. When the wood live for the Missy house, it heart can lay down good."

I coveted for the people of my country this feeling for a living tree. If a "begging from the heart" were made to every tree before it was cut in the United States . . .

When the swaying weight of the tree had torn the anchor of vines and lay on the ground it was amazingly large. The Bassaus have a saying, "Do not measure your tree in the jungle."

"Plenty good friend have to help we carry the stick high," said Willie, appraising its great girth. "Today we build the saw stand and make the small kitchen for cook chop while we work."

Willie and Moses cut good planks and made good talk when they stopped to rest and cook small chop in the kitchen. From the time that the pepper bird made his loud talk until the sun "sat down small" on the dead trees on the western hill, Willie and Moses lived with their work.

While they shared their roast cassava with me around the small kitchen fire, Willie told me about his pa who "could cut stick past all people."

"My-part work in the land of my people," I told him, "is also to cut stick. I like to see the way your pa can do."

"Tomorrow-time," Willie promised, "I bring you small thing from the hand of Chief Kondea, my pa."

The thing he brought me was a wooden rice spoon, smooth as satin, beautifully proportioned and balanced.

"How Kondea can make the wood smooth like the stone that live for the river?" I asked.

"Hah, Ma, you don't know that one? I show you." He was off to the bush and brought back a handful of leaves. The undersides were rough with thorny prickles.

"That one fine country sandpaper," he said. "When God make the world he make plenty thing for the people who cut stick."

The palaver-house studio progressed as slowly as the work bench. The poles for the uprights and roof were brought from the bush, and the palm thatch for the cone-shaped roof was laid in a long cord, but there was no rattan with which to tie the thatch onto the roof poles.

While I waited through the delays, I sorted all the wood beneath the house and stacked the largest solid pieces in a separate pile. I wanted to find a typical and characteristic head-type in each of the different tribes. Already I could identify most of the tribesmen by their head shapes and facial characteristics. But I wanted to make something more than a record of head contours, something more than portraits of individuals. I wanted to say something in wood about the lean weeks when the supply of rice in the rice kitchens is finished and the new crop has not yet come in; something about the patience with which native people fight the jungle; something about the quick joy that possesses a face when the dance drums throb; something of the reverence with which they listen to the wind.

"Fire must not catch this part," I told Buno Yardboy when I had sorted out the best wood.

Wheager was my first model. I first saw his tattered petunia-colored shirt rippling in the evening breeze while I stood at a window admiring the purples and reds of a sunset. It was as though a few shreds of colored cloud had been torn from the heavens by one of the stark branches of the big dead trees on the horizon, and had floated down to me. Above the fluttering shirt was an old, yellow American straw hat. The top of the crown was taking leave of the straight sides, so that as Wheager bounced along he was not only shaded, but also fanned, by the flopping circle of straw.

"Who lives under the hat?" I sent Johnny to find out.

"The hat live for the head of one boy named Robert Wheager Fisher Yardboy," reported Johnny.

Wheager had two interests: keeping his stomach full, and remembering the happy days he had spent with Mr. Fisher, who gave Wheager his old straw hat when he went back to the States.

Wheager vexed my coast Bassaus with his aversion for soap and water.

"Wheager is a Bush Bassau," Johnny explained, "and those people can't care for clean. All your other Bassau boys take three hot baths every day. Even the Kpuesi people take bath past Wheager. Sometimes water can't touch Wheager for a whole week together."

Sammi didn't want Wheager in his kitchen. None of the boys would let him sit on their beds. But when Wheager sat on the grass and told them stories about his pa and about Mr. Fisher, they rolled with laughter. Wheager was the court jester, a little gnome with knobby knees whose only contribution to the world was to make everyone around him laugh. Before beginning a story, Wheager always gathered up the tattered ribbons of his purple shirt which once had been the top part of one of Mr. Fisher's pajamas, stuffed the bulk of his silken rags into his negligible trousers, and affectionately patted the result. Then the story went on with elaborate gestures. Afterward when I tried to write down his tales, they did not seem good. Like the gift without the giver, Wheager's stories without Wheager were bare.

When the water was to be carried, Wheager was out looking for sweet potatoes. When there was wood to be chopped, Wheager was in the swamp hunting for bullfrogs. When the animal food was to be cooked, Wheager was gone to find cassava. He would eat his week's ration of rice in two days and spend the other five hunting food.

The more I saw of Wheager's impish face with its amazing prognathous jaw, the more certain I was that I wanted him for my first model. I explained to him that I wanted to make his photo in wood and all he needed to do was to sit still for a long time. This seemed to strike him as a pleasing occupation for which he was suited by temperament.

"I will wear my new trouser for the photo," he said.

"But the photo I make is for the head part only. Trouser can't show in this one."

"Oh, Missy, the trouser can show!" he said. "When a boy got new trouser, the heart can grow big with glad. And when the heart be glad, the glad can show in the face. So, you see, the trouser can show."

"But where you get new trouser?" I asked. "You never take pay from my hand, because the moon never finish, this time."

"Missy, one man die in my pa's town," said Wheager happily. "This man, he leff his trouser to me. It is necessary I walk one day to reach my people. That night, my people give me plenty rice, and I sleep for the town. Soon morning, I come again with the trouser in my hand."

When Wheager appeared in my living room with his inheritance rolled in a tight gray bundle under his arm, I gave him blue soap and sent him to the creek to beat the garment on the washing rock, wondering of what horrible disease his benefactor had died.

"Soap and rock can make new cloth fini soon," objected Wheager.

"Dirty trouser can make yardboy work fini soon," I said sternly.

When the gray pants came back from the creek they were, to my surprise and Wheager's delight, cream-colored with a black pin-stripe. They added greatly to his sartorial impressiveness.

As the Wheager head grew, Wheager talked to it constantly. He gave it detailed instructions about how to behave. He seemed to think of it as a sort of other self that might bring him into palavers.

When I had the mouth blocked out, he announced, "Now the head ready to take chop. Let me go find small chop for the head. It can no grow proper without small chop."

The head demanded increasing amounts of food to "grow proper" as the work progressed. Several stalks of bananas, many lengths of sugar cane, and a few unfortunate snakes, rats, and bullfrogs were consumed.

Wheager looked at the finished carving for a long time, and finally announced, "It be Wheager for true."

From New Song in a Strange Land, *by Esther Warner, Houghton Mifflin Company, 1948.*

What Is Negritude?

BY LÉOPOLD SÉDAR SENGHOR

Léopold Sédar Senghor, poet-president of Senegal, was honored in September 1966 by Howard University at the opening convocation of its Centennial. In appreciation of his leadership as a statesman, scholar and poet, he was awarded the degree of Doctor of Humane Letters.

As a young man, Senghor was a brilliant student in the schools of his homeland and in Paris. He was the first agrégé from Black Africa, an academic rank signifying that he had passed examinations higher than those leading to the doctorate. Steeped in French culture, he taught for years in French secondary schools and was imprisoned by the Nazis during the Second World War. Later, he represented Senegal in the French National Assembly and took a leading part in his country's independence movement. He was elected the first president of Senegal in 1960 and re-elected in 1963.

In awarding the degree to Senghor, the acting president of Howard University said: "In your poetry you have sung of Africa and the Negro, of your childhood in Senegal, of your homesickness as a young student in Paris, of African Masks, of the Black Woman 'clad in her color which is life, in her form which is beauty.' You have eulogized the Senegalese martyrs and American Negro soldiers. You have found poetry in the mighty Congo River and in the streets of New York City.

"Convinced that the Negro has made and will continue to make a significant cultural contribution to world civilization, you have become the spokesman of Negritude. Your unshakable faith in the Negro's cultural heritage and potential found its crowning justification a few months ago in the First World Festival of Negro Arts, which you sponsored."

The following speech delivered by Senghor in accepting the degree from Howard University explains why the poet-president considers the concept of Negritude so important in contemporary Africa.

For some thirty-five years I have known of the existence of Howard University. For thirty-five years I have pondered over its significance, imagining it to be the temple of Negritude in the U.S.A. Is it not the university of Alain Locke, the spiritual father of the Negro Renaissance? This is why, Mr. President, I could not be more sensitive to any honor than the one you are conferring upon me today.

I am convinced that my only merit is that of having been for thirty-five years a conscious and constant militant for Negritude. In the French-speaking world I did not invent the word. It came rather from my friend, the poet and dramatist Aimé Cesaire. And I surely did not invent the concept—that ideology which has enabled tens of nations, a whole race throughout the world, to recover its being, its strength, if not the taste for life.

"A tiger does not proclaim its tigritude," a Nigerian writer quipped. I was asked what I thought about that. I fear that it may indicate an inferiority complex inoculated by the former colonizer, a complex that the former "colonizee" has not yet cured.

My answer would be: The tiger does not proclaim its tigritude because it neither speaks nor thinks. It is an animal. To man alone the privilege is given to think and rethink his thought: the privilege to know himself. *Gnothi seauton,* Socrates advised.

The British speak of "Anglo-Saxon civilization" because they are men, and the French speak of "French civilization" or of "Greco-Latin civilization." We Negroes speak of Negritude, for we too are men—men who, forty thousand years ago, were the first to emerge as *Homo sapiens*, the first men to express themselves in art, the first to create the earliest agrarian civilization in the valleys of the Nile and of Mesopotamia.

Yet I must render to you, Negro Americans, what belongs to Negro Americans: the merit of having invented, before all others, perhaps not the word but, certainly, what is more important, the concept, the ideology of Negritude. To be sure, at the beginning of this century the French and Germans had made known and extolled first the artistic values, then the social and philosophical values of Negritude. The École de Paris, at the height of its triumph and

Young sculptor creates new designs from old materials. *(UNESCO/ Paul Almasy)*

Women traders in West Africa have always been the backbone of the huge markets which sell foods, clothing, crafts. People travel for miles to these mammoth trading centers. *(Mary A. McAlpin/Palmer)*

Women fill varied roles in family and community life.

Mother and child *(above left)* in Uganda are symbol of the extended family or clan. *(East Africa Tourist Agency)* Young women *(above right)* on the Ivory Coast take evening course in arithmetic. *(UNESCO/A. Tessore)* Woman delegate *(below)* in Nigeria practices her script. *(Nigerian Consulate)*

Farming *(top)* is the chief occupation in Ethiopia where old methods are still common. *(Marc & Evelyne Bernheim/Guillumette)* Workers on a community project mix cement for a model home in Ghana. *(UNESCO/Marc & Evelyne Bernheim)* Miners *(right)* working two miles down in South African mines are known by numbers only, not names. *(Margaret Bourke-White/Life Magazine © Time, Inc.)*

Women *(above)* in Ghana carry cement in rhythmic manner. *(UNESCO/Marc & Evelyne Bernheim)* Singing acts as stimulant to co-operative road-building in Nigeria. *(Nigerian Consulate)*

Educational aims are changing in Africa, but knowledge has always had a high priority. According to an old African proverb: "Not to know is bad: not to want to know is worse."

Social welfare *(above)* is the subject of a village meeting in Ghana which attracts men, women, and children. (UNESCO/*Marc & Evelyne Bernheim*) "I Will Try" is the motto of the Livingstonia School in Malawi, which Legson Kayira attended. *(Peace Corps/Charles Over-holt)*

Child care class *(above)* in Congo uses live baby as model. *(United Nations)* School fees *(left)* are paid in coffee beans by Ugandan student. *(S. G. Weeks)* Biology students use new equipment at Uganda Technical College. *(United Nations)*

Sports and games appeal to Africans of all ages.

Students *(above)* in the Central African Republic at Emile Gentil College practice broad jump. *(UNESCO/Louis Duré)*

Children's game *(above)* in the Congo needs no expensive equipment. *(Leon V. Kofod/ APA)* Ethiopian boy *(left)* learns about boxing from Peace Corps Volunteer at Haile Selassie University. *(Peace Corps/Phil Hardberger)*

Nigerian women carrying head loads with grace and dignity. *(Mary A. McAlpin/Palmer)*

*Traveling is popular
whether on foot, bicycle,
by air, rail, bus or
mammy wagon.*

Children *(above)* obey safety patrols on the way to school in Eastern Nigeria. *(Nigerian Consulate)*

Airport hostesses *(left)* in traditional and modern dress meet at Nairobi Airport, one of the busiest in the world. *(East African Airways)*

Family *(right)* travels by bicycle in Uganda. *(Uganda Information)*

Mammy wagons are the principal carriers in West Africa for passengers and produce. *(P. Larsen/Palmer)*

Tribal groups continue to live in the ways of their ancestors.

Pygmies *(left)* race through the Ituri Forest to see what their nets have captured. *(Leon V. Kofod/APA)* Women of the bushmen tribe in the Kalahari Desert store precious water in ostrich eggshells. *(Museum of Natural History)*

Masai tribesmen are proud nomads whose wealth and social standing are counted in cattle. *(P. Larsen/Palmer)*

Contemporary art has an important part to play in independent Africa.

Nigerian father and daughter *(above left)* display art pieces of their community. *(Nigerian Consulate)* Idah, *(above right)* modern craftsman, works in cement to create fresh designs for the palace at Benin. *(Nigeria Magazine)* Art class *(below)* in Ugandan secondary school encourages new talent. *(P. Latham)*

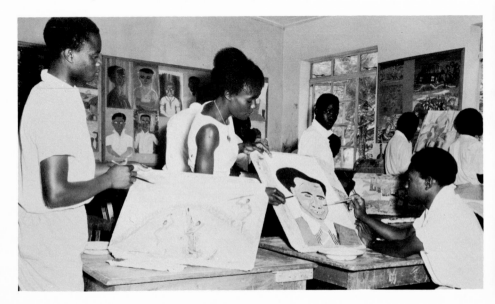

The Dakar World Festival of Negro Arts offered nightly programs of dance, drama, and music from more than twenty-five African states.

Dance group from Ghana gave outstanding performances. (*Courtesy Mercer Cook*)

Duke Ellington receives congratulations from President Senghor with U. S. Ambassador Cook (*center*) after concert at Dakar Festival. A Senghor poem reads: "Play 'Solitude' again, Duke, so I can cry myself to sleep." (*Courtesy Mercer Cook*)

Jomo Kenyatta, surrounded by his Cabinet, salutes crowd after announcing date of Kenya's independence. *(Kenya Mission)*

Noni Jabavu *(left)* is the distinguished Xhosa author. *(St. Martin's Press)* Legson Kayira *(center)* is the boy from Malawi who decided to walk to America for his education. *(Skagit Valley Herald)* Josephine, the mysterious columnist of the *Central African Mail*, is not one, but three people: *(left to right)* David Maango, Barbara Hall, and Kay Sufiniso. *(Simon and Schuster)*

while it was the pride of Western civilization had, by borrowing from us, given us a place at the universal banquet table. Without overlooking the role played by Haiti, the fact remains that you were the ones who, between the years 1920 and 1925, started the Negro Renaissance and gave birth to the New Negro, conscious of his Negritude, determined to *live* it: to defend it and make it famous.

Some years later, in the Latin Quarter of Paris, a few young men, a few students, found, on reading you, the remedy for their confusion and food to appease their hunger for dignity, or rather, an example to follow. For you were not only talking about Negritude, you were living it, you were Negritude.

I am pleased to render homage here to the pioneer thinkers who lighted our path in the years 1930–1935: Alain Locke, W. E. B. DuBois, Marcis Garvey, Carter G. Woodson. And also to pay well-deserved tribute to the poets whose works we translated and recited, and in whose footsteps we tried to follow: Claude McKay, Jean Toomer, Countee Cullen, James Weldon Johnson, Langston Hughes, Sterling Brown. I cannot forget the two magazines that we feverishly skimmed through: *The Crisis* and *Opportunity*. That was a time of fervor. At the First World Festival of Negro Arts I quoted a poem by Langston Hughes that I had translated thirty years before and that the poet himself no longer remembered. And how could I forget that one of those who initiated us to the New Negro Movement, along with Paulette Nardal, founder of the *Review of the Negro World,* was a Negro American, a student at the Sorbonne —Mercer Cook, who is present here today and once again a professor at Howard University.

But what is Negritude? As you may well guess, we have often been asked that question. It is neither a French engine of war, as has been charged, nor one of those brilliant abstract ideas which are so often born in Paris. Once again, though the word was coined in France— invented, moreover, by a West Indian, an American—the thing itself, the ideology, was indeed a product of the Negroes of the U.S.A.

And yet, before being an ideology, an ideal, Negritude is first of all a fact. It was Langston Hughes who wrote, shortly after World War I: "We younger Negro artists who create now intend to express our individual dark-skinned selves without fear or shame."

Yes, that's what Negritude is first of all, "Negro personality," the fact of being a Negro among other men who are not black. For you, as you have felt and still feel, this means being Negro Americans among white Americans. For us, Negro Africans, this meant, yesterday, being the colonized among the colonizers. Today it means being underdeveloped nations among the developed nations, being poor in the midst of the rich. Thus, in reality, the fact is a *situation*, a network of relationships.

It is because we are in a situation that the fact of being Negro solicited yesterday and requires today an ideology, in other words, an ideal situation in the future. Yesterday's ideology consisted in disalienation and in the resolve to be free, the equal of other men before the law. For you, it was a matter of getting rid of slavery and segregation; for us, it was a question of getting rid of colonization. The truth of this year 1966, this year of the centennial, is that though you have transcended slavery, you have not yet completely transcended segregation; by the same token, though we have gotten rid of colonization, we have not yet completely mastered underdevelopment. Thanks to your own efforts and to men of faith among your white fellow citizens, you are walking on the road to integration. Thanks to the efforts of the Negro African peoples themselves and to the aid of rich friendly nations, we are on the road to *development*.

These are the reasons which offer us in 1966, in this centennial year of your university, a new ideology, a new ideal to be realized. On the one hand, the abolition of slavery and the beginning of integration; on the other hand, decolonization and membership in the UN have become possible only through the discovery, under the Negro fact, of the values of Negritude. As early as 1808, Abbé Grégoire, the leader of the French abolitionists, in a volume entitled *On the Literature of Negroes,* had made Europe aware of Negro culture. Let us make no mistake about it: it is because one discovered men and a civilization under the Negro fact—under the black skin and the flat nose—that our situation has changed.

To repeat, because that situation is being normalized, we must set up a new ideal to be realized, a new world to be built. But, in truth, it has begun to be built, the new humanism of the twentieth century. It can be deeper and richer than the humanism of the Great Renaissance. For the latter, while resuscitating Roman and Greek ruins, massacred the Indians and organized the slave trade.

Twentieth century humanism will be the symbiosis of all human values if only all civilizations contribute to it. Negro civilization first and foremost. For there is, underneath the physical fact of being Negro, a mine of cultural—technical and spiritual—values, by which Negritude is defined. But why have I said "Negro civilization first and foremost"? That is what I should like to explain in my conclusion.

Forty thousand years ago, the Negroes then were the first men to create works of art, the first to give art, better than its techniques and rules, its deepest significance. It was because Western art, except during the Christian Middle Ages, had forgotten this significance that it degenerated until the twentieth century, when the values of Negritude came to reteach the West and the world not only the meaning of art, but also that of man.

But what is this meaning of art? Let us return to the first statuettes in soapstone and ivory, sculptured by the Negroids of Grimaldi. Let us remember two of them: the famous Venuses of Grimaldi and Lespugue. Their creation answers the fundamental needs of man, which the Grimaldian artist, the Negro artist, satisfies by the characteristics of his arts.

The first spiritual need of *Homo sapiens,* of the man who has crossed the thresholds of reflection and co-reflection, is to express his inner self in the form of an idea. This is what our sculptors do when they express the idea of fertility, that is to say, the idea of life everlasting. This is the very idea of the human being in all its fullness. Thus, the first characteristic of Negro art is always to turn its back to the anecdotic, to express an essential idea.

Here is its second characteristic. The idea is expressed concretely but not directly in the manner of a photograph; it is expressed by an image-symbol. Man translates his inner self by choosing the elements of his language in the dictionary of nature, the dictionary of external forms. The Grimaldian artist translates the idea of fertility by the image of a woman with rounded forms.

I should have said, by repeating curved forms. In order to acquire its strength as a symbol, the image must be rhythmic. I need not explain to Negro Americans what rhythm is. It is unity in diversity, asymmetrical parallelism, repetition in change. It is at once the most concrete and the most abstract expression of life: the most sensual because it is expressed in or by our senses; the most spiritual because it suggests rather than describes.

Starting from these characteristics of Negritude, you can guess what could be deduced from them, in the realm of thought, for a philosophy of life. Thus it is that, at the beginning of this century, without even waiting for our complete emancipation, we began to make our contribution to the civilization of the universal: in America, Europe, Africa, everywhere in this vast world.

Ever since a Negro mask appeared, like a phantom, in a Paris bistro, ever since the first muted trumpet sounded in the cemetery during the First World War, one no longer paints, sculptures, sings, or dances—I may even say one no longer thinks, at least one no longer lives—as one used to do in this world. Warmth has been communicated, dialogue has been established between man and man, who has regained the taste for life.

Mr. President, Ladies and Gentlemen:

Despite the trials which at this very moment are bearing down on the black community in the U.S.A., this is no time to be discouraged. It is, in large measure, by you and by America that the values of Negritude, that the values of life, have conquered the world. Your greatest strength lies not in material arms but in those of the spirit: the living values of Negritude.

Continue your work of humanism, and the rest—your fair share of temporal power—will be given you to boot.

From a speech delivered by Léopold Sédar Senghor at Howard University, September 1966.

Behind the Mask of Africa

BY ANDRÉ MALRAUX

The First World Festival of Negro Arts, held at Dakar, capital of Senegal, in April 1966, was a cultural event of the first magnitude. Its exhibit of traditional African art presented a once-in-a-lifetime display of Benin bronzes, masks, and other priceless items on loan from private American, African, and European collections and museums. An exhibit of contemporary art included works by Africans and artists of African descent from such countries as Brazil, Haiti, and the United States. An Artisan Village featured handicrafts by skilled craftsmen.

The value of Negro culture and identity, sometimes called Negritude, was interwoven in all aspects of the Dakar festival. It was the link between the collection of traditional African art, which Senegal's President Senghor called the "heart of the festival," and the nightly performances by drama, dance, and musical groups, representing more than twenty-five African states, the West Indies, Brazil, and the United States. The American participants—Duke Ellington and his orchestra, the De Paur Chorus, the Marian Williams Gospel Singers, pianist Armenta Adams, soprano Martina Arroya, and the Alvin Ailey Dancers—won enthusiastic and well-deserved acclaim.

Above all, the Dakar festival was an opportunity for people to meet people. It was an opportunity for younger and older devotees of African culture to meet and exchange ideas. It was a unique experience for the 2,000 Negro artists and 10,000 visitors who attended the three-week festival. Sponsored by the government of Senegal, UNESCO, and the African Society of Culture in Paris, the festival was stimulating and it was informative. Its guiding spirit was Léopold Sédar Senghor, the poet-president of Senegal, who said on the opening night that the purpose of the festival was "the elaboration of a new humanism which this time will include all humanity on the whole of our planet earth."

Highlight of the festival was a colloquium on "Negro Art in the Life of the People" which attracted artists, writers, and Africanists from all over the world. The keynote speaker of the colloquium was France's Minister of Cultural Affairs, novelist and art critic André Malraux. This distinguished author of *Man's Fate* and *The Voices of Silence,* who has been called the most representative humanist of his time, delivered the following thought-provoking and somewhat controversial speech on the artistic heritage of Africa.

So we step into history. For the first time, a mortal man, a head of state, has taken into his hands the cultural destiny of a continent.

Never before in the history of a continent—never in Europe, Asia or America—has the head of a state said: "Together we are going to try to determine the future of our culture."

What we are attempting today resembles the early councils of the Church. Our aim is to vindicate and illustrate the artistic creation of Africa. But before we begin, ladies and gentlemen, it will be as well to clarify certain distinctions which have become rather too blurred during the last ten years.

A culture is primarily a people's intrinsic response to the universe. But here, today, the word has two different, though complementary, meanings. On the one hand, we are speaking of the artistic heritage of Africa; on the other, we are speaking of its creative life. So, on the one hand, we are speaking of a past; and on the other, of a future.

The artistic heritage (I repeat *artistic*) of Africa does not include all the arts—not, for example, architecture; it includes dancing, music, literature, sculpture.

Africa has transformed dancing throughout the world. But there is also a field of dancing which is uniquely her own: I refer to her secular and sacred dancing. This is dying out and it is the responsibility of African governments to save it. But this second aspect of Africa's contribution to the art of dancing is quite different from the first. Sacred dancing is one of the noblest expressions of Africa, as of all the great cultures. The fact that no American, Englishman, or Frenchman now dances as his grandmother did is of quite another order.

As for music, here too we must be on our guard. Africa, ladies and gentlemen, has two musics. One is the music born of despair long ago in the United States; it is the great lamentation, the eternal voice of affliction which, with its searing originality, has passed into European music. I remember asking Yehudi Menuhin, "What does music most constantly convey to you?" to which he replied, "And to you?" I was moved to reply, "Nostalgia. The great music of Europe is the song of paradise lost." Menuhin said, "There is also praise . . ." Now observe this: The first great music of Africa does not sing of a lost or even an unknown paradise, but of very simple, very ordinary happiness in a world wrested forever from the unfortunate men who improvised songs on the banks of the Mississippi while the sun went down behind palm trees like the palm trees of Africa.

But this music is similar to our own; only it is physically more exciting.

And then there is jazz. It is a species apart by virtue of its rhythm; it is a musical invention. It is also a species apart by virtue of its musical content which we can relate to modern music but not to the classical or traditional music of the West. We can sometimes relate the content of the greatest jazz music to that of Stravinsky or Boulez. But jazz came first. Here Africa has invented, in a highly complex field of art, that of musical content, something which today reaches the entire world as powerfully as her contribution to dancing has reached dancers.

Music of this kind, working up sensation to paroxysm, seems deliberately self-destructive. I ask you to consider what, in another field, is the art of a painter like Picasso . . .

To conclude, jazz takes its origins from European or American melodic elements which have enabled Africa to rediscover her soul; or, more exactly, to discover a soul which she did not possess before; for although the blues perhaps express her soul of despair, what jazz expresses has no link with her past. She has really invented jazz.

And it is perhaps in much the same way that Africa, starting out from a poetry akin to Western poetry, has charged it with an emotional fury disrupting models and prototypes.

Finally, the greatest of African arts: sculpture. It is through her sculpture that Africa takes again her place in the mind of man. It has often been said that this sculpture is a sculpture of signs. But signs, let us add, charged with emotion and creating emotion.

It is also a sculpture of symbols, in the sense in which Romanesque art is an art of symbols. These works were born as magic works, as we all know; but they are experienced by us as aesthetic works.

It is said: "By you, Westerners." I don't believe this. I do not believe that there is one of my African friends—writers, poets, sculptors—who responds to the art of masks or ancestors in the same way as the sculptor who created these figures. I do not believe that any one of us Europeans responds to the kings on the main door of Chartres as the sculptor who created them.

The truth is that a magic or sacred art is created in a universe of which the artist is not the master. When the sacred element disappears, all that remains in the artist's creation is an obscure communion or sympathy. This sympathy, in the etymological sense of the word, runs very deep throughout Africa. But for the sculptor of Chartres, the statues which we call the kings, and are really saints, *were prayed to but not admired;* and for the Africans who sculpted masks, the masks referred to a religious truth and not to an aesthetic quality.

To believe that we—even Africans—can recover the world of magic is vain and dangerous for two reasons: first it is false, and secondly our mistake would prevent us from receiving from this august art all that it can bring to us, Africans and Europeans.

Metamorphosis has played a leading role here. Certainly African sculpture seems very closely related to modern sculpture. But the fact remains that when we look at a sculpture by Lipchitz or Laurens we know that we are not looking at a mask because, although our relationship with the mask is not that of magic, magic is *in* the mask. African sculpture had a sphere of reference which is not that of modern art: it referred to the supernatural, whereas modern art refers simply to art, whether we like it or not.

This brings us to the fundamental problem of this conference. When African sculpture took its place in the world, that is to say, when certain artists began to be aware that they were in the presence of a great art, the field of reference for sculpture of whatever kind was that of Greco-Roman art. Sculpture referred to what was then called nature, either through imitation or through idealization.

As you well know, African sculpture is not concerned with imitation and still less with idealization. What is less well known is that, in the slow but decisive process of establishing itself throughout the world, African sculpture has destroyed the field of reference of art. It has not established its own field of reference; the sculptor who created masks has not established magic. But African art has destroyed the system of reference which denied magic, and it has powerfully contributed to establishing the great epochs of art in the place of Greco-Roman antiquity.

The cultural heritage of mankind has become the great sculpture of India, the great sculpture of Persia, the sculpture of Buddhism, of Sumer and the pre-Columbians. From the day when Africa destroyed the old field of reference and opened up again for art what had once been the vast realm of the supernatural (including our Romanesque sculpture), on that day Africa made her triumphal entry into the artistic life of humanity.

It is not because this particular mask happens to be better than that particular Greek sculpture that the African phenomenon has established itself in the world. It is because from the day when Picasso began his Negro period the spirit which had reigned in the world for thousands of years and disappeared for a brief period (from the seventeenth to the nineteenth century in Europe), this spirit recovered its lost rights. Needless to say, we do not today approach art as we did in the twelfth century, but we have resuscitated the immense field of art which in the twelfth century covered all the regions of the earth.

This is where Africa's claim supremely rests and enforces our recognition. When Africa is in her own realm of spirit and form, we are no longer concerned with one more art or one less, or again with what was once called naïveté or primitivism. What concerns us, when confronted by the genius of Africa, is nothing less than the nature of world art. And inevitably world art acclaims the genius of Africa as one of its own.

Needless to say, the element of species remains: Africa is not India. Africa represents a very special power of communion with the universe; vehemence and pathos place it in direct opposition to the solemn ballet of Asia.

On the one hand, there is the European world which we all know; let us symbolize it by the Victory of Samothrace and leave it at that! And on the other, there is the vast domain which we call the great epochs of art: Egypt, India, China, and all the rest. But there is a difference between Africa and all the rest: this difference is her rhythmic urge and pathetic power. But we have to remember what we call a great epoch of art is nearly everywhere the negation of the pathetic principle, or, in other words, of emotion.

Egypt and Asia have created their style by implying emotion. On the contrary, Africa has created her style out of emotion itself, a style more arbitrary and perhaps more powerful than that of any other civilization. This perhaps will prove to be her decisive contribution to the cultural heritage of mankind.

This heritage will come to Senegal from her own artistic domain, from that of the African continent, and from that of the world. But who is to enjoy it? I need hardly say: All those who want it.

Ladies and gentlemen, there are two ways of furthering culture: One can try to bring it to all; one can try to bring it to each.

In the first case you have to accept an intellectual totalitarianism; you have to accept political domination; you have to accept methods which are the most efficient, but also the most absolute. In the second hypothesis—culture for each—you have to insist that your government gives to each an opportunity.

But in that case, you can also insist on liberty, because it is a question of what the state must give, not of what it can impose.

This leads us from Moscow to Paris, from the Soviet to the French Maisons de la Culture.

Gentlemen, many of you are university men. It is important to clear up the confusion which at present exists between universities and Maisons de la Culture. The aim of the universities is to spread truth. Truth, in its precise meaning, is what can be demonstrated as true. The university develops knowledge, it is qualified to do this and it is our duty to assist it in its task. The Maisons de la Culture do not develop knowledge; they develop emotions. They make works of art come to life for the people who behold them. The aim of the university is to teach what it knows. The aim of the Maisons de la Culture is to make loved what they love.

Here lies an essential distinction. If we fail to draw it, we shall throw the university off its bearings and destroy the Maisons de la Culture.

What is the problem of culture? We think of it as a heritage, if you like. But it is not only that.

Since the beginning of this century the world has undergone a greater transformation than in the previous ten thousand years. Both Einstein and Oppenheimer in turn have said that there are more research workers in science alive today than the sum total of past researchers since the world began.

What is the cause of this transformation? Humanity has decided that the purpose of thought is to discover the laws of the universe and no longer to answer the question "For what purpose is man on earth?" The search for the law of the universe has, in some measure, taken the place of religious questionings.

On the other hand, the transformation of the world is evidently due to the operation of the machine.

For twenty years we have been talking about the materialism of our machine age. Yet neither the civilizations which claim to be Marxist nor those which claim to be anti-Marxist have, save in words, been materialistic.

Russia has said: "The main point is to liberate the proletariat." America has always proclaimed religious or idealistic values.

Note how our machine civilization has multiplied the dream life of humanity in a way hitherto unknown: there are machines to transport us physically, there are also machines to make us dream. Dream factories have never existed before our day. We are in the presence of the radio, the television, the cinema. A hundred years ago, three thousand Parisians a night went to some form of entertainment. Today in the Paris area there are several million television sets. Thus the problem of culture is not to establish a realm of the mind in opposition to a realm of the machine—which is impervious to the mind. On the contrary, the machine is the most powerful means of diffusing the imaginary that the world has ever known. The principal object of culture is to discover what the mind can bring to bear against the multiplication of the imaginary brought about by the machine.

The cinema was not born to serve humanity; it was born to make money. It relies therefore on those very elements of emotion (the comic alone excepted) that are most suspect. Our task, then, must be to combat the power of dream factories for generating money by setting up dream factories for generating spiritual values. In other words, to combat sex and death images by projecting immortal images. Why immortal? We do not know; but we do know that when our soul discovers those great memories which we ourselves have not implanted there, it discovers within itself forces as powerful as its own organic elements. And let us not forget that the African genius is itself partly organic.

Culture is that endeavor; it is not the utilization of leisure.

What I earlier called lamentation, when speaking of the songs of the Mississippi, is part of the heritage of mankind. But it is not despair which is part of it; it is the genius of that despair. Even the most terrifying civilization, once it is dead, no longer bears witness to what made it terrifying. The most atrocious civilization the world has ever known—the Assyrian civilization—has left to memory only the admirable token of the wounded lioness. And if in future times something remains of the concentration camps, it will be images not of the tortures but of the martyrs.

Gentlemen, what we call culture is that mysterious power of things so much older and deeper than we ourselves, things which, in the modern world, are our strongest allies against the power of the dream factories. That is why each country of Africa needs its own cultural heritage, needs the heritage of the African continent and needs too to create its own world heritage.

It has been said: Let us try to recover the African soul which conceived the masks; through it we shall reach the African people. Ladies and gentlemen, I don't believe a word of it. What once inspired the masks, no less than what once inspired the cathedrals, is forever lost. But this country is the heir to its masks and can say: "I have an affinity with them that nobody else has. And when I look at them and ask them to tell me their message of the past, I know that they speak to me, and that it is to me that they speak."

Take into your hands all that was Africa. But take it knowing that you are in the throes of a metamorphosis. When the Egyptians believe themselves to be the descendants of the Pharaohs, that is unimportant; what is important is when they relate themselves to the Pharaohs and say to themselves: How can we be worthy of them?

We Frenchmen have spent so many centuries believing ourselves to be the heirs of the Romans. What were the Romans to France? They were the people who once killed us. But France has become the greatest Roman power. . . .

Make no mistake about the ancient spirits. They are truly the spirits of Africa. They have greatly changed; yet they are there for you to question them. But you will make no communion by studying the ceremonies of the bush. It is indeed for Africa to vindicate her past; but it is still more important for her to be free enough to conceive a past in the world which belongs to her. Men believe themselves less strong and less free than they really are. It is not necessary for you to *know* how you will make your imaginary museum. Did you know how you would create your dance? Did you know what jazz would be? Did you know that, one day, those trifling fetishes which used to be sold like firewood would cover the world with their glory and be bought by our greatest artists? There you have the supreme mystery of metamorphosis.

Africa is strong enough to create her own cultural domain, present and past, provided only that she dares to try. Nothing more is needed.

My country has had, on two or three occasions, its share of greatness: it was when she tried to teach liberty. Ladies and gentlemen, let me end by repeating her ancient message in the realm of the spirit: May Africa conquer her liberty!

Translation of a speech delivered by M. André Malraux at the Dakar Festival, April 1966.

Ibo Music

BY W. W. C. ECHEZONA

William Wilberforce Chukudinka Echezona is a musicologist who spent several years traveling from village to village in Nigeria, studying the indigenous music of the Ibo people. The Ibos are the largest ethnic group in the Eastern Region of Nigeria, where they number more than five million. Mr. Echezona collected this material in partial fulfillment of the requirements for a doctorate in music from Michigan State University. He borrowed special scientific equipment from the physics department at the university in order to measure different pitches and scales of the various Nigerian instruments. While he was making his study, he received a grant from the United States A.I.D. (Agency for International Development) program and conducted village choirs for a mission organization. He is now on the staff of the Department of Music, University of Nigeria, at Nsukka.

Music has always been an important part of African life. Storytellers use music to accompany their stories, just as minstrels did during the Middle Ages in Europe or during the Golden Age in Greece. Songs and dances are a natural part of African weddings, funerals, and tribal ceremonies. They are part of making love and making war. Work parties in the fields or forests would not be complete without music. So it is all over Africa, just as it is with any people where oral tradition is strong.

To every Ibo, life has a melodic and rhythmic orientation. Songs act as a stimulant to cooperative work. Any type of work, whether it can be performed in a rhythmic manner or not, is accompanied by singing. On occasions when men march, they keep time with songs. One of the songs for marching means "Let the unfortunate clear out of the way." In the olden days when wars were rampant, war songs were sung to work the Ibo up to fury for battle. One such song may be translated: "We are so superior physically that we lord it over the enemy."

Frequent marriage ceremonies are a source of folk singing. One common song at this time is "Our daughter is a charming young lady." At funeral obsequies people sing "We are looking for the young man who died, nzomalizo." (Nzomalizo serves the same purpose as "fa-la-la" in madrigals.)

When there are feasts, many masqueraders parade through towns singing special masquerade songs. For paddling canoes, the paddlers sing rhythmic songs to help them in their work. For tapping the national drink of palm wine, the tappers sing *gbenchikichiki*. This is the sound that the tapping knife seems to make as parts of the palm tree are being scooped out.

Again, when a cooperative work group assembles in the morning to go to work on a farm, a flautist, whose shrill notes have meanings, provides the workers with music for their farm labor—even from a long distance away. Often the songs and the accompanists stress the work rhythms.

Another way in which songs are put into use is as an aid to remembering historical deeds, especially in telling a tale containing an account of a chronological list. For instance, a storyteller at one point may forget an important name in an event he is narrating. He stops and begins to sing a song. When he has remembered all the names, he picks up his story where he left it. The song has helped his subconscious mind to remember the names which he had forgotten.

Music, vocal or instrumental, plays a large part at initiation ceremonies of youths to manhood or to the tribal mysteries. Dances and songs of a religious or ceremonious nature play a large part in religion where they constitute acts of worship or accompaniments to such acts. The extemporized words of the songs, the swell of the music, rhythmic motions of the dance, and the gregarious feeling that everybody is taking part in the same action heighten the religious sentiment. Other acts of a ritual nature, such as processions around the town before the actual burial processions, are largely musical.

People who specialize in performing either instrumental or vocal music are held in high honor. They are thought to be very clever.

Music plays a very important part in civic life. Wrestling matches are a common occurrence in the dry season after the harvesting season. When civil ministers of one town visit another town, usually the town being visited provides music of drums, xylophones, flutes, and gongs to meet and accompany the ministers into the town. Likewise, when they are going back, musicians lead them out of the town with music. Should the musician not lead the ministers in and out of the town, it means that the ministers are not welcome.

Ibo poetry is made to be sung. There is no conception of poetry without a tune and no tune exists without words; words determine the time of a song. This is the reason why certain European hymn tunes do not fit the Ibo words despite the fact that the Ibo words are the correct translation of the English, French, or German words of the hymn.

Generally all words and tunes are extemporized in making up songs, but some songs have stood the test of time by being passed on from generation to generation with very little variation. To this class belong most fable songs and historical war songs. These are mostly of the nature of a rhythmic vocal flowing melody in which the singer sings in a declamatory and rhetorical manner. The bard steadfastly repeats his melodic line with certain charges and then immediately the chorus repeats the entire song or part of the text.

As a general rule, most fable songs are unaccompanied, but there are songs that are accompanied either by playing the drums, striking sticks together, slapping the body, clapping, beating the ground, stamping with foot or a piece of stick, making explosive sounds with the lips, or by humming.

Often stories contain metrically recurring formulae which serve as antiphonal responses to the storyteller's singing, which is called "antefable." Most tales all over the world have this characteristic. It is found not only among the Ibos, but also among the Eskimos, Bantus, and Europeans.

Upon being given a musical and verbal subject, the Ibo often extemporizes poetically and his listeners respond by singing fragments of his melody as a refrain.

If the people of any country are gifted with a sense of rhythm, it is the Ibo people, and there is no doubt that their musical abilities have developed from this rhythmical sense. Rhythms dominate the Ibo. He begins to practice the playing of his rhythms, supervised by older children, as soon as he can sing. When the Ibo presents his rhythms in tones, he makes music; when he presents them in gestures, he dances. The Ibo loves his complicated and strong rhythms. They constitute the most important element in his music and it is on them that he builds his music. The complicated and difficult set of rhythms from an Ibo band are sometimes very difficult for well-trained musicians to write. The Ibo assembles the rhythms in melodic fashion, he combines them in harmonic style, each instrument beats an interesting melodic set of rhythms which when combined produce counterpoint of rhythms.

To a person who has not been introduced or oriented to Ibo music, or African music for that matter, the sole aim of the music makers seems to be to generate noise. The foreigner cannot appreciate the Ibo's love of his drums and rhythms, but when he understands the Ibo man and lives with him in his village, he not only appreciates them, but adores them. If the foreigner is a learned musician, he soon finds that most of what "modern composers" try to force into their music has been in Ibo music for centuries. He finds that deep down in the strange sound of *tum-piti* of the drums are some compositions in dual modality, asymmetric meters, asymmetric divisions, principles of cross-rhythms, nonaccented rhythms, shifted accents, changing meters, and ostinato resulting from the use of instruments. For this reason "modern" music appeals to the Ibo more than does a fugue by Bach.

The musical instruments of the Ibos have not been standardized and are limited as to ranges and techniques that can be employed in the performance of them; still the Ibos achieve skill, dexterity, and ingenuity with what they have. They make their own instruments and extemporize both melodies and rhythms with profound inventiveness. The music produced serves as a means of communication; for in a dance certain specific instruments at appropriate times give specific directions to individual dancers. To most non-Ibos all the sounds produced are the same and therefore they are not aware of the instructions; but any intelligent observer cannot fail to notice that a certain instrument at one point or the other is louder than the rest, and by watching the dancers he can see one person or the whole group physically responding to the rhythm of the solo instrument.

Two short observations on the uses of musical instruments in Ibo culture ought to be made here. The first is that in the Ibo country it is common to find both instrumental soloists and instrumentalists in groups; the second is that although it is common to find solo instrumental performances, accompanied songs are the most significant. This is substantiated by the fact that almost no song exists without words, whether those songs are actually performed or not. Therefore, when a musical instrument plays a song, a mental image of the words is invariably formed, although they may not be expressed. In short, the uses of musical instruments are dependent upon the originality of the performers.

Although there are many instruments, it is the drum that is most important to Ibo music. Drums have assumed a position of greatest social importance. Any occasion whatsoever, be it funeral, marriage, or naming ceremony, is unimaginable without the drum. It is on the drum that these social ceremonies are built. In contrast to European music, which is built on chords and which uses the drum to ornament the music played by other instruments, the Ibo treats his drumming as music in its own right subordinate to no other instrument. The various rhythms and accents of the drums direct the movement of dancers and excite them to a frenzy.

The Ibo has organized in a scientific way a rhythmic principle which the Western ear recognizes as being different from his own and which seems very complex but which, on analysis, is very simple. He achieves this by the interweaving of complex, contrasting rhythmic patterns on drums and other musical instruments. In most cases the drum derives its rhythms from the rhythms of the words of the song; these rhythms are accentuated and varied by other drums and by the rest of the musical instruments. It does not matter what instruments are used to express the complicated rhythms; the result is always a conflict of rhythms in a highly organized rhythmic contrapuntal development. For example, a song which appears to have only one main rhythm will prove on examination to have at least two rhythms: one in the melody and one in the accompaniment.

Drums are to Ibo music as strings are to classical compositions. It is in the drumming that all elements—melodic, harmonic and rhythmic—are exhibited. All these elements are found in all the other media of Ibo music whether in singing, clapping, or in the medium of other instrumental displays, but were we to study music without adequate reference to drums and drumming, we would be missing the most important element.

In Ibo music the drums supply the melody and a harmony of free uncalculated pitch relationships as well as the timbre and a free rhythmic counterpoint. That is why there are usually more than two drums performing at the same time.

The master drummer first establishes his rhythm, the second drummer bears in mind where the original strong beats are and he then plays another rhythm which is both melodically and rhythmically as interesting, but he avoids as much as possible having the main beats correspond with the original. In order that the main beats do not fall together, the second drummer makes full use of suspensions. Another means he uses to achieve the same effect is to have rests where normally a strong beat would occur.

After he has invented his rhythm, he maintains it throughout unless there has been a very good reason why it should be changed; but the master drummer who is the leader of thematic material frequently varies his rhythms because he has something specific to say. He does not begin from the beginning and say everything at once. He says something and repeats it three or four times; he says something different, and repeats that three or four times and continues thus.

Since Ibo music is so closely related to language, it is evident also that Ibos themselves must be responsible for the perpetuation of their musical heritage. To be able to do this effectively, Ibo musicians must be trained for the task. But since the days of apprenticeship to masters in the art and of imitation by younger ones are gone, a new approach is now inevitable.

Music schools and colleges manned by qualified staff specially devoted to training Ibo musicians so that potential Ibo composers will become musically literate is the only worthwhile answer. The course of study in these institutions should include the expert usage of musical notations, an intelligent appreciation of Ibo musical heritage, and a broad and detailed study of European music.

"Ibo Music," by W. W. C. Echezona, Nigeria Magazine, *March 1964.*

Land of Darkness

BY MARGARET BOURKE-WHITE

Margaret Bourke-White was a pioneer in combining professional photography with journalism. She started her career in 1930 on the staff of *Fortune* magazine, bringing a new artistic skill to photographs of steel mills, glassblowers, and other industrial subjects. She went on to photograph people during times of great emotional stress: famine, poverty, floods, and war. She traveled around the world, interviewing and photographing the great and the near-great.

Always Margaret Bourke-White was as much concerned with the "little" people as with the leaders. She interviewed and photographed families who lived in rural, poverty-stricken areas during the Depression, Korean peasants whose sons were killed by roving guerrillas, and miners who even today work like slaves in South African gold mines.

"Land of Darkness" is part of a chapter from her autobiography, *Portrait of Myself*. The dreadful conditions of African labor in the gold mines of South Africa have been described by Peter Abrahams in *Mine Boy* and by other African writers, but there is a special poignancy to this account of a visit to the mines, made not so long ago, by a sensitive, trained observer from the world outside Africa.

There is a kind of magic about South Africa. I had always longed to go there, and in 1950, *Life* sent me to the Union of South Africa to do a photo essay on its problems and its people. I had always wondered what the veld looked like. I have seen the steppes in Russia, the *Hortobágy* in Hungary, and the prairies in our own central United States. The veld has a little of all three, but it has a special enchantment all its own.

The land is spacious, under an enormous sky. Around the entire ring of the horizon is a perpetual drama which you watch as though you were following the action on a revolving stage. Clouds build up to noble proportions. Hail falls. Stabs of lightning give way to rainbows. Squalls dissolve. The softest golden sunlight follows each storm.

When you drive around the Rand, where one gold mine follows another, the modern buildings of Johannesburg rise from the strangest landscape in the world. The road to the metropolis passes through a chain of man-made mountains, cone-shaped and in startling colors: warm shades of ocher to orange; cold shades of bilious yellow, off-whites and sickly tan. In the soft center of each cone is a crater of sludge. This is mine waste, and the core is treacherous as quicksand. From time to time, children playing unwisely close to the slimy rim are sucked in to a terrible death.

Glimpsed above these strange hills, the skyline of Johannesburg shimmers in the noonday sun like a mirage in the desert. Many times in the weeks to come, I thought of the country as a mirage; things are not what they seem.

The entire economy of South Africa is geared to gold. Johannesburg is literally built on gold. Under this modern city, under its splendid department stores, tall office buildings, its sturdy Dutch Reformed churches, the gold mines plunge directly down to the awesome depth of two miles.

I got my first glimpse of one of the oldest gold mines, Robinson Deep, on a Sunday. I had driven to the entrance, not expecting any activity on the Sabbath but just to get the feeling of the place. I was delighted when I found some very photogenic activity. In the mine compound, the miners were putting on a weekly show of their tribal dances.

I was struck by two of the native dancers who moved with such lively grace that I decided I must use them in further pictures. I am always looking for some typical person or face that will tie the picture essay together in a human way. I asked their names. I learned that black miners aren't known by their names; a miner is a "unit," with his number tattooed on his forearm.

Next morning, I explained to the superintendent that the two gold miners, Nos. 1139 and 5122, had impressed me so much that I would like to carry through with the pair, photographing them where they worked, where they ate, lived, slept. The superintendent told me the men were working very deep down in a "remnant area," where visitors were never taken.

"What is a remnant area?" I asked. The superintendent explained that it is a spot so honeycombed with old workings that cave-ins are a constant hazard, and with so little gold left that it has been abandoned. However, recent revaluation of gold had made it profitable for the company to send men back for scrapings.

The officials said, "We will move them up to a more convenient location, where you can take your pictures more easily." I said, *"Life* magazine doesn't do things that way; either I photograph them where they really work, or we'll forget the whole thing." They consented.

I was told to return the next day and put on proper mine clothes. I was astonished to find that these were heavy and warm, as if I were dressing for the frigid top of the world rather than for the hot depths of the earth. The superintendent explained to me that unless the body is thoroughly conditioned to the abrupt temperature changes under the earth's crust, a visitor might go through the heat of the lower depths, get wringing wet and catch pneumonia on the slow return to normal temperatures above ground. My costume was topped with a crash helmet, and I wore a whistle hanging round my neck to use if we were trapped.

To me it was a solemn moment when I stepped into the mine cage and started the slow two-mile descent into the hidden space of the world. I felt something of the excitement of my first snorkeling in tropical waters: my first look into a new world. With snorkeling, all was sparkling and bright; here it was all gloom and obscurity. As the elevator lumbered downward, the darkness was broken only by occasional eerie cracks of light as we passed the mine stages.

At the bottom of the first mile, which is the halfway point in this vertical journey, you change to a smaller mine car which shoots down an incline. You travel that second downward mile in the sober realization that you are now below sea level.

When I stepped out, I felt no discomfort, for the air circulation system close to the elevator shafts was adequate. As soon as we started walking along the lateral passages, the atmosphere became very hot and humid. When we reached the little sloping pocket where the two men were working, I could hardly recognize my dancers. With rivers of sweat pouring down their bare chests, and with sad eyes and perspiration-beaded faces, they hacked away. I was in the midst of making photographs when a strange depression and lassitude overcame me. I could hardly raise my hands; I had lost the power of speech.

The superintendent, noticing my distress, led me quickly to a more open mine passage, gave me a little water, directed me to wash out my mouth, but not swallow it; then he took me to the foot of the shaft, where I was revived by the better air. Later I learned a man had died from heat prostration two months previously on this mine face.

I left the mine realizing that I had spent only four hours underground, and I would not have to return if my pictures were all right. But these men, who had danced so gaily and happily in the upper air, were destined to spend the better part of their waking hours underground with no hope of escaping the endless routine.

Although he works an eight-hour day, a miner is often underground as many as eleven hours. The white-skinned foremen must come up first, before the elevators take up the blacks. On each landing stage, as I made the ascent, I saw the black gold-miners clustered in large groups, awaiting their release to the outside air and the open sky. They would see little of this sky. They would sleep in concrete barracks without windows, rolled up like sausages on the floor, forty to a room, crowded into compounds surrounded with barbed wire. At night they were locked in. Over their windowless bunkers arched the jeweled night sky, inlaid with the glorious Southern Cross and other celestial diamonds not mined in South Africa.

In a country where 8,500,000 blacks are, in effect, ruled by fewer than 2,500,000 whites who own nine-tenths of the land and all the mines, an efficient pass system is used to recruit cheap labor on a titanic scale. The finest reasons are given for the pass laws: "to protect the ignorant native" . . . "to prevent crime." The native African must carry four to eight passes on his person at all times. He needs a traveling pass to move from one area to another, a permit to seek work, an employment certificate when he has found work, a tax receipt, and a "special" pass to be out after dark. Only the man with a white skin can come and go as he wishes.

The coming of white civilization to South Africa was outstand-
ingly successful in channeling the black man into the service of the
white, but it does little to fill the vacuum created by the disintegra-
tion of tribal civilization. The villages are sucked dry of able-bodied
men, family life disintegrates and the land erodes. The men are recruited to work eighteen months in the mines; then they are given
six months to go home and till the soil—and presumably breed more
miners. A man's tribal homeland may be so remote that when he
reaches his village, it is time to go back to the gold mines on a renewed contract.

Of course the legal niceties are observed. The contract is read
aloud to the mine recruits. No one can deny that the men heard the
contract, saw it, and even touched it long enough to leave a thumb-
print. And if a man wanted to do something else with his life, what
could he do? His bondage begins at the age of eighteen, when he is
old enough to pay taxes. He cannot pay in cows or in grain—which
measure his wealth in an agricultural society—but must pay in the
white man's currency, which he has to work in the mines to earn.
Without the all-important tax receipt, he cannot get passes, and
without passes, he cannot travel, work, exist. The tax receipt is just
the first link in the paper chains which will bind him all the days of
his life.

From the venerable gold mines of Johannesburg I went to the
Orange Free State, where the big mining companies were prospect-
ing for new gold. Borings had been made to a depth of several thousand feet.

The mining company which led the gold rush was just sinking its
first shaft and had reached 2,000 feet. There wasn't much to see
above ground, and as for seeing anything below ground, no regular
elevator machinery had been installed yet. The only way to go was
the way the tools and men went: in a bucket.

And so, within the week, I found myself in an oversized bucket—
large enough to hold the foreman and two helpers, all of us dressed
in white oilskins and white helmets. My cameras were wrapped in a
raincoat. The system worked from a pulley, like buckets in a well. As
one went down the 2,000-foot drop with a load of tools and miners,
the other came up with sludge.

We had reached the halfway point when we heard a loud rattling
sound coming up out of the darkness, like a train rushing toward us.

With a deafening clatter, it scuttled past us and up and quickly died away. It was the other bucket going up with its load of sludge.

"Do they ever break loose?" I asked the foreman.

Several weeks ago one had. It was carrying only tools, no men, but it hurtled down, killing seventeen men on the floor of the shaft.

"It must go off like a gun," one of the men said. The foreman said, "Yes." And then speech was suddenly made impossible.

We were entering the region of the underground rains. There never was such a rain above the surface of the earth. We were swirled around as though we were in a giant champagne glass, or in the heart of a tropical storm. Water came from everywhere at once and bit and tore at us. The foreman was looking cautiously over his side of the bucket now. I ventured a look over mine.

Far below was a disk of light the size of a dime. It grew to the size of a quarter, a silver dollar. It seemed to rush up toward us as though threatening to engulf us, and I realized that this was the bottom of the shaft—our destination—rising up to meet us. The curious loss of perspective when there is no frame of reference is something I had experienced in planes at high altitudes, but I was surprised to find it underground at the foot of a 2,000-foot well.

Thirty feet above the floor of the shaft, we swung to a stop so that I might have a good elevation for taking pictures. It was a little while before I could see what was going on. My eyelids seemed to be pasted together by the torrents which never ceased, but when I was able to open my eyes, I looked down on a crew of forty black men in white shiny oilskins crawling like ranks of white maggots over slabs of glistening rock and gravel and sludge.

Our bucket was rotating in the most disconcerting way—round and round, and no way to stop it with the cable from which we were suspended a couple of thousand feet long. There were wonderful subjects, but snatching a picture when you are constantly being swept past what you've seen is like grabbing the brass ring on a merry-go-round. The extra raincoat we had brought to be used as a sort of umbrella over me and the cameras whipped and flapped in the torrent. I had brought four Rolleiflexes, and as fast as one became soaked and useless, I started on the next. We had to go up now; our bucket was needed for tools. This was once in my life when I didn't say, "Just one more."

It was a great comfort to look above as we ascended and see that little square of daylight over our heads expand and grow. Suddenly it stopped growing. We came to a dead stop. Something was stuck in the braking machinery. We were only 25 feet from the surface, but to me that meant there were 1,975 feet of the void under us. I wished the foreman had not told us of that accident with the bucketful of tools, or that I had not heard still another story about a bucket filled with miners, which tore loose, hitting another bucket filled with miners, sending both downward in the fatal plunge.

We dangled for a long twelve minutes. Then the machinery performed once more, and we stepped out on the crust of the earth safely and gratefully.

From Portrait of Myself, *by Margaret Bourke-White, Simon and Schuster, 1963.*

Joy and Woe in Jo'burg

BY FATHER TREVOR HUDDLESTON

Father Trevor Huddleston is a notable exception among Europeans who have lived and worked in South Africa. Anthony Sampson, Editor of *Drum,* describes him as "a tall, dignified figure, wearing his long black cassock, with a worn leather belt around his waist." He went to South Africa in 1943 to be priest-in-charge of the mission of the Community of the Resurrection in Sophiatown. He stayed in South Africa for twelve years, serving also as superintendent of St. Peter's School in Johannesburg, the only school where an African could receive a superior liberal education at that time.

Sophiatown, where Father Huddleston's mission was located, was the oldest of the black African townships, established in 1905 on the outskirts of Johannesburg. As the gold mines turned Johannesburg into a boom town, Johannesburg expanded and eventually encircled Sophiatown. It became the busiest, most crowded, most publicized of all the townships, or locations, situated on the Reef.

When the Bantu Education Act was passed in 1954, it provided for complete government control of education, with a special syllabus to train Africans along tribal lines and to insure that "there is no place for the Native in European Society above certain forms of labour." Father Huddleston closed St. Peter's School rather than conform to the government restrictions. On his return to England, he wrote about his mission to South Africa in *Naught for Your Comfort,* from which the following episodes are taken.

Every morning in the Rand *Daily Mail* there is a column or two headed "Crime List." It reminds Johannesburg and the Reef that there are violence and terror in plenty in their streets. Unfortunately it also reminds the fearful and the prejudiced that a high percentage of such crime as it records is African. Few stop to ask themselves the reason. For in South Africa you soon get into the habit of thinking with your blood.

Three or four years ago a great deal was being said and written about juvenile delinquency among the Africans, and it was pointed out that the Africans themselves were the chief sufferers. In the ill-lit locations and in the dark alleys and side streets of places such as Alexandra Township there was plenty of opportunity for gangs or individual thugs to operate. This sudden surge of indignation against the juvenile delinquent, however, seemed to me to have possibilities of exploitation in another direction. If people were so concerned about it, perhaps they might be prepared to take some positive action of a preventative kind. It was worth trying.

Our swimming bath at Sophiatown had proved itself over the years. All through the long South African summer it was packed with children from the dusty streets, free even of swim suits, abandoning themselves to the unutterable joy of cool if murky water and an hour on the sunbaked concrete surrounding the pool. But it was the only public bath for Africans in Johannesburg which was accessible to the vast population in the west. And indeed the only other bath at all was sited in a municipal compound in the city itself.

Christmas was hotter than usual in 1951. It was a good psychological moment. I wrote a letter to the *Mail*, linking delinquency with the lack of recreational facilities and appealing to the European public for a swimming bath at Orlando. I have learned from long experience that nothing is less predictable than the Johannesburg public conscience. The most needy project may fail to stir it in the least. The most unlikely cause may rouse it to heights of generous response. And always there is the possibility of a loss of interest, of a new excitement to replace the old halfway through. But from the start the swimming-bath appeal rang the right bell. Money poured in from all sides in the first two or three months.

I was not too ambitious at first. I felt that anything, even a paddling pool, would be a start. And I have always believed very strongly in the plan of doing the job first and asking permission afterwards. I did not even consult the City Council before launching the appeal, for I could foresee that if I did so I should be caught in a mass of red tape and bogged down (to strengthen the metaphor) in a sea of committees.

It took three years to raise the money. And I could never have done it without the help of three Johannesburg businessmen, one of them the director of a very large building firm in the city. They were enthusiastic. Nothing less than an Olympic Games-size bath would do! "Build first and worry afterwards" was their motto, and they did just that. We had only about half the cash we needed when the bulldozers went to work. And then, too, there were more tricky problems to overcome.

One of them was the reaction of the African Advisory Board in Orlando. I knew that I must give them the fullest and most complete confidence in the project if it was to succeed. Too often the authorities had gone ahead with plans for the "improvement" of the location and its people without consulting the Board: the representatives of the people themselves. Yet I dared not approach them until I knew that we were sure of completing the bath. So it was with some fearfulness that I attended a meeting, specially summoned, to see the plans and to hear the exposition of them.

Mpanza was there. Mpanza, who had led the great squatter movement ten years before and whose Sofasonke Party had remained in control of the Advisory Board ever since. I did not know him except by repute. But I knew that what he said and the attitude he adopted would decide the future of the swimming bath. It may seem strange to those who know nothing of urban Africa to be told that any place, any group of people would lightly refuse a present of such quality and purpose. But it is not surprising to those of us who know the humiliation of that paternal, official attitude which constantly assumes the African to be incapable of responsible action. Mpanza came in and the proceedings began. It was a hot afternoon and Mpanza himself was hot and perhaps unwilling to bestir himself. I unrolled the plans.

"Here are the change rooms: and here, you see, is a special shallow end for the little kids. . . . Yes, it's fifty meters long . . . Olympic size . . . filter plant. . . ."

Everyone except Mpanza seemed impressed. He sat back in his chair, silent and apparently unconcerned. When everyone else had given his opinion or asked a guarded question, the chairman turned to Mpanza: "And what do *you* think?"

All attention, including my own, was focused upon that squat, silent figure. Slowly and with great deliberation he said, "Swimming baths? . . . Swimming baths? . . . We men do not need swimming baths."

I felt a wave of despair sweeping over me. How could I hope to persuade them, in face of that?

But Mpanza had not finished. "The Father is throwing sweets to the children," he said.

"Very expensive sweets," I said, hoping to relieve the tension in that stuffy room. "That bath is costing us about twenty-five thousand pounds."

"Sweets to children," he repeated. "And *if anyone else except Father* threw those sweets, I would say to the children, 'Don't touch them. They're poisoned.' But if the Father throws them—why! They're all right."

It was perhaps the greatest compliment I have been paid by an African. It also meant that the bath was approved. I thanked God.

The mayor of Johannesburg, a hundred Europeans, and two or three thousand Africans assembled on a March day for the opening ceremony. And when the speeches were all over there was a rush and a scramble. Five or six hundred children, not waiting to strip, were in the water, splashing and shouting: enjoying for the first time in their lives one of the pleasures that white Johannesburg had always taken for granted. It was a good moment.

Three days later the phone rang on my desk. "It's Andrew, Father" (the superintendent of the bath). "There's been an accident here, Father. A boy. Please come." I knew in those few seconds what it meant: the thing I had dreaded above all else. And it had happened so terribly soon. When I got there his father had already arrived, a municipal policeman, standing quietly by the still, stretched figure in the shower room. John Matlanyane. Aged twelve. Drowned. I never saw his face, though I have imagined it countless times. He was their only son, but they did not blame me or reproach me once. And when I met my African Committee a few days later: "You mustn't worry, Father. You must understand. Our people don't know how to swim yet. They have to learn, and they have to make mistakes. Look how many children are drowned each year in the dams! Please don't be sad."

Perhaps—no, surely—John and I will one day meet again. And I believe that we shall know each other, for I pray for his soul every day of my life: that little African boy I have never seen, for whom the bath was to have been a place of joy and freedom, a window opened on to a wider and more exciting world than he knew. And perhaps, after all, it was.

One afternoon at St. Peter's School, school ended, the door of my office opened, and Hugh came in. That was not unusual. I have always kept open house for the children, and they drift in and out, read the magazines on my table, or just hang around for a chat. To me, incidentally, that is the logical answer to apartheid—just that. And when a boy or girl feels sufficient confidence in me to use my office as their playroom, then I know that there is a relationship established which will make its mark upon their whole life. In the years that lie ahead there may be many opportunities for being completely at ease for an African boy, completely at ease, I mean, in a European house. But at least those who have been to St. Peter's will have known it, and maybe their children and their children's children will remember that even in 1955 love and friendship were possible between the two peoples: it was possible to meet and to talk on the level.

So Hugh came in. He sat on the arm of my chair and began to crack his fingers—a sure sign of some embarassing but important request. Hugh was fourteen then, more than usually attractive, with clear and unclouded eyes, the eyes of innocence and childhood which I love. I had always found him hard to resist, so I braced myself to meet what I guessed would be a request. He took hold of my hand and wrapped his fingers round mine.

"Father . . ." he began. "Father—I—want—to—learn—the—trumpet." He paused for my reaction.

"Well, that sounds all right, son, but trumpets are pretty expensive things. You'll have to wait a bit before you can get one, I expect."

He ignored that statement entirely. "You see, I *love* music, all music. But my father won't believe in me. I want to prove I can do it."

"But why the trumpet? Why not the piano?"

"Well, I listen to the trumpet; I hear Louis Armstrong—he's a Negro, Father. . . . Anyway, I love it. *Too much.*"

I don't remember now how I brought the conversation to a close;

probably with the half-honest assurance that I would "see what I could do."

A few weeks later Hugh was ill in bed. Not very ill, really, but he lay there looking listless, and those great eyes of his had an added magic. I took my decision without telling him. On my way back from town that morning I stopped at a musical-instrument store, descended nervously to the basement, and said, "How much is a trumpet?" It seemed to surprise the salesman quite a bit.

"Well, as a matter of fact, a young man has just brought back a new trumpet because his mother couldn't stand the racket. You could have it for fifteen pounds. It's worth twenty-five."

I took it. I sat on Hugh's bed and opened the case. But I watched his eyes. It was a sufficient reward.

If I had to choose a motto expressing just one truth that has served me well in South Africa I would say, "*Always* act on impulse." And after twelve years' experience I would still say the same. You will make mistakes, of course. But as Chesterton said somewhere, "The man that never made a mistake never made anything." Anyhow, Hugh got his trumpet because I acted on impulse. But it wasn't a mistake—not at all. It was the best thing of its kind I ever did. It is true that for the first three months I wondered. Nothing is more agonizing to listen to than a boy learning a trumpet. I wondered, too whether Hugh would persevere. He did. Then his friends came and asked if they could learn. I managed to get an African brass-band trumpeter to come and help. Lessons were held on a Saturday morning in the carpentry shop, and I feared complaints from the neighbors. One trumpet wasn't much use now, and I realized I had started something I could not stop. I had started, in fact, the "Huddleston Jazz Band," now worth above five hundred pounds, and including every instrument that any really good jazz band can want.

It took me two years to beg or cajole those instruments, and I have never enjoyed anything so much. It became almost an obsession with me, when I went into the city, to see what instrument I could bring back: a selfish obsession it was—just to have the joy of *their* delight, to hear the chatter and the exclamations as they handled a new and gleaming saxophone or plucked the strings of the bass. And I remembered what Yehudi Menuhin said to me that day we drove to Sophiatown: "Don't forget, Father, it was the Negro jazz bands that first breached the color bar in the States."

The day came when the band was complete except for one instrument, and that the most expensive—a tenor saxophone. Again I acted on impulse. Mr. Spyros P. Skouras, chief of Twentieth Century–Fox, was in Johannesburg negotiating a big deal. I happened to have met him three or four years previously at a meeting of social workers in the city. I rang him up. It was always a secretary who answered the phone and always a polite excuse. This went on for three or four days, but at last I managed to reach Mr. Skouras himself.

"What do you want, Father?"

"I want a saxophone!"

"A what?"

"A tenor saxophone for my African jazz band."

"How much does it cost?"

I took the plunge. "Eighty pounds, at least."

He paused. "Well! You're a gold digger, but you can have it!" Within an hour that saxophone was an object of worship to twelve African boys.

I have always felt sorry when I have come to read again that passage in the Old Testament about Absalom: "Now Absalom in his lifetime had taken and reared up for himself a pillar, which is in the king's dale: for he said, 'I have no son to keep my name in remembrance': and he called the pillar after his own name: as it is called unto this day, Absalom's place." I have felt sorry, for, after all, a pillar is not much use to anyone. I think I am more fortunate than Absalom, for I have a swimming bath *and* a jazz band. That is better than a tombstone.

From Naught for Your Comfort, *by Trevor Huddleston, Doubleday & Company, Inc., 1956.*

Who Killed Mr. Drum?

BY NORMAN COUSINS

"Mr. Drum" was the pen name for Henry Nxumalo, editor of the African magazine, *Drum*. He personified the editorial policy of the magazine which was established in Johannesburg during the 1950's as the voice of black Africa. Starting with news coverage of sports, jazz, crime, and tribal culture, *Drum* eventually included political and social reporting.

When the editors of *Drum* were recruiting African staff members, Henry Nxumalo was their first choice. He rapidly advanced from sports reporter to feature writer on current political affairs. As Mr. Drum, he investigated conditions of farm labor and of prisoners in the local jails.

The following profile of Henry Nxumalo was written by Norman Cousins, American author and editor of *The Saturday Review,* who stopped off in South Africa in 1956 on his way to interview Dr. Albert Schweitzer. At that time South Africa was still a member of the British Commonwealth of Nations. It was known officially as the Union of South Africa, or simply as "the Union."

My decision to stop over in South Africa had the encouragement of Alan Paton who, on his visit to New York some weeks earlier, said that even a brief visit would be well worth the journey. The trials of more than a hundred South Africans under the new, extreme "treason" laws were coming up in Johannesburg and this was a good time to see history in the making.

I was to meet people who were intimately involved in the problems of the Union. This would include persons of varying political opinions and backgrounds—all the way from owners of large gold mines to African writers and nationalist leaders.

One of the first persons I was scheduled to meet was Henry Nxumalo, one of Africa's leading journalists. His writings appeared regularly in *Drum,* a monthly magazine, and in *The Golden City Post,* a newspaper, of which he was news editor. *Drum* was written by Africans and claimed the largest circulation of any non-European magazine on the continent.

Several people referred to the fact that Nxumalo was presently writing a book on South Africa for an American publisher. His growing importance, I was told, was largely the result of his crusading articles. Everyone I met who knew him said he was one of the soundest and most courageous among African observers. His achievements in journalism were prominently described in the book *Drum* by its former editor, Anthony Sampson.

Consequently, I looked forward to meeting him at dinner the first night of my visit in Johannesburg.

Nxumalo didn't come to dinner. He had been murdered earlier in the day.

Right then, I learned one of the main facts about life in the Union of South Africa. I learned that there are two worlds. One is the world of graciousness, spaciousness, and infinite natural beauty and color, heightened in its loveliness by crisp air and sparkling sun. Then there is the other world, made entirely by people. It is taut, harsh, violent. The charming villas by day become places to be closely guarded at night. When two men approach each other after dark, each is apprehensive about the color of the other. Thus, passing a person on the street at night takes on the aspects of an encounter. For when the sun goes down the coolness seems to enter the human soul and the mood of the land hardens.

I knew I could never begin to understand South Africa unless I could understand the nature of this change, unless I could comprehend the proximity of the loveliness to the terror, and the interrelationship between the two. Perhaps if I could find out about Henry Nxumalo—why he wrote as he did, why he was feared and why he was murdered—I might learn a little about the two worlds.

The newspaper obituaries established that Henry Nxumalo, thirty-nine, lived with his wife and five children in the "location" called Orlando, some miles outside Johannesburg. (Africans are not permitted to live in the city itself; they live in "locations"—most of which are slum areas consisting of old huts and shacks and some of which are

new housing developments with their well-built though fairly small
homes. Orlando was one of the earliest of such developments.)

Nxumalo was born in Port Shepstone, on the East Coast near Durban. He came from a Zulu family. Both his parents died while he was
a boy. Henry's first job was as a kitchen boy in Durban. Like thousands of Africans, he found himself lured to the big city, Johannesburg; and he became part of a giant paradox. Once having left the
way of life of the village or the small town, the Africans who come to
Johannesburg seldom want to return. They resent the white man's
world not because they are forced to stay but because they are not
fully accepted. What they seek is not freedom to return to the village
but freedom to live decently and honorably in the city.

Henry Nxumalo came to Johannesburg as a youth and worked in a
boilermaker's shop. After hours he wrote poetry, which he sent to the
magazine, *Bantu World,* and much of which was published. This led
to a job as messenger for the *Bantu World,* of which he later became
sports editor. He enlisted during the war and became a sergeant.
This brought him to North Africa. At the end of the war he went to
London. When he returned to Johannesburg, he resumed his writing
for the *Bantu World.* In 1948 he married a nurse. In 1951 he joined
the staff of a new magazine called *Drum.* The same publishing house
also put out *The Golden City Post,* of which he became news editor.

His exploits on *Drum* and, to a lesser extent, in *The Golden City
Post,* made him perhaps the best-known non-European journalist in
South Africa.

Why was he murdered?

The facts of the killing were elusive. The body had been found on
the dirt sidewalk of a crowded location. Heavy footmarks indicated a
struggle. Several persons apparently had been involved. A trail of
blood showed that Nxumalo had crawled more than fifty feet from
the scene of the attack before he died. Robbery did not appear to be
a motive for the killing; his valuables were untouched. The police
had no theories.

Most of Nxumalo's friends were reluctant to talk; they looked
away and said nothing. I spoke to a leader in the YMCA who had
known Henry Nxumalo as a boy. He said that from the beginning of
their acquaintance Henry had talked about wanting to be a journalist.

"He came to see me after he got the job on *Drum* and told me the kind of thing he wanted to do. He wanted to expose the brutal conditions of the jails. He wanted to write about forced labor on the farms. He was not a revolutionary. He believed that many white people who were in a position to effect basic reforms really knew very little about what was happening. And he had confidence in his ability to reach their consciences with documented facts."

I learned that after Nxumalo started his series of articles under the byline "Mr. Drum" he began to get threats of various sorts. But not until now had any of them materialized. At that, no one could say that any of these threatening letters had been received recently. Two close friends, however, mumbled their suspicion that it had been a political killing but would say nothing further.

I paid a visit to the publication offices of *Drum*. It was located just off one of the main streets in the heart of Johannesburg. *Drum's* reportorial staff was African, though the editor, Sylvester Stein, was white.

The arrangement of the office and the general atmosphere were more suggestive of a daily newspaper than that of a monthly magazine. I chatted with several men on the staff. They spoke freely about Nxumalo and his contempt for danger. They spoke, too, about his heartiness, his ready sense of humor, his joy of living.

"Despite everything that man went through, and it was quite a bit," said Zeke Mphahlele, himself one of the leading African writers, "Henry never became embittered. That's the most important thing for any writer, not to become embittered. Bitterness enters the eyes and keeps you from seeing the full story. It turns you away from the people you have to reach. All of us here envied Henry because he wasn't bitter. But we never knew how he managed it."

I met William Modisane, the music critic on the staff, who had been with Nxumalo only a short time before the murder. Mr. Modisane spoke about Nxumalo's part in building up the circulation of *Drum* until it became the biggest magazine by Africans for Africans on the continent. He told of the time Nxumalo committed a minor law violation in order to be put in jail, served his sentence, and then wrote about the actual conditions. There were official denials, but the reforms he called for came about.

Then there was the time that Nxumalo, disguised as a laborer, got a job on a farm in Bethal. He had heard that prisoners were being sent to Bethal in what amounted to forced labor. At Bethal Nxumalo was beaten up along with the prisoners. He worked alongside young men, not prisoners, who had been "recruited" on the understanding that they would be taken to an entirely different place but were shipped to Bethal and deprived of the right to leave. The legal pretext for keeping them was that they had "held the pen." It is not necessary for Africans to sign their names to labor contracts. If they "hold the pen" over the contract, witnessed by a white man, the contract is considered to be binding.

The big need in South Africa is for human labor, and intensive efforts are made to recruit the Africans from the villages. Nxumalo was concerned both about the dishonesty of the recruiting and the dreadful conditions under which the men worked and from which there was no legal recourse. He escaped from Bethal, and presented the documentary evidence of what had happened. A large part of the continent was stunned by the disclosures and, once again, there were denials; but the basic reforms were made just the same.

Mr. Mphahlele and Mr. Modisane offered to take me to see various parts of Johannesburg that were indispensable for any understanding of the place. But first I wanted to talk to *Drum's* editor, Sylvester Stein.

They brought me to Mr. Stein's office. Mr. Stein is a "European," as all white men, regardless of their geographical origin, are designated. I judged him to be about thirty-six. He was in the middle of a magazine deadline situation not unfamiliar to me. I watched sympathetically as he worked quickly to keep the production machinery moving. I could see that he knew his business.

Then, the copy cleared from his desk, Stein sat back and talked fully and openly. No, he didn't think the government had engineered the killing or was implicated in any way. Whatever *Drum's* political and social differences with the government—and they were substantial—he didn't feel that it would sanction murder as a technique for disposing of troublesome people.

Stein went on to talk about Nxumalo's work for *Drum* and how, by exposing brutality and callousness, he had helped to effect important reforms. There was still some responsiveness to honest and dramatic fact-finding in the community at large. The executive and legislative branches of the government were responsible for the apartheid repressive legislation and restrictions. But a large part of the judiciary was still rigorously honest. And there was a considerable section of the white population which, even though it might go along with apartheid in general, balked about some of the specific aspects of apartheid in practice.

This was one of the many complexities that one came to recognize and respect in South Africa. Despite the iron will of the government about apartheid, the old forms of parliamentary government and judicial machinery were in large part preserved. This seemed at odds with the practices of the other branches of government, but you accepted it as part of the puzzle. Nor was the grand picture simplified by the sharp divisions among the whites—especially between the English and the Afrikanders (Dutch), with the latter now enjoying a preponderance in government. And even among the blacks, there were factions and frictions that not infrequently resulted in violence. This, too, was something that had to be taken into account before accepting or making any generalizations about the situation in South Africa.

Apartheid was more than a wall of color separation. It was a declaration of white ownership and control. It meant that the Africans, who constituted 90 per cent of the population, were limited to ownership of 15 per cent of the land. It meant that Johannesburg was out of bounds to blacks except for daytime working purposes. In order to commute to work from the locations, the Africans often had to spend four or five hours a day, much of it waiting for buses.

Apartheid meant a license just to live. An African needed a license to identify himself. He needed a license to work. He needed a license to be out of work. A passbook sometimes contained as many as six or seven separate items, each of which had to be countersigned regularly and kept up to date. Irregularities in passbooks—indeed, just leaving a passbook at home—could mean a prison sentence. It was in this way that Henry Nxumalo got himself arrested in order that he could write about the wretched conditions at the local prisons.

"I could never forget about apartheid," Sampson wrote [when he was editor of *Drum*]. "It cut across nearly everything I tried to do. It made the job of a white editor on a black paper awkward. I could never travel with Henry in the same train, taxi, bus, or lift. We could not be together in a restaurant, a bar, a theater, or a park . . .

"Even in the contents of the magazine, apartheid intervened. We were ticked off for showing a picture of Eleanor Roosevelt shaking hands with Mrs. Edith Sampson, a Negro woman. We could not print photographs of a black boxer pummeling a white boxer. Mixed boxing is forbidden in South Africa, and photographs of mixed fights were frequently held up by the South Africans as constituting 'incitement.' "

Sampson had also written about the time that Nxumalo saw a white woman fall down in the street.

"I was just going up to help her," Nxumalo told Sampson, "and then I stopped and thought: what will the whites think? They'll think I'm trying to rape her. If I pick her up it means I'll actually have to touch her. A native touching a European woman! Oooh! Terrible! I couldn't risk it, so I walked on."

Ironically, it was the fearful reluctance of the Africans to become involved in difficult situations that may have cost Henry Nxumalo his life.

For his body lay on the sidewalk five hours before the police were summoned. It is possible that he bled to death during that time. Across the street was a hospital.

If Henry Nxumalo's own doubts about helping a fallen woman seem unjustified, it may be helpful to consider a statement made by Alan Paton, who for millions of white people around the world has served as their conscience in South Africa. Paton was speaking at a public meeting about both the ostracism and physical danger involved in direct contact with Africans under the existing strained circumstances.

"Who is there who would not hesitate to come to the aid of an African who stumbled in the street?" he asked. "And if you say that no one would hesitate, I must tell you that there is at least one, and he is speaking to you from this platform now."

From Dr. Schweitzer of Lambarene, *by Norman Cousins, Harper &*
Row, 1960.

The Progress of Man in Africa

BY LOUIS SEYMOUR BAZETT LEAKEY

Dr. Louis S.B. Leakey, curator of the Coryndon Museum in Nairobi, is the distinguished anthropologist who has stirred up a world-wide controversy concerning the origins of ancient man. Convinced that Africa, not Asia, was the cradle of the human race, Dr. Leakey started digging many years ago in the Olduvai Gorge in Tanzania, which he considered a likely place. For thirty years he and his wife, also an anthropologist, painstakingly sorted through fossil beds nearly two million years old, without finding any relics of man. Then, in July of 1959, Mrs. Leakey made the first dramatic discovery—the jaw of a hominid whom they named *Zinjanthropus.*

Further excavations uncovered hundreds of fragments of fossil bone nearly three times older than any previous discovery. The age was verified by the carbon dating process, and the National Geographic Society sponsored further excavations, including the building of dams in the vicinity so that the neighboring Masai tribesmen could water their cattle without destroying any of the precious relics now being uncovered.

The discovery of *Zinjanthropus* was followed by the discovery of other jawbone fragments, more closely related to modern man, classified by Dr. Leakey as *Homo habilis,* the first "handyman" or man who used tools. Dr. Leakey places the approximate date of *Homo habilis* at about 1,750,000 years ago, making him the earliest known ancestor of man. Dr. Leakey is not satisfied to stop work with these remarkable discoveries but continues to work on at Olduvai Gorge, with his wife and sons and a team of skilled scientists. He says: "There are still so many gaps, so many questions."

As a social anthropologist, I naturally accept and even stress the fact that there are major differences, both mental and psychological, which separate the different races of mankind. Indeed, I would be inclined to suggest that however great may be the physical differences between such races as the European and the Negro, the mental and psychological differences are greater still.

Such differences, however, are emphatically not a matter of superiority or inferiority and it is a very great pity that probably ninety out of every hundred people try to measure difference in terms of "better" or "worse," using their own particular code as their yardstick when so doing.

On the other side of the picture there are people, both European and American, who firmly believe that the only mental and psychological differences between an African Negro and a white man are those which can be attributed solely to education and to cultural background. This is just as foolish as the opposite point of view and just as baseless.

These people apparently believe that an African who is given a European or American education will at once become in all mental, intellectual, and psychological aspects "a white man with a black skin." They believe, therefore, that given an adequate degree of so-called Western education, modern Africans, in spite of major racial differences, many of which are psychological, will become so like Europeans and Americans that it will be fair to judge their actions as though they were Europeans.

Herein to me lies one of the biggest calamities of the twentieth century and the major cause of nearly all the burning problems of racial conflict which torture Africa today.

I have spoken earlier of Africa's age of darkness, the period when the greater part of the continent was cut off from the rest of the world at the very time when civilization was dawning there. Because of this isolation and stagnation, that part of Africa which lay to the south of the Sahara Desert remained, to all intents and purposes, in a cultural state very similar to that of Britain at the time of the coming of the Romans. It was only when the great period of European maritime exploration (starting with the Portuguese adventurers and sea captains and continuing until the end of the nineteenth century) combined with such feats of territorial exploration as were accomplished by men like Livingstone, Stanley, Speke, and Baker, that this period of cultural stagnation was gradually brought to an end. I stress cultural in connection with this stagnation because, as we shall see, in other respects there had been major advances, and the peoples of Africa, while backward in some respects, were very advanced in others.

During the last hundred years the greater part of Africa has at long last got beyond the awakening stages after its long slumber and is really stirring into action again. This awakening has been brought about by many different agencies: explorers, administrators, traders, missionaries, settlers, and even mere adventurers. Nearly all of these people (at least until very recently indeed) were fully convinced that they were in contact with an inferior type of humanity which was certainly wholly different from themselves. Inferiority in material things was of course a demonstrable fact. Major differences in such things as political ideas, social structure, family customs, law, justice, and religion were also very very numerous. It was, however, wrong to assume that such differences necessarily indicated inferiority.

In certain ways Africans were perhaps superior to their white invaders, even though their superiority was not linked with such manifestations of mental achievement as Europeans are apt to regard as clear evidence of *their* superiority—I refer, of course, to our Western pride in such achievements as pictorial art, the theater, writing, higher mathematics, and skills in devising methods of mass killing in wartime.

When we talk so glibly of the "superiority" of the white races at the time when the Europeans arrived to introduce Western civilization to the peoples of Africa, we should do well to reflect that in many ways the Africans had already reached a position which we, the so-called civilized races, are only just beginning to comprehend.

The importance of family planning, as it is now called, is at long last beginning to be fully recognized in Europe and even in such Asian lands as India and Pakistan. The spread of this idea stems from a realization that if there are too many children in a family the children, as well as the mother, will suffer, be less healthy, and less useful members of the community. Long before the Europeans arrived in Africa, many Bantu tribes had already recognized the need for family

planning. In my childhood days, Kikuyu Elders would explain to
young candidates for initiation into adult status their law that a
woman must not bear a child more than once in three years by saying
quite simply, "If a woman starts another child before the previous
one is more than two years old, then the child that has thus been conceived, the growing child which she is nursing, and the mother herself, will all suffer. Therefore, our law forbids a woman to have a
child until three years after the previous one, unless the previous one
has died in the meantime." Could anything be more physiologically
and psychologically sound or more advanced than this? Does this
point of view really seem to be that of an inferior people?

Let us take another example. In the so-called civilized world we
are just beginning to do away with the death penalty for some forms
of murder. What is more, it is only relatively recently that we abolished this extreme punishment as a penalty for such lesser crimes as
sheep stealing! Yet in most of Bantu Africa, long before the arrival of
so-called Western civilization, only a person who was a persistent
murderer was put to death. It was generally accepted that in all like-
lihood a person who committed one murder had suffered some extreme provocation and was most unlikely to act in such a violent way
again. He and his family were then required to make the fullest possible restitution to the bereaved family, but the murderer himself
was not put to death. This is surely more logical than killing one person because another is dead, in accordance with the old Biblical concept of "an eye for an eye and a tooth for a tooth."

Or again, at a time when most so-called Western civilized races still
held that a man had such strong legal rights over his wife that he
might with impunity force her to live with him physically, against
her will and within the law, most African tribes gave women far
greater freedom and greater rights to live their own lives as they
chose, even to considerable sexual freedom, provided they remained
with their husbands and looked after their children properly.

To give yet another example, at a time when drunkenness was a
major curse in many parts of Europe and America, in Africa the laws
of a number of tribes forbade all except the very old to get drunk at
all.

Let me remind you too that before the coming of the white man,
social organization in many African tribes was such that tragedies
such as destitute widows and orphans, unloved lonely spinsters, un-

married mothers, and aged and uncared-for elderly people were un-heard of and indeed could not occur, while prostitution was unknown.

I have cited these few examples simply to show that Africans, who had certainly stagnated culturally and in the matter of material things for so long, and who had been so cut off from this aspect of civilization which was developing elsewhere, were by no means necessarily inferior in some respects to the so-called civilized races, al-though certainly different, and in some respects even superior.

In matters relating to religious and other beliefs also, most Euro-peans have for many years taken the view that the Africans were in-ferior, or held false views. They have forgotten that what we call truth is always relative and depends upon our state of knowledge at any given point in time and space. We have, moreover, too often worked on the strange assumption that "what I believe is the truth but what the other fellow believes (unless he happens to believe as I do) is merely superstition."

It may be of interest in this connection to recall that years before Ross claimed that he had discovered the cause of malaria, a European traveler in Abyssinia wrote the following passage: "The Natives hereabouts say that Malaria is caused by the bite of the mosquito, but, of course, we know better—it is caused by the miasmas of the swamps!"

As I stated earlier, the many different categories of white men who came to Africa during the past hundred or so years (in some parts of Africa much longer of course) and who have influenced it so much, have (almost without exception) been imbued with a sense of their own superiority and have consequently treated the Africans as infe-riors. They have tried—by precept in some cases, by example only in others—to turn the Africans in the short space of a century from an Iron Age community, with many high mental as well as moral at-tributes and a well planned social and political organization adapted to their own way of life, into inadequately trained, black-skinned, imitations of European politicians, artisans, and professional work-ers.

It is all too easy to forget that the undoubted intellectual superi-ority of the white races in certain branches of, shall we say, science, stems from a long heritage of training and represents only one facet of mental quality.

Moreover, those very people who have been responsible for thus attempting the impossible (impossible because racial differences are as real on the mental and psychological plane as they are on the purely physical and prevent such speed of change), these people, I say, then turn round and, on the one hand, condemn the Africans for "trying to go too fast" and, on the other, accuse them of having gained little "from the education we have given them."

We should remember, too, that many of the present-day problems and troubles in Africa stem from our own failure to recognize that difference is not necessarily linked with superiority or inferiority. We must realize that differences of race involve fundamental differences in mental make-up and in psychological approach in respect of all the day-to-day problems of mankind.

What is happening in Africa today? Why is the ferment of nationalism giving rise to such dangerous situations all over the continent?

In the first place, it seems to me, man's progress in Africa has recommenced after a long period of stagnation which, as I have tried to show, was not caused by racial factors so much as by those of geographical and climatic accident. This has happened at a time when the rate of progress throughout the world has, as a result of a natural law, reached an alarming speed. Consequently, the Africans have had too little time to adjust themselves to the changed way of life, but this is neither their fault nor ours.

Secondly, the Western races, in endeavoring to bring what they believed to be civilization to Africa, imagined, in all good faith but in serious error, that racial difference did not involve such great mental and psychological differences as it did physical ones and that they could, therefore, by means of classroom "education" turn men of the black races of Africa into model Europeans, albeit with black skins and curly hair. (It is, of course, open to doubt whether this aim was in any case a wise one.) Those who attempted this educational approach usually forgot that classroom education represents only a tiny fraction of real education.

Thirdly, the immigrant races believed that ideas and methods which they had developed for themselves and which work (in part at least) in Europe and America must necessarily, therefore, work in Africa also. This is a most doubtful proposition, but we have so thoroughly persuaded the Africans that the Europeans have achieved perfection in political matters that nowadays the Africans themselves not only demand "independence" but also require that this independence be achieved through the so-called democratic principle of "one man, one vote."

In Africa, prior to the coming of the white man, most African tribes were ruled by those people whom they chose as their rulers, but the choice was not made by elections on the basis of "one man to one vote." Rulers and leaders were chosen by popular acclaim. Today, throughout Africa, Europeans have introduced so-called modern democracy. However, only a very few of the potential voters have even enough knowledge to get themselves recorded on the voters roll, let alone knowledge of how to exercise their rights if they do get a chance to vote. Those who do register often belong to the ranks of the clerks and petty shopkeepers and so, naturally enough, when the time comes to exercise their vote, they elect a man of their own group and caliber. When such a man finds himself in the position of a cabinet minister without having had any training for such responsible work, he naturally has difficulty in doing his duties properly.

Under purely African conditions only the mature and experienced men ever reached the top; but such men today are usually not even registered as voters, nor could most of them qualify to stand for election to Parliament since in many cases, although wise and experienced, they are illiterate and have no knowledge of a European language, which is now held to be a prerequisite for political advancement.

There is one more aspect of the present-day situation in Africa upon which I wish to dwell briefly.

It is most unfair to judge what is being done by Africans who hold political power today solely by our very different European standards. To do so is to perpetuate the fallacy that our type of academic education can alter a man's racial characteristics either at once or even in a few generations. This is no more possible than it would be to train a pack of Pekingese to excel in the duties we give to foxhounds, or to expect a greyhound to become an efficient police dog simply because we had given it a police-dog training.

It is essential that we should remember, moreover, that what is happening in Africa today occupies but a very brief moment of time in the long story of man's progress in Africa.

Against our own limited background of day-to-day living, much of it appears to be far worse than it actually is, while some of the exaggerations of the less reputable sections of the press do not help us to get, or to maintain, a balanced point of view. But against the background of the million or more years during which man has lived in Africa the incidents of today look less serious.

Let us hope, then, that those who are attempting to guide Africa in its present political awakening will show more understanding than they have done in the past, and that the African leaders for their part will try harder and more sincerely to be good and wise African leaders, rather than unsuccessful black copies of white politicians.

Africa led the world in matters of progress throughout the early years of man's development. Africa is again awakening and is destined, I feel sure, to play a major part once more in world progress. A better understanding of the problems is therefore vital.

From The Progress and Evolution of Man in Africa, *by Louis Seymour Bazett Leakey, Oxford University Press, 1961.*

Part 3

THE WIND OF CHANGE

"The wind of change is blowing through this continent."

Prime Minister Harold Macmillan
in a speech in Capetown, South Africa
February 3, 1960

The Role of the Writer in a New Nation

BY CHINUA ACHEBE

Chinua Achebe, author of several novels, was born in 1930 in Eastern Nigeria. While studying at a government secondary school, he received a scholarship to study medicine, but abandoned this in favor of the liberal arts and became one of the first to follow a full-degree course at the University College in Ibadan. As an undergraduate, he studied the work of English literary stylists—Conrad, Hemingway, and Graham Greene. He also read Tolstoy in English, and began writing his own first novel while still in college. This novel, *Things Fall Apart*, was widely praised by critics. Gerald Moore in his *Seven African Writers* calls it "the first West African novel in English which could be applauded without reserve."

Aside from his writing, Mr. Achebe has made a career for himself in broadcasting. He joined the staff of the Nigerian Broadcasting Corporation in 1954 as a producer, took additional training in London with the British Broadcasting Corporation, and returned to Nigeria to become the director of External Broadcasting, a position he still holds.

In a television interview in 1964 Mr. Achebe said, "I belong to a very fortunate generation in this respect: the old hadn't been completely disorganized when I was growing up." He speaks for this generation in the following article, a lecture delivered to the Nigerian Library Association in April 1964.

Although I have cast the title of this lecture in rather general terms, I hope you will permit me to talk specifically of the role of the writer in a new African nation and, even more specifically still, the role of the writer in the new Nigeria.

It is natural for a people at the hour of their rebirth to cast around for an illustrious ancestor. The first Negro African nation to win independence in recent times chose the name of the ancient kingdom of Ghana. Then Mali followed Ghana's example. Here in Nigeria, as you know, there was a suggestion to change the country's name to Songhai, the third of the great empires of the Sudan. Historians everywhere are rewriting the stories of the new nations—replacing the short, garbled, despised history with a more sympathetic account. All this is natural and necessary. It is necessary because we must begin to correct the prejudices which generations of detractors created about the Negro. We are all familiar with the kind of thing I mean.

This presents the African writer with a great challenge. It is inconceivable to me that a serious writer could stand aside from this debate, or be indifferent to this argument which calls his full humanity in question. For me, at any rate, there is a clear duty to make a statement. This is my answer to those who say that a writer should be writing about contemporary issues—about politics in 1964, about city life, about the last coup d'etat. Of course, these are all legitimate themes for the writer, but as far as I am concerned the fundamental theme must first be disposed of.

This theme—put quite simply—is that African peoples did not hear of culture for the first time from Europeans; that their societies were not mindless but frequently had a philosophy of great depth and value and beauty, that they had poetry and, above all, they had dignity. It is this dignity that many African peoples all but lost in the colonial period, and it is this that they must now regain. The worst thing that can happen to any people is the loss of their dignity and self-respect. The writer's duty is to help them regain it by showing them in human terms what happened to them, what they lost. There is a saying in Ibo that a man who can't tell where the rain began to beat him cannot know where he dried his body. The writer can tell the people where the rain began to beat them. After all, the novelist's duty is not to beat this morning's headline in topicality, it is to explore in depth the human condition. In Africa he cannot perform this task unless he has a proper sense of history.

Let me give one small example to illustrate what I mean by people losing faith in themselves. When I was a schoolboy it was unheard of to stage Nigerian dances at any of our celebrations. We were told and we believed that our dances were heathen. The Christian and proper thing was for the boys to drill with wooden swords and the girls to perform, of all things, May-pole dances. Beautiful clay bowls and pots were seen only in the homes of the heathen. We civilized Christians used cheap enamelware from Europe and Japan; instead of water pots we carried kerosene tins. In fact, to say that a product was Ibo-made was to brand it with the utmost inferiority. When a people have reached this point in their loss of faith in themselves their detractors need do no more; they have made their point.

A writer who feels the need to right this wrong cannot escape the conclusion that the past needs to be re-created not only for the enlightenment of our detractors but even more for our own education. Because, as I said, the past with all its imperfections never lacked dignity.

The question is how does a writer re-create this past? Quite clearly there is a strong temptation to idealize it—to extol its good points and pretend that the bad never existed.

When I think of this I always think of light and glass. When white light hits glass one of two things can happen. Either you have an image which is faithful if somewhat unexciting, or you have a glorious spectrum which though beautiful is really a distortion. Light from the past passes through a kind of glass to reach us. We can either look for the accurate but maybe unexciting image or we can look for the glorious technicolor.

This is where the writer's integrity comes in. Will he be strong enough to overcome the temptation to select only those facts that flatter him? If he succumbs he will have branded himself an untrustworthy witness. But it is not only his personal integrity as an artist which is involved. The credibility of the world he is attempting to re-create will be called to question and he will defeat his own purpose if he is suspected of glossing over inconvenient facts. We cannot pretend that our past was one long, technicolor idyl. We have to admit that like any other people's past ours had its bad as well as its good sides.

What I have said must not be understood to mean that I do not accept the present day as a proper subject for the novelist. Far from it. My next to last novel is about the present day and the next one will again come up to date. But what I do mean is that owing to the peculiar nature of our situation it would be futile to try and take off before we have repaired our foundations. We must first set the scene which is authentically African; then what follows will be meaningful and deep. This, I think, is what Aimé Cesaire meant when he said that the short cut to the future is via the past.

It is clear from what I have said so far that I believe the writer should be concerned with the question of human values. One of the most distressing ills which afflict new nations is a confusion of values. We sometimes make the mistake of talking about values as though they were fixed and eternal—the monopoly of Western civilization, and the so-called higher religions. Of course values are relative and in a constant state of flux

Even within the Western civilization itself there is no unanimity; even within one country there are disagreements. Take the United States which is the most powerful country in the so-called Free World and whose constitution has inspired many a movement for equality and freedom. Does freedom there mean the same thing for everyone? For the late J.F. Kennedy and for the school children who shouted "we are free" when they heard of his assassination or their elders who celebrated with champagne?

Now if there can be so much spiritual confusion in an almost homogeneous culture, how much more in an African country trying to build a modern state with tools fashioned in the tribe or clan? Some years ago—in 1958 or '59—there was an accident at a dance in a Nigerian city. Part of a wall collapsed and injured many people— some seriously. Incredible as it may sound, some car owners at that dance refused to use their cars to convey the injured to hospital. One man was reported saying that his seat covers would be ruined.

The African writer may ask himself: Why was such callousness possible? Is this an example of what some people have called the elemental cruelty of the Negro? I am afraid it's nothing so fanciful. It merely shows a man who has lost one set of values and has not yet acquired a new one—or rather has acquired a perverted set of values in which seat covers come before a suffering human being. I make bold to say that such an incident could not have happened in a well-knit traditional African society. Of course, it would have been quite permissible to treat a stranger and an enemy with such cruelty. But then you were not obliged in those days to live next door to an enemy—as you have to do today. In fact, the whole concept of enemy and stranger has changed. So we need a new set of values—a new frame of reference, a new definition of stranger and enemy. The writer can help by exposing and dramatizing the problem. But he can only do this successfully if he can go to the root of the matter. Any incompetent newspaperman can report the incident of the seat covers. But you need a writer to bring out the human tragedy, the crisis in the soul.

Take another example. Anyone who has given any thought to our society must be concerned by the brazen materialism one sees all round. I have heard people blame it on Europe. That is utter rubbish. In fact the Nigerian society I know best—the Ibo society—has always been materialistic. This may sound strange because Ibo life had at the same time a strong spiritual dimension—controlled by gods, ancestors, personal spirits, or *chi,* and magic. The success of the culture was the balance between the two, the material and the spiritual. But let no one underrate the material side. A man's position in society was usually determined by his wealth. All the four titles in my village were taken—not given—and each one had its price. But in those days wealth meant the strength of your arm. No one became rich by swindling the community or stealing government money. In fact, a man who was guilty of theft immediately lost all his titles. Today we have kept the materialism and thrown away the spirituality which should keep it in check. Some of the chieftaincy titles and doctorate degrees we assume today would greatly shock our ancestors!

Let me mention just one more example of the crisis in our culture. Why is it that Nigerians are content with shoddy work? Put a man to sweep this room and in nine cases out of ten he will scamp through it, leaving most of it unswept. Why? Because it is government work, and government is alien, a foreign body. When I was a boy, strangers from another part of Iboland were coming for the first time to our village during the planting season to work for the villagers for so much money and three meals per day. One day one of these strangers came to plant my mother's coco-yams. At the end of the day he received his pay, ate his last meal, and left. About two or three weeks later the coco-yams began to sprout and the whole village saw what this man had done.

When he had got tired of planting he had simply dug a big hole in the ground and buried a whole basket of coco-yams there. Of course by the time his crime was discovered he had left the village and was not likely to come back. Now this sort of crime was only possible when societies that were once strangers to one another suddenly began to mix. Apply this on the national sphere and you will begin to understand our problems. The village code of conduct has been violated, but a more embracing and a bigger one has not been found.

The writer in our society should be able to think of these things and bring them out in a form that is dramatic and memorable. Above all, he has a responsibility to avoid shoddiness in his own work. This is very important today when some publishers will issue any trash that comes out of Africa because Africa has become the fashion. In this situation there is a real danger that some writers may not be patient enough and disciplined enough to pursue excellence in their work.

This brings me to the linguistic question. In this discussion I am leaving out writers in the various Nigerian languages. It is not that I underrate their importance. But since I am considering the role of the writer in building a new nation, I wish to concentrate on those who write for the whole nation, whose audience cuts across tribe or clan. And these, for good or ill, are the writers in English.

For an African, writing in English is not without its serious setbacks. He often finds himself describing situations and modes of thought which have no direct equivalent in the English way of life. Caught in that situation he can do one of two things. He can try and contain what he wants to say within the limits of conventional English or he can try to push back those limits to accommodate his idea. The first method produces competent, uninspired, and rather flat work. The second method can produce something new and valuable to the English language as well as to the material he is trying to put over. But it can also get out of hand. It can lead to simply bad English being accepted and defended as African or Nigerian. I submit that those who can do the work of extending the frontiers of English so as to accommodate African thought patterns must do it through their mastery of English and not out of innocence. The good writers will know how to do this and the bad ones will be bad anyway.

In closing, let me remind you of a theme that has been recurring in Sédar Senghor's thinking of late. He says that Africans must become producers of culture and not just its consumers.

African societies of the past, with all their imperfections, were not consumers but producers of culture. Anyone who reads Fagg's recent book *Nigerian Images* will be struck by the wealth and quality of the art which our ancestors produced in the past. Some of this work played a decisive role in the history of modern art. The time has come once more for us, artists and writers of today, to take up the good work and by doing it well enrich not only our own lives but the life of the world.

"The Role of the Writer in a New Nation," by Chinua Achebe, Nigerian Libraries, *September 1964.*

The Children's Clinic

BY ROBERT COLLIS

During the decade before World War II, medical students from all
over the world came to the famous Rotunda Hospital in Dublin to
study pediatrics under Dr. Robert Collis. Some of these students became his life-long friends and associates. Among those he admired
most for their keen intelligence was a young doctor from Nigeria,
Ade Majekodunmi. One thing led to another. Dr. Collis met several
eminent Nigerians and, when their University Hospital in Ibadan
was completed in the 1950's, Dr. Collis was invited to head up their
Pediatrics Department. He couldn't refuse. It was partly friendship,
partly the fascination of Africa which reached out to him even in his
familiar and comfortable Irish homeland.

Wherever he went, in Europe or Africa, Dr. Collis was concerned
with the health of children. He says: "Of all the children I have ever
known, the Nigerian child is the most endearing." After his experiences in Nigeria, he wrote about the country and its people with
deep sympathy and insight in *African Encounter,* from which the
following episode is taken. His introduction to the children of Nigeria took place at the old town hospital at Adeoyo, just before the
new University Hospital was opened at Ibadan.

It had been arranged that for the good of my soul I should do the
sorting-out clinic at the Adeoyo Hospital the following morning,
starting at 8:30 A.M.

I arrived on time at the hospital gate, which was surrounded by a
shouting mob of people, largely women, many with children tucked
in on their backs. With some difficulty I got my car inside and drove

along a paved road which ran round inside the compound which was
bordered by low hospital buildings on each side. There were a few
fine trees, giving some shade from the sun which seemed to strike
down here and come back up at one from the hot road beneath with
particular sizzling fierceness. Just before I reached the gate again I
came upon a number of buildings in and around which seemed to be
gathered an enormous number of women and children—hundreds!
This was the children's clinic.

I stopped, got out, and entered a sort of lean-to shed with a tin roof
slanting from a high wall and open on the other side except for
wooden pillars supporting the roof. The floor was made of earth. Inside the shed were arranged a great many wooden benches on which
were seated about one hundred women and children. Outside in a
very loose queue were another one to two hundred more.

An extremely efficient-looking man dressed in a long white coat
came forward and brought me in to a chair. There was no room for a
desk, only a low table to one side on which were numbers of containers holding different types of tablets and some bottles of liquid
medicine.

We started work at once, the male nurse standing and I sitting. A
mother would come forward pulling a baby off her back or leading
an older child. She would pour out a volume of words in Yoruba to
the male nurse. He would turn to me and say "fever," "diarrhea,"
"vomiting," "worms," "rumbles in the stomach," or just "sick, I
don't know." I would look at the child, feel its head, estimate how ill
it was, listen to its chest, and then make up my mind. If it wasn't
really sick but had a fever, probably malaria, it got chloroquin; if
diarrhea another standard treatment; if it was really sick, or I
couldn't make up my mind, I sent it to the consultant clinic which
was going on in a semibasement close by. If the child was burned,
had ulcers, or needed a penicillin injection he was sent into the treatment clinic and dressing room behind. It was necessary to carry out
this process in an average of less than two minutes per patient.

Hour followed hour. The numbers seemed in no way to decrease.
The temperature rose steadily till the midday sun beat down directly
overhead and the humid atmosphere reached 95° Fahrenheit. What
struck me most was the extraordinary patience of everybody—the
doctors, the nurses, and the mothers, who had been there since dawn
in extreme discomfort. Mostly they did not complain but came for-

ward in turn, quietly, their soft brown eyes pleading for their children.

The latter, except those who were so sick that they had lost interest in living and looked at one silently without facial expression, or those who cried in pain, came along smiling, without fear, presenting themselves for examination with far less fuss than children in Europe. Maybe the reason is that African children have much more security in their subconscious than ours, all being breast fed for many months, sometimes years, and all carried on their mothers' backs till they are two or three years old. Or maybe it is because African children just have better nerves and a happier disposition than ours. But whatever the reason, Yoruba children are the most entrancing in the world. Indeed, it comes as a shock to all of us Western doctors and nurses when after looking after these beautiful black children we are suddenly called upon to attend a white one again. Now the latter looks insipid, horribly pale, and sweaty. We find usually that it is spoiled and not very lovable.

Of course not all the mothers were quiet all the time. About halfway through, a fierce lady with a face like a man and a startling red and blue headdress of several yards of material tried to jump the queue. At once a yell of anger arose from the others. She began to shout back. She pushed herself forward past a number of other mothers. The baby on her back leant out and yelled abuse also. Then everybody began to shout. Suddenly the male nurse left me and dashed into the now struggling mass. He raised a huge male fist, he roared in a deep male voice, drowning the high female screams. He seized the man-faced lady and sent her staggering backwards. Calm returned instantly and everybody smiled again.

Then there was a very fat lady in a blue blouse and a silk skirt who seemed to feel she belonged to the upper classes and should therefore be given preference. She said a lot in what I supposed was a refined accent. Anyway, it sounded different to me, though I couldn't understand a word. The male nurse, however, appeared completely unsympathetic, maybe because the blousy lady wasn't really upper class, or maybe because she was and hadn't dashed (tipped) him, but his lips curled up in a nasty way and he spat out a couple of words at her which it seemed to me no male should probably say to a lady. Anyway, she answered him back and he said one more word whereupon she took herself off very testily, her enormous buttocks shaking with rage, their contours clearly seen under the silk skirt.

Three hours passed; four hours passed. Gradually I became light-headed. The sweat had been pouring down inside my shirt so that I was soaking. I was dehydrated, slightly nauseated, and my head was aching intolerably. The smell was horrible. And yet . . . this was no horror, no frightful nightmare like the concentration camps in 1945 in Germany, though the sickness, overcrowding, and the smell reminded me of those days. Indeed, as the hours passed a sort of peace came into my mind, a kind of patience. Perhaps it was the beginning of a love for those gentle suffering people.

Suddenly, quite unexpectedly, the male nurse said, "It is finished!" The illusion that it would last forever had been created by the queue moving forward to the dressing room getting all mixed up with the one moving out from our shed and collecting their things.

I got up. Somebody came forward and said that there were four mothers with five children needing admission to the new hospital one and a half miles away. Would I give them a lift over? I said, "O.K." They all got into my car. We drove there. They all got out. Each woman picked up a child and either wrapped it on her back or carried it on her hip. There was one over, a little scared, round-faced boy of two or three years old. He hadn't a mother. One of the other women was his aunt. She had her own sick baby to carry.

Rather gingerly, for he was the first African baby I had ever picked up, I held my arms out to him. He waddled forward, a funny entrancing smile enveloping his face. His eyes were all black pupil, but they were shining. I raised him up and pressed him to me above my hip. Suddenly with a kind of reflex his legs and little thin arms shot out and clasped onto me like an Australian bear, and he buried his face in my shoulder. At that moment I lost my heart to Africa.

We proceeded to a lift, a very modern lift whose doors opened and shut automatically at the pressing of a button. None of the mothers had ever seen a lift before but all entered the "funny-looking cave" without question and were silently shot up a hundred feet. The pupils of their eyes seemed to get a little larger, I thought, but none of them screamed or showed any outward emotion. They just seemed to accept it as another male contraption for getting about, like motor cars and airplanes, a much less alarming business than real juju.

A few days later I saw the different reactions of the female and the male mind to this sort of thing. I brought in a Hausa groom from the polo stables where I had found him lying in the stall with his horse. He had pneumonia. On reaching the hospital he, too, had to go up in the same lift. He nearly died of terror. He yelled to us to stop. He fell down and got up several times and had to be helped out. Obviously this kind of levitation was too much for his male make-up without some decent male explanation.

On leaving the lift we now passed along a spacious veranda and came to one of the children's wards. But even its magnificence did not seem to upset or astonish the mothers. They settled down at once on chairs by their children's cots in the large, cool, green terrazzo-floored ward with its wide french windows opening on to the balconies on each side, high up above the ground. None of them could ever have imagined that a house could possibly look like this. Indeed, the majority had probably come from mud and galvanized iron shanties. Yet they took it for granted.

Like all African mothers they had come to stay too, for African mothers don't leave their children in hospital. They come with them and stay beside them most of the time, feeding them, doing some of the nursing, and above all giving them confidence and security. You might think that they would be a nuisance. They seldom are. Often if a doctor has to stick a needle into a child he gets the mother to hold him. In this way the child is much less frightened than he would otherwise be, for he accepts it. Mother is there; she wouldn't let him be really hurt or killed by these white-robed people. It may hurt a bit but terror is avoided. And it is terror followed by panic which matters much more than pain.

For many years, during his all too short life, Sir James Spence, the beloved Northumbrian children's physician, preached the doctrine of getting mothers to come into hospital and nurse their own children there. His ideas were vehemently opposed by most doctors and pretty well all matrons, the usual grounds being that the mothers would "upset" the children and prevent them from settling down. Of recent years this attitude has been changing, due to the psychiatric work of Bowlby and others, and now in most hospitals in Great Britain and Ireland there is no longer a single visiting afternoon a week, or none at all, as was the practice in some children's hospitals, but the mothers are encouraged to come in every day. I have often felt that James Spence would have been very pleased if he could have visited our wards in Ibadan and seen the principles for which he had fought so hard demonstrated so clearly here in darkest Africa.

From African Encounter, *by Robert Collis, Charles Scribner's Sons, 1960.*

Interview in Accra

BY PETER ABRAHAMS

Peter Abrahams is a distinguished modern writer, born in 1919 in the slums of Johannesburg. His father was an Ethiopian; his mother was a Cape-Colored. He is the author of numerous short stories, articles and novels. His best known works are *Mine Boy* and his autobiography, *Tell Freedom*.

As a boy, he worked at various trades and snatched a little schooling when he could. It was always casual labor,—in hotels, in the markets, on the farms. A friendly clerk introduced him to *Lamb's Tales from Shakespeare* and aroused his ambition to become a writer. In 1939, at the age of twenty, he signed on a ship as stoker and worked his way to England. A backlog of 300 short stories which he had written were lost at sea. Another group which he salvaged were published in England two years later under the title, *Dark Testament*.

In London, he began to make his living by writing. He was one of the growing number of educated Africans living abroad, who rebelled against colonialism and formed a group called the Pan-African Federation. Later, he moved to the West Indies where he now makes his home, along with other exiles from South Africa.

It was a hot, humid, oppressive August day in Accra, capital of the Gold Coast that was to become Ghana. The air had the stillness of death. I walked down toward the sea front. Perhaps there would be the hint of a breeze there. As I neared the sea front I was assailed by a potent stench of the sea with strong overtones of rotting fish.

In about eight minutes of walking, some fifteen "taxis" pulled up beside me: "Hi, massa! Taxi, massa! Me go anywhere you go cheap!" They are all private taxis with no meters and driven by strapping young men with flashing teeth. The place is full of taxi drivers willing to go anywhere and do anything cheap.

The street traders here are women. "Mammy traders" they are called. They trade in everything. They sell cigarettes, one at a time; round loaves of bread and hunks of cooked meat on which the big West African flies make sport. They love bargaining and haggling. They are a powerful economic factor in the life of the country. The more prosperous ones own their own trucks, some own fleets of trucks. These "mammy trucks" are the principal carriers of the country. They carry passengers as well as produce and go hurtling across the countryside with little regard for life or limb. Each truck has its own distinctive slogan, such as: REPENT FOR DEATH IS ROUND THE CORNER, or ENTER WITHOUT HOPE, or THE LAST RIDE or IF IT MUST IT WILL. My own favorite—and I traveled in this particular truck—pleaded NOT TODAY O LORD NOT TODAY.

I passed many mammy traders, many mammy trucks, before I reached the sea front. I crossed a street, jumped over an open drain, and there was the sea. But there was no breeze, and no shade from the terrible sun. In the end I gave in to the idea of "taxi, massa, taxi" and looked about for one. But now there was no taxi in sight.

Instead, I saw suddenly a long procession of many women and a few men. The procession swung around a corner and came into full view, twenty or thirty yards long. The women wore white flowing robes and white kerchiefs on their heads. Their faces were painted into grotesque masks made with thick streaks of black, red, white, and yellow paints. The heavy thud of bare feet rose above the hum of the sea.

Then, all at once, the drums burst forth and there was no other sound about me. The marching women began to jig, then dance. As the tail of the procession passed me the drums reached a frenzy. A thin, pure note from a reed rose above the drums. The whole procession became a shivering, shaking mass. The reed note held longer than seemed human. And then, dramatically, there was silence. The thudding feet faded away out of sight and sound. There was silence and a slight racing of my heartbeat and the hum of the sea, and, of course, the overpowering fishy stench.

My thoughts shifted to my forthcoming meeting with Kwame Nkrumah, Ghana's first prime minister. It was well over seven years since I had last seen him, in London. Then he was a poor struggling student; now he was the head of a state and the spokesman for the great Pan-African dream of freedom and independence.

I remembered our past friendship and wondered what changes I would find in him. Anyway, it was now 9 A.M. and my date with him was for 9:30. I would soon know.

A few minutes later I flagged a taxi and simply said, "Kwame's office."

A pale-brown West Indian miss was the prime minister's secretary. She welcomed me as though I was a V.I.P. The prime minister had not come back from a conference yet. This tribal business was taking up a lot of his attention. She told me with indignation how members of the Ashanti tribe had to crawl on their bellies for some twenty yards into the presence of their king, the Asantehene, and how tribalism had to give way or there would be no progress. If she was any indication, then Nkrumah was very worried about the opposition the tribesmen were offering his Western-style Convention People's Party.

A number of officials came in. The lady stopped assailing the tribes. Then there was some bustle and the prime minister arrived. In something just over five minutes he had seen and dealt with these officials and I was ushered into his office. It was a big, pleasant, cool room.

Nkrumah came round his big official desk, took my hand, and led me to a settee near the window. The now famous smile lit up his face. As we exchanged greetings, felt each other out with small talk in an attempt to bridge the gap of years, my mind went back to our London days. This poised, relaxed man, with the hint of guarded reserve about him, was a far cry from the friend I had last seen nearly eight years earlier.

For me, the most striking change of all was in his eyes. They reflected an inner tranquillity which was the one thing the Nkrumah in Europe never had.

Even his name had been subtly different then. He had been our friend Francis Nkrumah, an African student recently arrived from the United States, and he had not seen Africa for a decade and more.

He had quickly become a part of our African colony in London and had joined our little group, the Pan-African Federation, in our protests against colonialism.

He was much less relaxed than most of us. His eyes mirrored a burning inner conflict and tension. He seemed consumed by a restlessness that led him to evolve some of the most fantastic schemes.

The president of our federation was an East African named Johnstone Kenyatta, the most relaxed, sophisticated, and "Westernized" of the lot of us. Kenyatta enjoyed the personal friendship of some of the most distinguished people in English political and intellectual society. He was subtle, subtle enough to attack one's principles bitterly and retain one's friendship. He fought the British as imperialists but was affectionate toward them as friends.

It was to this balanced and extremely cultured man that Francis Nkrumah proposed that we form a secret society called The Circle, and that each of us spill a few drops of our blood into a bowl and so take a blood oath of secrecy and dedication to the emancipation of Africa.

Johnstone Kenyatta laughed at the idea; he scoffed at it as childish juju. He conceived our struggle in modern, twentieth-century terms with no ritualistic blood nonsense. In the end Francis Nkrumah drifted away from us and started his own little West African group in London. We were too tame and slow for him. He was an angry man in a hurry.

Then he went back to his part of Africa, and Francis Nkrumah became Kwame Nkrumah. He set himself at the head of the largely tribal populace and dabbled in blood ritual. There was some violence, a spell in prison, and finally Nkrumah emerged as the first African prime minister in a self-governing British African territory.

Tribal myths grew up around him. He could make himself invisible at will. He could go without food and sleep and drink longer than ordinary mortals. He was, in fact, the reincarnation of some of the most powerful ancestral spirits. He allowed his feet to be bathed in blood.

By the time I visited the Gold Coast the uneasy alliance between Nkrumah and the tribal chiefs had begun to crack. A week or so before my arrival he had threatened that, unless they cooperated with his government in turning the Gold Coast into an efficient twentieth-century state, he would make them run so hard that they would leave their sandals behind them. This was a calculated insult to the tribal concept that a chief's bare feet must never touch the earth.

That was the beginning of the secret war. Nkrumah thought he would win it easily. He was wrong.

And the chiefs have, negatively, scored their victories too. They have pushed him to a point where his regime is, today, intolerant of opposition. The tribal society brooks no opposition. Nkrumah's government banishes its most active opponents. As a modern socialist leading a Western-style government, he justifies this as a temporary expedient. But his less sophisticated ministers frankly talk the tribal language of strength, frankly express the tribal impulse to destroy those who are out of step.

There was an air of delicacy about our conversation and we were both aware of this. We touched on local politics. He let off at full blast against the tribalist. I told him I had heard that the Accra Club was still exclusively European. His eyes lit up. "You wait and see," he said. Then, in relation to nothing either of us had said, he leaned toward me and exclaimed, "This place is rich! God, man there's so much riches here!"—as though the revelation had just been made to him.

From An African Treasury, *edited by Langston Hughes, Crown Publishers, Inc., 1960.*

Modern Artist of Benin

BY ULLI BEIER

Ulli Beier, critic of African literature and art, is a professor at the University College at Ibadan. Austrian by birth, he has lived in Nigeria for more than fifteen years and now makes it his home. In 1956 he founded the literary magazine *Black Orpheus* and became its first editor. One of his chief concerns is to encourage the creative talents of African authors and artists.

During the early days of independence, some Nigerians took the stand that "art is a luxury we cannot afford." Mr. Beier opposes this viewpoint. In his book, *Art in Nigeria,* published in 1960, he wrote: "At no stage in the history of Nigeria has the artist a more important function than now. For to define and create the Nigerian personality is to give meaning to independence. . . . The new Nigerian generation must come to terms with its past before it can pass on to a creative future. Only then can we hope that Nigeria will have another contribution to make to the world of art that is as important and revolutionary as that of its traditional woodcarving and brass-casting."

In the following article from *Nigeria Magazine,* he discusses the work of the woodcarver, Idah, who has worked in ebony and developed the use of decorated cement blocks and cement sculpture.

The fame of Benin City rests largely on its traditional culture. The visitor to the historical city is likely to look for the museum, the palace, and some of the beautiful ancient houses that survived the great fire of 1897. Although several thousand of the famous bronzes were carried away as loot after the destruction of the town, and even though many valuable antiquities were stolen from Benin in recent years and sold to unscrupulous art dealers in Europe and America, many beautiful works still survive in the city.

The art of Benin is not entirely a matter of the past, however. The guild of brassworkers is still in existence and numerous brass casters and woodcarvers are at work in the city. Nearly all this work is rather mediocre, however. The constant stream of foreign visitors to Benin is anxious to have copies of traditional Benin art and in this way most of the artistic energy in the city has been diverted to the tourist trade. Some of the younger people, of course, have found their way out of this tradition altogether. They were able to leave the city and learn Western techniques in the Zaria Art School or elsewhere, and become modern artists. Bruce Onobrakpeya and Colette Omogbai come to mind. But among those who carried on the traditional arts and crafts in the city hardly any have been able to survive the corrupting influence of the tourist market.

Perhaps the one brilliant exception is O. Idah, an old illiterate woodcarver. Idah was trained strictly in the traditional styles of woodcarving, and he has had no schooling and really no outside influences on his work. Yet he has not succumbed like others to the routine of perpetually copying traditional work. His strong and imaginative mind has retained a freshness and originality that make him one of the most colorful personalities and one of the most attractive artists not only in Benin but in the whole of Nigeria.

Idah was born in 1908. At the age of seven he was sent to stay in the palace with the late Oba Eweka II. Here he learned to carve in the traditional manner. He began with carving coconut shells, palm kernels, calabashes. Later he proceeded to the carving of coral beads, wood, and ivory. When he was thirteen, one of his wooden panels won first prize at an exhibition in Benin.

At the age of fifteen Idah left for Lagos to learn carpentry in the Public Works Department. During his training he found time to continue with his art. He started ebony carving in Lagos, a medium which has since been taken up by so many Nigerian artists, both good and bad. A great deal of "airport art" is being produced today in ebony. It is worth while, therefore, to look at some of Idah's earliest ebony carvings, which are sensitive and delicate and show no resemblance to the dreary cliché work that is hawked around the airport and the big hotels in Lagos today.

When Idah's talent was discovered in Lagos, he was engaged to teach woodcarving at the King's College, Lagos. During his nine years at the college, he taught many boys that have become well-known artists, important public figures, statesmen, and civil servants.

After spending a total of twenty-four years in Lagos, Idah fell seriously ill in 1947 and returned to Benin. After his recovery, Oba Akenzua II persuaded him to stay in his native city to teach art there. At first he taught in the Divisional Council Secondary Modern School. Later on he was put in charge of the Council's Arts and Crafts School, where he is still teaching.

The years since 1947 were in a sense his most productive and original years. Soon after his return to Benin, he started once more to experiment with new media. He developed a very successful form of cement sculpture, which has all the power and virility of traditional mud sculpture, but is more resistant to the effects of weather. He mixes cement with laterite soil, to give it a very beautiful texture and color. Outside the palace of Benin one can see his statue of Ozolua, an ancient Oba of Benin.

At the present time Idah is working on six cement reliefs for the palace—which are perhaps the most interesting works he ever made. These reliefs are to replace some ancient mud reliefs that were made on the outside of the palace wall in the time of Oba Eweka II, but which have since crumbled and practically disappeared. Other cement works by Idah can be seen in the house of Chief Iyamu, for which he molded two large elephants.

As a woodcarver Idah will be chiefly remembered for his carved doors on the Benin Divisional Council and for the carved panels and large figures in the Oba's palace.

Another monument to Idah's ingenuity is the yet unfinished Aruosa Cathedral in Benin. This new church, which Oba Akenzua II of Benin undertook to build himself, was designed by Idah, who cast specially decorated cement bricks for the building. The cathedral, though not completed, is one of the most interesting sights in Benin. Idah's decorated cement bricks will interest all architects working in Nigeria. Cement blocks have so far proved to be a bit of a disaster in Nigerian architecture. Its cheapness and handiness have made it an irresistible medium, but we all know the dreariness and drabness of buildings erected with it. To my knowledge Idah is the first person to liven up the surface and texture of this material. Idah has here opened up new possibilities that are just waiting to be picked up and used and developed by others.

Perhaps the most fascinating and charming monument Idah has created is his own house. I cannot think of any other dwelling in Nigeria which reflects and projects the personality of the owner so completely. The house is built on one of the remaining sections of the ancient city wall of Benin. Running at right angles to Oba Market Road in the city, the wall has been steeply cut some thirty yards from the road. Idah has planted an attractive garden between the road and the wall. A flight of steep cement steps are built into the wall and lead up to the house. Nothing would be more like the studio of some internationally famous surrealist artist on the Left Bank of Paris than Idah's house—except that the house is a great deal more genuine, charming, and less affected than most studios I have ever seen. The entrance of the house is flanked by a series of lively cement sculptures and reliefs covering a great variety of subjects. There is a sculpture of an elephant trampling on a man, and a relief of Oba Akenzua II shaking hands with Queen Elizabeth. As one is walking up the steps towards this colorful entrance, faces stare at one in flat relief from the steps themselves. Entering the circular vestibule of the house, one is confronted by one's own life-size image, because a large old-fashioned mirror has been placed opposite the door.

As the artist takes one around the house, which he built himself, one is continuously delighted by the wealth of ideas and the inventiveness of the owner. Practically every room in the house is on a different floor level, little steps leading up and down from the one to the other. The house is filled not only with Idah's own carvings but with traditional Benin art he has collected. It has excitingly exotic furniture he has made or collected and all kinds of weird old colonial "period pieces" for which Idah has a liking, like an English artist collecting Victorians. Among his chairs are some curious wrought iron structures, which once formed part of the furniture of Lagos's first cinema. The chairs are in the style known as "art nouveau," the most famous examples of which are the older Paris metro stations. Idah replaced the wooden seats by new ones which he carved himself. There are Victorian gilt picture frames on the wall and there are all kinds of curious brass ashtrays and stands for flowerpots that Idah welded together from bits of scrap metal and dismantled brass chandeliers which he acquired at Lagos auctions.

There is a bedstead in the middle of his living room. Just over the pillows Idah has painted his own head on the wall, so that on entering one has the impression that someone is lying in bed. Idah's house is filled with quaint and humorous ideas like this.

Idah has a sensitivity towards materials, a feeling towards old objects, and a sense of humor in building them all together into a curiously surrealistic atmosphere that will make the artist from London, Paris, or New York feel immediately at home with this charming, old, illiterate craftsman in Benin, whose English is quite limited and who has never heard of the "isms" and movements of the West with whose exponents he has so much in common.

A visit to this delightful and ingenious old man is an exciting and precious experience. His work and his life are a living testimony to the fact that the creative potential of Benin is not dead, that it has not been entirely killed by the tourist trade, and that it is fully capable of making the transition from traditional crafts to modern individual art.

Without knowing it, Idah is a great pioneer. One would hope that others will recognize this in time, and that his wonderful house will be acquired and preserved by the City of Benin or the Department of Antiquities. In times to come it could be a fine monument to the spirit of an outstanding son of Benin and to these vital years of cultural transition.

"Modern Artist of Benin," by Ulli Beier, Nigeria Magazine, *March, 1964.*

To School with Love

THE AUTOBIOGRAPHY OF A UGANDAN SCHOOLBOY

COLLECTED BY SHELDON WEEKS

This autobiography is one of twenty collected by Sheldon Weeks, a sociologist doing research on education in Uganda, who spent nearly two years with a group of over 300 students at a secondary day school. These personal histories proved to be provocative human documents and gave overwhelming evidence of the strong drive for education felt by many boys and girls in this area.

Although each life story is unique and individual, certain trends appear throughout the twenty autobiographies. The most common factor is academic excellence, as only one out of fifty could have secondary schooling. A second is the outstanding insecurity due to lack of money and the resulting hunger, disease, and lack of school fees. These conditions often resulted in appeals to the extended family or friends for economic support. The constant insecurity involved many new personal and social relationships: living away from home, dependence on odd jobs, conflicts of responsibility and interruption of school work.

In the account which follows, personal and place names have been changed or modified to preserve anonymity, but the student's language and mode of expression have not been edited. The simplicity and sincerity which are retained more than compensate for any slight awkwardness in the use of English.

I am a Muganda boy approaching nearly eighteen years of age. I was born in a village called Bira. Bira is a small village in a valley enclosed by lofty hills. On the hills one can see the immovable huge stones covering each and every hill. Here and there are groups of trees on which early in the morning birds used to sing merrily. Short grass grows at the lower regions of the hills and it is such places that the villagers inhabit. At the foot of certain hills streams meander towards banana plantations.

In the year 1945 in the month of June I came to dwell in a country which differed in every way from that I came from. I did not dream at all of the new country that was comforting me. I could never guess to visit a new land and I thought that my mother's cavity was my home forever. Although I was safe here I felt desirous to find rather a larger room where I could romp. The need became so strong that I started to stretch my body out from the dark, secret room, where nothing could be felt but organs of every shape, and among these I wriggled.

My mother felt my struggle, and perhaps she became aware of the fate that lay before her. My search for a way out became so continuous that she was forced to leave everything she was doing aside to prepare for the stranger. I was in despair when I found my way out. I was born at last. It might have been a sunny day since the glare of the sun struck me sharply and I screamed at that very instant. My delicate bag was removed from me and I remained naked. As it is the Kiganda custom, *Luwoneko: Lukulike, Katonda Yebale,* were words of praise. The whole family remained in great joy for most of the hour. Their gratitude for my birth was supreme.

This peaceful period could not last long, and everything went sharp upon me. After my mother left home I lived with my grandmother. At the age of two, my mother came back again, but she found me already attacked by a horrible disease of which I cannot tell its name. The disease together with the bad food I ate made me so weak that if the wind blew a little harder I could be rolled along the ground. The doctor paid more attention to me and I soon recovered from my shocking need.

I was very fond of the goats. Every morning I went to cheer them up and to sympathize with them after the long night of displeasures. I talked to them, telling them that we were being treated in the same way. However, they took no notice and sometimes they seemed to rebel as I undid their ropes and they ran away.

Under the consent of my grandmother, and at her expense, I was finally sent to school, a co-ed school known as the Lulu Mixed School. This was in 1950 when I was five years old. I was very much pleased at the idea as I was then dispensing with the laborious works at home. I also would escape grazing animals on rainy days.

The first day at school created astonishing impressions in my mind. I had never come in contact with a place where people of various ages collected. I wondered where all these chaps lived, and at first I thought they lived at the school, and perhaps I was also to live with them. They eyed me superficially and boastfully. They wore a pair of shorts made out of khaki and blue shirts out of cotton. They were very smart but they had no shoes. I wore a pair of pocketless shorts and a shirt called *kapere kungulu* (ticking cloth). My uncombed hair was something to notice, and my presence divided me from my hopeful new friends.

I was taken to the headmaster in a narrow room furnished with a wooden table and a wooden chair on which the headmaster sat. On the table was an inkpot and pen inside the inkpot. There was also a pile of long thin books and these were the registers. He pulled out one and in this I was enlisted under a continuous list of names headed "Class I." My grandmother was told to pay ten shillings * for my school fees for the whole year, and to buy me a school uniform during the following fortnight. Only two exercise books were to be bought and a pencil.

My Class II work was at first hard, but as the term drew to a close I was able to catch up. I was fourth at the end of the term in a class of thirty-two pupils. At the end of the year I had passed and was to join Class III the following year. It was now time to look for another school, as the Lulu School was comprised of two classes only.

Five miles from my home was another private school called Kitabu Memorial School, which now is a Buganda Government school. I became a pupil at the school in 1953 in Class III. The school fee there was thirty-six shillings a year, excluding the school books and school uniform. We were taught a little English, but nevertheless it was English, arithmetic, English grammar, geography, history, and religion that we studied. My work was good and I succeeded in making the first position, surpassing the others in a class of thirty pupils.

Everything went at right angles during my studies in primary four and I was on top throughout the year. I was the master of studies at that time. My sixth year was spent at the private school, Mutesa Memorial. I stayed with Mr. Kibirige's two sons, who went to the same school. Mr. Kibirige was our neighbor at Bira and perhaps is the one who advised my grandmother to take me to Mutesa Memorial

* One East African shilling is worth fourteen cents.

School. Katumba, his elder son, was my classmate; Wadda was two classes lower. We made good company, we three men. We prepared our meals every day after school and on Saturdays we dug in our small garden of cassava. We stayed in the house all alone. Mr. Kibirige came only occasionally with heaps of matoke, cassava, pumpkins, and potatoes for our diet.

When we were preparing our meals, each of us did a different job and this made the work easy for us. I fetched water from a distance of about a mile while Katumba peeled the bananas and Wadda ground the nuts. There was a gentleman to whom I fetched a tin of water daily and he paid half a shilling for every tin and at the end of the month I collected fifteen shillings. With the money I sometimes bought fish from Kasulu, for these were cheaper, so every Friday I went to Katwe to purchase them. With the rest of my money I bought a few textbooks. Some of it I used to buy fried groundnuts at school.

I studied very hard so that every time I sat for my examinations I won first position. My work impressed all my teachers and then they selected some pupils to sit for the special entrance examination at a government day secondary school (GDSS) in Kampala. We were four to sit. Two of us failed while Kiwana and I passed and were offered vacancies in the school.

Since I had to leave Mr. Kibirige's house near the Mutesa Memorial School, I was to hire a room somewhere near the GDSS. As I had no relative to stay with, I had to stay all alone. My father was now eager to educate me, but he had incurred financial difficulties. The school expenses seemed too high for him to afford. The fee was fifty-eight shillings per term with a few other things to be bought. However he strived to get the money for my first term.

Because we had just entered the school, we were given no examinations at the end of the first term; therefore no one knew his position or the state of his studies. During my holidays after the first term, I went to my father. It was a disappointing holiday because my father told me that in his opinion I should stop studying. He said that it was a good idea for me to discontinue my studies so as to give my younger brothers a chance at an education. He said that unless I was to stop studying, my brothers were to remain illiterate.

On hearing what my father said I went to my aunt Nabingo, who lives at Kakande village, a few miles from Bira. I told her all that my father had said. She grieved at the news and she asked me to stay with her for the rest of the holidays. She had a few shillings at her disposal which she hoped could be used to buy enough bananas to brew beer. She suspected that we could raise money if we brewed beer. We bought bananas for several times, brewing beer which as a result made what we started with high enough to cover my school expenses. My heart was furnished with joy and no more worries dwelt in my mind.

My second term began. I was as happy as the rest of the pupils and never told my friends my difficulties.

We sat for our mid-year examinations. I became first out of thirty-two pupils in my class at the GDSS.

My holiday as usual was very oppressive. I meditated over the ways of how I was to obtain my school fees for the coming terms. In some ways fortune lay before me. My aunt, Nabingo, had loved a man; the man was old but rich. He possessed a lorry, a shop, a shamba of coffee, and a large plantation of bananas at Singo County. Mr. Kizza was very kind, and loved every relation of Nabingo, his sweetheart. I spent my holidays at his home with my aunt. We did a lot of work. Every morning we cultivated and in the evening we picked coffee. He was very much pleased with our labor, so pleased that he offered me one hundred shillings. This amount was quite enough to cover my school expenses.

My "uncle" came to me and asked me to go to his home as he proposed to finance me for the whole year. Mr. Kizza had a shop at Mugongo; it was a small shop; he had some coffee trees and a small area of banana plantation. I was in charge of the shop and occasionally picked coffee. At the end of the holidays I was given 150 shillings of which 65 shillings was for school fees. The rest was for house rent, food, books, and other miscellaneous essential things. I received a new school uniform and a pair of shoes. Besides these I got a white pair of shorts and a blue shirt. I had now become rich.

In 1960 I had reached Class A Junior II. This was a very happy year when all my financial troubles were settled. Everything went perpendicularly. However, things changed. Mr. Kizza had also planned to grow fourteen acres of maize. He hired a tractor and employed more on the maize farm. As he paid more money to the men, his purse could not stand upright, it was no longer heavy. He had gone bankrupt. There was no money left even to run the shop.

I told him that I would go to town where I would find a job. He gave me fifteen shillings to use while searching for a job and off he went. My search was always in vain and I passed my holidays with no job. Despite the fact that I had not any assistance, when the holidays were over I went to school to begin my new term. Every Saturday and Sunday I looked for any kind of work. I was determined to do anything if only I could get money out of it. But I did not steal.

Most businessmen could not believe my words, so they would not dare employ me. Some despised me because of my youth. It was essential therefore to have a well-known person to assist me in my search. I consulted Mr. Kiwanuka, my neighbor, and requested him to help me. He was kind and at once we left for Nakulabye, a major crossroads near Kampala.

Moving from shop to shop, garage to garage, in all directions, we asked each and every one whether there was a job for me, but the answer always was a negative one. In spite of the unsuccessful attempts we made we continued to search for a job. Reluctantly we strolled to a man's garage where there were only a few workmen. They were busy hammering and screwing different parts of the cars together. We asked him, almost hopelessly, if he could employ me at any kind of job he might have. In his answer he expressed that the job he could provide was unsuitable for me. But when we told him all my financial affairs as a schoolboy, he willingly consented to employ me. But he was still not sure whether I was capable of guarding his garage at night. I assured him that I could. He suggested that my pay be fifty shillings a month. At all costs I was determined to work. It was a nighttime job. It was really difficult and a risk to one's life.

The time was a season of thieving. Day after day there were reports of the theft of vehicles in the town. Reports about the removal of car tires and housebreaking. Such news threatened me, but I was bound to face my fate.

The first day I passed a sleepless night. I had nothing but my clothes which I wore, nothing with which to fight my assailants. I had no weapon to chase whoever interfered with me. However, I thought of collecting some stones. I placed stones in heaps in every corner of the building, outside along the veranda. I knew that a stone blow was more effective than any other blows issued by me. I stayed heavy-eyed every night for fear that the kings of the night might come to steal my master's properties.

Every morning I went to school. Every night I attended the garage. The job was very sharp and cruel, but nevertheless I liked it very much. I was very proud of it. I could always feel my pride. One morning, Sunday, just as I had a break in the job, I was told that my aunt Nabingo was very sick. I decided to go to Kakande to see her. My whole aim was to spend only a few hours away so that I might return to attend my job.

It was a long journey with many troubles; I did not return to my night watchman job until ten o'clock that night. My master had been to the garage earlier to find out if I was there. After inspecting, looking in every car in the garage to see if I was sleeping, he saw I was not there and went away. The following morning as I was passing he called me and told me that it was my duty to look for another job.

I went back to school deeply upset. I had already paid my school fees. The fifty shillings I had been paid was at my disposal. I completed my term's work without bothering to look for a job. As soon as we had our holiday I visited the town continuously. I was roaming thoughtlessly in the town when I saw a friend. He was my recent classmate, but was now working. I told him all my troubles but he did not seem interested. However, he advised me to convert myself from my religion and become a Muslim. He said, "If you are a Muslim, you can easily obtain a scholarship from the Muslim Society." I thought this to be sensible advice, but to whom was I to go for conversion? I went to Kibuli because I was told that there I could find somebody who could fulfill my needs.

On the other hand I remembered that my family hated the Muslims; they always strongly warned that if any member of the family becomes a Muslim, he ought to be canceled out of the family. Since the family had no solution to my troubles, what would be the effect to me if I was canceled out of it! I went reluctantly to Kibuli, where I inquired of the responsible man. I was taken to him. He concluded that if I was seeking financial assistance he was unable to do anything. I was shocked at his answer. This was the only route I thought would solve my problems. I was overcome by despair. So I proposed to die and preferred death to a life which was just like that.

I therefore went to a Mutoro Shop where I bought poison which was designed for the killing of wild animals. I paid him two shillings for a packet. I was sure a packet could do well in my plan. This was the best way to dispense with my friction forever. It was my aim to obtain such a peaceful time. I started to clean everything, my room, my clothes, above all to say good-by to my friends.

I had many friends, some were my classmates, others were those whom I studied with in previous schools. I was eager to see them before I had to depart. Among my friends at school the dearest were Miss Kalema and Master Kazibwe.

Kalema Becca was a beautiful girl, charming in every way. Her sharp eyes set my thoughts at random. Her absence from me was very poisonous. I loved her more than words here can reveal. One day I prepared to go for my holidays to Mityana. I wished her a glorious holiday and bade her goodby. She could say nothing, but her face was swept with tears. Life was unpleasant at the least absence from her. Her father had a car which brought her to school and back to home. On certain days she preferred walking with me to going in her father's car. This was a hard time for both of us. I was going away never to be seen again. I was to die. We would never see each other again. When I told her that very soon I was disappearing forever, it was to set her to the mercy of tears. She cried so much that day and never attended classes. She devoted her time to talking to me to try and persuade me so that I may curse my plan for once and for all. My love towards her was intense. I gave heed to whatever she had to say. I remained happy and found it best to conceal my worries when I was with her. Her words were as sweet as honey. I was content not to commit suicide. My sweetheart had settled me.

I was making my way to town after sunrise. All along the streets ran swiftly cars, motorcycles, hurrying towards the city. Pedestrians were complaining about the terrible state at which the vehicles sped.

On the way I met Mr. Sentongo. He owns a shop at Nakulabye. He is a kind man, middle-aged. I used to pass by his shop going to and from school. I always saluted him. Mr. Sentongo became my friend. When I met him he asked me why I was not going to school that day. I explained to him plainly that I had been chased out of school because I had failed to pay my school fees. He wanted to know the amount which was due. His questions meant something hidden in him. I told him that it was 125 shillings. He paused. He told me to come on Sunday night to collect seventy-five shillings, which I could pay to the school so that I might continue my studies. The other fifty shillings I could collect some days later.

When I had my holidays, I then spent the whole of them at his home helping him with his business. I worked zealously to please him. I worked all day long without showing any sign of fatigue. He praised my service and he decided to continue to support me if I could be able to assist him every day after school. I agreed. I worked under this agreement until I finally had to give up.

Fortunately enough at this time I obtained 125 shillings from the Buganda Government for the clearance of my school fees. The money I had paid to the school was given back to me. I could not keep the money, so I decided to give one hundred shillings to a certain man, my neighbor, a fruitseller, who promised to give me a profit of ten shillings a month. I then remained with 25 shillings for my personal use. He used the money for two months, keeping to our agreement. But it happened that he fought a woman who had come to buy tomatoes at his stall. He was accused, but realizing that he was guilty, he dislodged himself from where he lived and never turned up again. My hundred shillings was gone.

I spent most of my time, even during the weekends, serving at Mr. Sentongo's shop. I had little time left for my studies. I could not do well at school. For fear that my friends would despise me if I did badly at school, I decided to discontinue my studies so that I might just work. On an unknown day in the month of April I left school and started working full-time at Mr. Sentongo's shop. However, I joined the British Tutorial College to take a bookkeeping course. I told Mr. Sentongo about it. He was pleased and promised to pay 180 shillings for the full Stage-A Bookkeeping L.C.C. I paid the amount and started my studies, which I found very interesting. I can now make sensible work of bookkeeping. I know how to enter business transactions in a cash book, and then to balance the cash book, and keep records of purchases and sales and prepare the profit-and-loss account.

Sometime later I visited many schools in search of a vacancy. The way was quite open in private schools, but they demanded more money than I could afford. At African High School the school fees were six hundred shillings a year. I went to an Asian-run school in town, which also asked a great deal of money. Finding that these schools were financially unsuitable for me, I went back to my former school, GDSS. I hoped to be admitted, but was not, for all the classes were full. I then went to another GDSS. I begged for admission to the headmaster's office. He was an Englishman, a reasonably tall man, sharp-nosed with sharp eyes. He was on the whole a kind, gentle man. Eager to hear from me, he asked me what I wanted. I placed my application before him. After he had read it he sent me to his secretary. The secretary wrote my name on a long form. That was a form granting a place to me in the school in Senior II. I was to join the school the following Monday. On my way I went laughing to myself as I was very joyous. I had the supreme gratitude towards my new headmaster. I went and washed my clothes and made ready for the morning. I told my master where I am working that I had obtained a place in a school and to have my pay ready.

It then became necessary for me to attend my master's shop for my service there in the evenings. Always after school from 5 P.M. I attended the shop. It was not easy to do this because I met many disadvantages. My studies were oppressively affected by the work; I had not enough time to devote to my studies. Then on the 30th of April my master dismissed me from my work. He said that his profits were not enough to continue to pay me fifty shillings a month. As you know, I could not work for nothing, so I stopped. Now I am increasing the number of unemployed in the city. I am a boy who was born unlucky and perhaps what is confronting me is misfortune.

"To School with Love: The Autobiography of a Ugandan School-boy," collected by Sheldon Weeks, Africa Today, *September, 1963.*

The Road to America

BY LEGSON KAYIRA

The motto at Livingstonia Secondary School in Nyasaland, where Legson Kayira graduated in 1958, is "I Will Try." For a long time Legson had had a dream of going to America for further study. He knew that other Africans from Kenya and Uganda went across the sea, so he decided to go too. He had heard that Abraham Lincoln, born in poverty, had worked his way up in the United States, and he believed that he could do the same.

He thought he would walk across Africa to Port Said (he did not know that it was more than three thousand miles) and then work his way across the Atlantic on a boat to the United States. He told his mother it would take five days, although in his heart he knew it would take longer.

His mother helped him get ready to go. His head was shaved, and he wore a clean school uniform, with the badge of Livingstonia on the pocket of his khaki shirt. His feet were bare. His mother handed him a bag containing flour for his five-day trip to the United States, an extra khaki shirt, a blanket, and two books—an English Bible and a copy of *Pilgrim's Progress*. Legson Kayira stamped his bare foot on the ground before he left, for he knew that every morning his mother would come and stand there, and she would look at his footprint and say, "I know who stood there."

It was almost two years later that Legson arrived at the city of Khartoum in the Sudan, still a long way from his goal—America.

I arrived in Khartoum on Sunday afternoon, September 25, 1960. The sun was low, the day calm and clear. The city stood before me in a remarkable dignity. Here and there I saw buildings, some beautiful, others ugly, some big, others small, some old, others new or under construction, but all combining to give the city a peculiar beauty.

I was tired and weak and hungry. I did not know anybody in the entire city. Everywhere I looked I saw men and women, some men riding donkeys, some standing or walking; a few places here and there I saw donkeys tied to posts and braying quietly and unconcernedly. Here and there I saw men, now kneeling, now standing, murmuring their prayers to Allah. The Arabic language was as strange to me as the city itself. "What am I going to do now?" I sighed. I picked up my bag and went about the streets as if I knew already all the directions, but my whole purpose at the time was to look for a place where I could sleep.

In front of me stood an ancient building, which, in point of fact, turned out to be a hotel, and an expensive one, too. I went straight to it. As soon as I entered, an old man, looking no younger than his building, came forth to ask me, "What do you want here?"

"I am a stranger here, sir," I trembled the words, "and I am looking for a place to stay for the night."

"This is a hotel, all right," he said in a rather friendly manner, "but I am afraid it's too expensive. I have another one in town here, and I'm sure it will suit you."

He drove me to his cheap place. It was a clean place, though no less ancient than the other. I stayed there for the night in the company of a few Egyptians, who, it appeared, were living there regularly. We slept outdoors, surrounded by a brick fence, because it was hot.

The sun had just risen, bringing with it the active rushings common to all big cities. The mercury on the wall was rising, and I was sitting at a table sipping a hot cup of tea that the manager of the place had just given me. The manager, awed by my tale, was sitting opposite me with his mouth half open in amazement. On my right were two Egyptians, one of whom kept saying, "Is that so?"

The manager asked me if I needed any more tea. I did not. He then suggested that I take a good shower and gave me a piece of soap, thus reminding me of my Indian friend at Itigi more than a year before. After taking my cold shower I put on my khaki shorts, my shirt, and a pair of the soon-to-be-no-more shoes, and I can say that I looked my best, better indeed than even my own mother had been used to seeing me. I took the necessary documents and went about in town hunting for the American Embassy. I would try for a visa there, and if they refused I would go on and try again in Cairo.

For some reason, mostly language barriers, I refrained from asking others the direction to the American Embassy, but walked here and there as if aimlessly, sometimes even coming back to the streets where I had been before. Then one time, looking at a far distance, I saw with extreme delight the Stars and Stripes. The flag was waving gently.

"There it is," I shouted to myself, pointing to it as though I had suddenly become possessed. With much haste I ran over.

I took the stairway and in no time at all I was panting before a rather bewildered lady in the office. Luckily the phone began ringing, and while she was attending to it, I regained my breath.

"Yes, sir," she said as soon as she had put the receiver back, "what can I do for you?"

"I am going to America," I breathed out. "I want a visa."

"Do you have Form 1-20?"

"What?"

"Form 1-20."

I did not have it; indeed, I did not even know what she was talking about. She began explaining to me, saying that I could not be granted a visa until I had this form, among other things. The college should have sent me that form.

"I am sorry," she said. "I can only help you if you get the form."

I was disappointed and angry. I hesitated a moment, then stood up to go. I looked at the map of the United States hanging on the wall, a row of magazines on the shelf, and back at the lady, but she had already said she could not help me until I got the form. Cairo, I was sure, would tell me the same story.

A gentleman came into the office. His name, as I later learned, was A. Salam Yausif Hamid, and he was working in the embassy. The lady, who probably thought it was funny for someone just to come into the office and ask for a visa while not in possession of Form 1-20, began relating my case to him. It appears he did not take it as funny, for he came to me, asked me a few questions, and then asked me to wait. A few moments later I was shown into another office. It was very tidy. A map of the United States hung on one wall, and that of Africa on the other. There was the Stars and Stripes again, not too far from the desk. The gentleman behind the desk motioned me to sit down, and slowly I perched myself on the chair.

"Your name is Legson Kayira?"

"Yes, sir."

"And you want a visa."

"Yes, sir."

"Where are you from, Mr. Kayira?"

"Nyasaland."

"And to which school are you going in the United States?"

"Skagit Valley College, sir."

"Any correspondence with you from Skagit?"

"Yes, sir," I said. I unfolded two letters from my passport where I had kept them, and handed them to him. He read them through rather carefully and slowly.

"All right," he said. "How do you intend to get to America?"

"Walk to Port Said and work my way on a ship to New York," I said.

"Walk?" he asked. "How did you get here from your home?"

"Walked most of the way," I said.

He took a piece of paper and wrote something on it.

"When did you leave your home?"

"In 1958," I said.

"What time in 1958?"

"October."

He looked at the map on the wall, then he wrote something on the paper.

He went into the other office, leaving me sitting uneasily in the chair, wondering how I was ever going to get the magic form. I waited until he, Mr. Emmett Coxson, vice consul of the U.S. Embassy, returned.

"Do you have any money?" he asked as soon as he sat down behind his desk.

"Five pounds, sir."

"Anything else?"

"Two shirts, a pair of short trousers, and two books."

"Any shoes?"

"These," I said, raising one foot up and pointing.

He said that it was cold in America and that he did not see how I could expect to walk on snow with my holed shoes. I said I would, but it was because I did not know what snow was that I said so.

He glanced at the map of Africa hanging on the wall, then asked where my home was. I said it was Karonga and we looked for it, but it was not there.

"Well," he said, "you do not have Form 1-20. Also the regulations require that an applicant for a visa should have sufficient money for a round-trip ticket, and you do not have that."

Then he said that he thought it was only reasonable that I should just go back home. I did not say a word, but in my heart, "Never, no, not now."

Another gentleman came into the office. He was asking for a visa too, saying he was going to work on his Ph.D. A visa was issued him, and I looked at him enviously.

Mr. Coxson then handed me a piece of paper and a pencil, and asked me to write what I had told him. I wrote the following:

In October in the year of our Lord 1958, having completed my Junior Leaving Certificate at the Livingstonia Secondary School, I left my poor mother and a brother and a sister, the only people in the family. I walked all the way to Tanganyika. My aim of leaving the country was to go out and look for schools. There are only four secondary schools in Nyasaland and there are hundreds of boys and girls who do not find schools yearly and eventually they just stay at home. No work for them and no doubt these are the people who will soon become thieves and damage the country.

With this view in mind, I therefore left the country and embarked on a journey, a long and difficult journey, a journey to glory or death. I crossed Tanganyika, worked on the way to get some cents for food. In January this year I crossed Lake Victoria and reached Kampala. It was very difficult to find a job but I had some little money to keep me alive. I used to pass time in the libraries and happened to apply to U.S.A. On being told that I could be offered a course of study there. I applied for a passport to the Nyasaland Government. I got the passport from the Commissioner for Rhodesia and Nyasaland, P. O. Box 1612, Nairobi, Kenya. On September 5th I traveled fifty miles, then got a lift by van to Lira. The next day I traveled to Gulu. At Gulu I stayed with police for three days, waiting for a bus to Nimule. On September 10th I was at Nimule. On the 13th I walked for thirty-two miles, then got a lift by a van for fifty miles. The next day I walked for twenty-four miles, then the same lorry picked me to Juba. In Juba I stayed with Mr. Andrea Taku, Box 51, for three days. On Sunday morning, I left Juba by boat to Kosti, a voyage of seven days. I had no food but, by the mercy of God, on the boat was an American tourist, Mr. George from Chicago. When he was told that I was on board too, he immediately called for me. I went to him and when I told him all about my adventures, he asked me to be getting food from him for the whole way up to Khartoum. I did so. On Saturday 24th I reached Kosti, the same night I left for Khartoum and arrived on Sunday afternoon, September 25, 1960.

After I had written this, and after he had carefully read it, he wrote the following:

American Embassy
Khartoum, Sudan
September 26, 1960

Mr. George Hodson, Dean
Skagit Valley College,
Mount Vernon, Washington

Dear Sir:

The Embassy was visited today by Mr. Legson Kayira who presented two letters from you dated February 29, 1960, and April 19, 1960, regarding his application for admission into Skagit Valley College.

Mr. Kayira has told me a story which I have no reason to doubt. Mr. Kayira's story is true—it is a classic example of a person's desire for education and, as such, warrants more than routine attention and assistance.

In short, Mr. Kayira is walking and hitchhiking from his home in Karonga, Nyasaland, to Skagit Valley College in Mount Vernon, Washington—approximately halfway around the world. So far he has traveled the approximately 2,500 miles from Nyasaland to Khartoum and so far appears undaunted by the prospect that his journey has barely begun.

Mr. Kayira's optimism notwithstanding, the Embassy is faced with the unpleasant and perhaps inpossible task of discouraging Mr. Kayira from continuing on his way from Khartoum.

As you are aware, certain conditions must be met before a student may be issued a visa to study in the United States. The only way that these conditions can possibly be met in Mr. Kayira's case is with the financial and moral support of your school and/or individuals in your community who may be interested in helping. I am writing this letter on the chance that someone may be interested in providing the assistance required to allow Mr. Kayira to continue on his way.

The assistance that would be required is substantial. Someone would have to undertake to guarantee his round-trip passage from Khartoum to Mount Vernon and guarantee that he would not become a public charge in the U.S. I notice in your letter that the school has available a scholarship that will cover his room and board also and to provide adequate clothing. Mr. Kayira's personal possessions consist of two extra shirts and the clothes on his back plus five pounds sterling as capital.

When Mr. Kayira presented himself my first reaction was that the whole thing was out of the question and I should tell him to go back home. Perhaps this is the correct thing to do under the circumstances. After glancing at the map, however, and seeing what he has done in coming this far over half the continent of Africa, my conscience would not permit me to drop the affair without first satisfying myself that there is indeed no hope. Your school has indicated to him that you have some interest in him and this interest has been sufficient to impel him on a journey of unbelievable hardship with only the faintest real prospect of reaching his goal.

I shall try to induce Mr. Kayira to remain in Khartoum at least until I hear from you. In any case a visa cannot be issued without the guarantees outlined above and the Form 1-20 from your institution. Mr. Kayira tells me he wrote you before he left Kampala, so I am confident you have some knowledge of his story. I am enclosing Kayira's account of his journey thus far. Your earliest reply is requested.

> Very truly yours,
> Emmett M. Coxson
> *American Vice Consul*

Mr. Coxson then asked me to check with the embassy in a few days.

Three days later I called at the embassy again. Mr. Coxson asked me to return in the afternoon, and when I did he introduced me to a tall, strong, and rather reserved gentleman. He was Mr. Harry Stuart Hudson, the Public Affairs Officer of the United States Information Agency. He took me into his big office, where we talked for several minutes. He pulled a one-pound note sterling from his wallet and handed it to me.

"Go pay your hotel bills," he said. "Bring your things here and I will take you to my house where you will stay until we hear from Skagit."

Mr. Hudson was living alone, as his family was back in the States. In a few days I got acquainted with his cook and his houseboy, especially the latter since he spoke English well, and especially since I often listened to his radio. In the morning I would sometimes ride with Mr. Hudson to town so I could read in the Information Service library and I would ride back with him or just walk. Later on he gave me the job of washing the car once a week and he gave me five shillings as pocket money. With this money I would buy stamps and write home.

My transit visa was about to expire, and Mr. Hudson advised me to go to the Immigration Office and have it renewed. When I went there they told me that they did not renew transit visas.

They even told me to leave the country before my visa finally expired, which would be in two days. I did not leave the country. I lived in the country illegally.

All this time, we were waiting for word from Skagit. It was already mid-October. Often Mr. Hudson would take me for a boat ride on the Nile, or sometimes he would take me to some of his friends. I had thrown away my shoes, and for several weeks I had been walking barefoot. This was what I was used to, but it was always a fight to walk on the burning sand outside the fence. He gave me a pair of canvas shoes to wear when walking back from the library.

About this time, Mrs. Hudson arrived from the States. She was a very kind lady, and she told me as much as she could about what I would expect to find or see in America. Then one day the telephone rang. It was Mr. Hudson. He said that they had received a cable from Mr. Hodson, dean of Skagit Valley College. The cable had said there would be help.

"Now," Mr. Hudson said, "you must begin reading about the State of Washington."

While I was reading whatever materials I could find on the State of Washington, and while Mr. and Mrs. Hudson were briefing me on the United States, Dean Hodson and Mr. Myron Mickey, the Student Body President, were forming the Legson Kayira Fund. Mr. Mickey was addressing clubs. Mr. Hodson was addressing the students and the faculty members. While I was washing a car or reading a book in Khartoum, they were staging a coffee hour at Skagit to raise funds. The Rotary Club, the Lions International, and the Kiwanis International were raising funds at their regular meetings. Churches and townsfolk in Mount Vernon and neighboring communities were responding. The Bayview Community Club was staging a dance with all the proceeds going to the Legson Kayira Fund, and they raised over three hundred dollars in one night. The radio and the local papers publicized the fund. And so it was that the small community of

Mount Vernon and the surrounding area, inhabited by kindhearted folk, raised money to help an African student stranded in Khartoum.

Mr. and Mrs. William Atwood and their seven children responded by offering me free room and board in their seven-bedroom home. just outside Burlington. "We, as a family," they wrote me in a letter in which they had enclosed their pictures, "would like to help too, and, as such, we would be honored to have you as a member of our family."

The date was November 15, 1960. The time was just a few minutes after eleven in the morning, and the sun was approaching its zenith. The sky was still as clear as it had been when I first arrived in this mother city of the Republic of Sudan, but this time the city and I were no longer strangers to each other. I had wandered to almost every corner of it, and so it was that on that day I had just returned from my wandering, and wiping the sweat off my forehead with an open palm, I entered the library, and there the librarian announced to me that Mr. Hudson wanted to see me. His office was just upstairs, and I hurried up. Judging from his smile I could guess that something was cooking.

He handed me a letter to which was attached a check for $650, which was to be used to cover the cost of my transportation. I read the letter, which was signed by Dean Hodson. I read it again, and it said that I should leave Khartoum in mid-December. I looked at the check. It looked very unreal. My lips quivered, my fingers, indeed my hands trembled, and so overjoyed was I that I felt sad and almost to the point of breaking into tears. The best I could say, indeed, the only words I could say were, "Thank you!" Two years I had wandered from strange place to strange place. Now I would wander no more.

Mr. Hudson took me to a tailor one evening to have me measured for a suit. He bought me a pair of black shoes and a suitcase. On another occasion he came into my room carrying a paper box. To my surprise, it contained nine shirts, a pair of gray trousers, two sets of underwear, one long underwear, three T-shirts, six pairs of socks, and five neckties. In just one short minute I had more clothes than all the clothes I had ever owned in my entire life. They all came from Mr. Coxson, Mr. Friedmann, and Mr. Hudson himself.

I had my medical examination and my smallpox vaccination.

Form 1-20 had been sent along with the check. On the twelfth of December Mr. Coxson finally issued me a visa.

I could not leave Khartoum without having an exit visa, or whatever it is. I went to the Immigration Office. No sooner had I entered than the man who had previously refused to extend my visa, surprised at seeing me still in the city, called out: "Didn't you leave yet?"

"I am leaving tonight," I said proudly.

"No, you won't." he said. "Your visa expired over a month ago, and you have been living here illegally."

"Well, but I couldn't leave then," I said. "This time I am really leaving the country."

"No, you aren't," he said.

"I don't understand," I said. "When I wanted to have my visa extended so I could stay here, you refused and you wanted me to quit the country. Now when I want to quit the country, you say I can't. How so?"

"You will have to pay one pound for each week that you have been here since your visa expired." He examined my visa and then said, "It will be about four pounds."

Four pounds! I would not pay it. I did not have that kind of money.

I went back to Mr. Hudson and told him about it. He then took me to the airport to see one of the immigration officers stationed there. Mr. Hudson talked to him in the diplomatic language, and the gentleman stamped my passport thus: "Seen on Departure."

I took a warm bath, brushed my teeth, combed my hair. Did I shave? Mr. Hudson inquired. No. He helped me put on my first suit, a brown one, with a necktie and a new white shirt, a pair of black shoes, and I never looked so funny and so strange to myself, but I wished my family could have been there to see me transformed. Mr. and Mrs. Hudson were going to a dinner party, but he would drive to the airport to see me off. Mr. Friedmann would drive me there, since I would have to get there early.

Some thirty minutes before departure time Mr. Hudson arrived. A few minutes later the big BOAC jet came thundering in the dark of the night. Trembling and awed, I stood watching the lights from the big lifeless bird as it touched the ground. I did not know what to do. I was afraid, afraid of the thing that would take me to my destination. I was afraid the pilot would not see the airport since we were flying at night. We would be lost. Maybe he forgot to get some fuel. Maybe he forgot to check his engines. There were a thousand things to that plane. Did he check every single one of them?

I shook hands with both Hudson and Friedmann, and walked timidly to the plane. I climbed the steps and waved back at them.

"A parachute, please," I said as soon as I had been seated in the very front row of the cabin.

"Just sit down," the stewardess commanded.

The big bird roared and thundered and swung itself forward, and when I opened my eyes, which I had closed the minute the engines began thundering, I saw Khartoum lying below us as if it were only a football field seen at night, and lighted by a million candles.

From I Will Try, *by Legson Kayira, Doubleday, 1965.*

Education for Tomorrow

BY GARRY FULLERTON

When the Congo became independent in June 1960, it not only inherited a tangled political situation, but also suffered from a lack of trained or educated leadership. In the whole country, almost one third as large as the United States, there were fewer than twenty college graduates.

In addition, the existing schools were oriented toward Europe as they were in all other African countries during the pre-independence period. Teachers and textbooks too were focused on European life and culture, not on African or Congolese history and culture.

Top priority was therefore given to changing both the quality and quantity of education. A crash program was begun, not to educate the few but the many. For this all-out effort, help was requested from the civilian agencies of the United Nations. The major responsibility for schools was undertaken by UNESCO (United Nations Educational, Scientific and Cultural Organization) with strong support from other UN agencies in the fields of health and communications.

Beginning in 1961, UNESCO recruited help from more than a dozen nations. By 1963 there were nearly eight hundred foreign teachers in the Congo, providing a "bridge" to the time when enough young Congolese are trained to staff their own schools and training centers. The following report explains some of the steps taken to provide the kind of education which will meet the specific needs of this newly independent African nation.

Nearly fifty years ago, Stanislas Kotynski and his older brother set out from their home in Warsaw on a journey to Africa. They did not get very far, however. At the city limits a kindly policeman picked them up and returned them to their family. Stanislas was seven years old at the time, his brother ten.

Now, half a century later, Stanislas Kotynski has finally realized his ambition to go to Africa. He and his wife, Mrs. Wanda Kotynska, are two of the nearly eight hundred teachers which the Congolese government has recruited with the help of UNESCO to staff its secondary schools.

Mr. Kotynski, a construction engineer and an internationally known expert in the economics of the building industry, was recruited to teach mathematics but has since become the director of the Congo's new Institute of Building and Public Works. Mrs. Kotynska, who completed her university education in Paris, teaches French at a nearby Protestant school.

At the present time [1964], foreign teachers are an essential part of the Congo's secondary education system. Before independence there were virtually no Congolese trained as secondary school teachers, and the handful which had been trained by 1960 were desperately needed for high administrative positions in the new nation's government. With UNESCO's help, a National Institute of Education was set up to train teachers, but its first classes will not graduate until 1964. Meanwhile the Congo must have foreign teachers to staff its expanding school system.

When I visited the Congo in April 1963, there were 556 of these UNESCO-assisted teachers, representing twenty-five different nationalities. Although employed by the Congolese government, they were paid one-third of their salaries in foreign currency by UNESCO.

Haitians were the most numerous of these teachers in 1962–63. There were 123 of them. Other principal nationalities were Belgians (99), French (85), Lebanese (60). But there were also teachers from Spain, Italy, United Arab Republic, Syria, Greece, Afghanistan, Poland, Canada, Honduras, Viet-Nam, United States of America, Norway, Switzerland, Netherlands, China, Luxembourg, Mexico, Rwanda, United Kingdom, Colombia, and Sweden.

What made these teachers come to the Congo? Their motives are as varied as their nationalities and professional qualifications: "wanted to travel," "good salaries," "spirit of adventure," "desire to see a different part of the world," "always interested in Africa."

Also, while they generally do not talk about it, most of the teachers are imbued with a genuine desire to help the Congo and its people.

This leads them to devote an incredible amount of spare time, evenings and weekends, to extra activities with their students. Their wives often volunteer to give homemaking classes to girls and women in the community.

At least one seeker of "adventure" probably found more than he was looking for. He is Emile Lejeune, a French high school teacher at Albertville, who was appointed in May 1963 to coordinate flood relief operations when Lake Tanganyika rose five feet above normal and threatened the city. On the job daily from 6 A.M. until late at night, Mr. Lejeune directed more than one thousand relief workers, including an entire battalion of the Congolese national army, several Boy Scout troops, volunteers from the Christian Young Workers organization, and medical teams of the World Health Organization.

Housing is one of the main difficulties facing the foreign teachers, especially in the bush—the Congo's vast interior. Often two or three families must share a house and this occasionally leads to friction. Food, too, is a problem except in the region of Goma and Bukavu, where the people enjoy strawberries all year around. In Kasai, for example, meat is a rarity and fresh vegetables bring premium prices, when they can be had.

Difficult living conditions are matched by difficult teaching conditions in many places. In the larger cities there are some well-equipped schools, but at Kabinda the students bring their own chairs from home because the classrooms are bare. There is also a tremendous shortage throughout the Congo of textbooks, laboratory equipment, visual aids, and school supplies in general.

Faced with these conditions, how well have the teachers been able to do their job? With a few exceptions, they have done well, and some have been outstanding.

"UNESCO's aid has been extremely precious to us in the difficult years following independence," said Michel Colin, the Congo's minister of education. And other Congolese authorities acknowledge frankly that without the foreign teachers under the UNESCO and Belgian technical assistance programs there would be no secondary education in the Congo today.

Merely keeping the schools open was not enough, however. It was also necessary to expand them by making maximum use of the teachers and classroom space available, for secondary schools have been the major bottleneck in the Congo's educational system. In 1960, for example, the official figures showed 1.5 million pupils in the primary schools, and there were two universities capable of receiving a large number of students. But only 152 Congolese completed their secondary education that year. (In fact, Congolese had been admitted to official secondary schools only since 1954.)

With UNESCO's help, therefore, the government embarked on a national emergency program to boost secondary school attendance. The results have been impressive. Total enrollment rose from 28,900 in 1959–60 to 54,000 in 1961–62 and to 65,000 in 1962–63. At the same time, a number of secondary school inspectors have been recruited in an effort both to improve the quality of teaching and to train Congolese inspectors for these functions.

Foreign teachers are still being recruited for Congo schools, and the Ministry of Education has estimated that the need for them will continue to grow until 1967, reaching a peak of 7,000 before leveling off as Congolese are trained to take their places. It seems unlikely, however, that this many can be provided, even with the combined efforts of the Congolese government and bilateral and international assistance. Thus, Congo secondary schools may be short-staffed for some years to come.

While the Congo must rely on foreign teachers to staff its secondary schools at present, eventually they will be replaced by Congolese. At independence, however, there were virtually no Congolese teachers at the secondary level and no facilities for training them. To fill this gap, the new government gave top priority to the creation of a National Institute of Education.

The institute, which opened its doors on December 5, 1961, is a prime example of international cooperation. Headed by a Congolese director, its staff includes UNESCO experts from twelve different nations. It receives financial assistance from the Congolese government, the United Nations, the United States AID program, and the British Council.

At the same time, as the institute's first director noted in his inaugural address, it is very much a national institution by the recruitment of its students, by its program of studies, and by the nature of the needs it seeks to satisfy.

Students come to the institute, better known as IPN (Institut Pédagogique National), from all provinces of the Congo. They are admitted regardless of ethnic origin. sex, or religious beliefs. The

sole requirements are high scholastic standing and a pledge to teach
or work in educational administration for at least ten years.

Its program of studies, in addition to the normal teacher's college
subjects, lays heavy emphasis on African linguistics, African and
Congolese societies and institutions, cultural anthropology and soci-
ology. By stressing the Congo's own heritage, it hopes to become
what Joseph Ngalula, former minister of education, called "an instrument of mental decolonization."

René Maheu, director-general of UNESCO, sees the institute's
task as "not so much to satisfy the legitimate demand of every nation
to be master in its own house, but to seek out and bring to light the
creative forces of culture and civilization which every people carries
in itself."

At present there are only two young women among the 207 students enrolled at the school. However, the decision to admit women
on the same basis as men is of prime importance, for teaching has
traditionally been a male monopoly in the Congo. Until recently,
few girls received more than two years of primary education, and far
fewer received enough to become teachers.

"We believe in equality for women," said pretty Maria Dacruz,
one of IPN's two coeds.

"The boys say they do, too," she added with a twinkle, "but I
think some of them are a little afraid that if women get too much
education, wives won't obey their husbands any more."

Miss Dacruz, nineteen, and her colleague, Fidélie Mianda, twenty,
are among the youngest students at the institute. The average age is
twenty-five to thirty. Most of the students are also married and have
had several years' experience in teaching primary grades. Many of
them have been directors of primary schools.

The man chiefly responsible for IPN's courses of studies is Antonio
Chiappano, an intense, hard-working Italian who was formerly educational director of the Societa Humanitaria at Milan. Mr. Chiappano feels very strongly that the curriculum must combine the best
experience of all nations and yet be adapted specifically to the
Congo.

"We know that our experience is not directly transferable to this
situation," he said, "but we don't know yet what can be saved and
what must be thrown out. We are in a process of constant revision
and self-correction. This school is, above all, experimental. What we

learn here will be applied when additional teacher-training institutions are set up."

To Mr. Chiappano, the fact that the faculty represents twelve nations is both an advantage and a disadvantage.

"Each of these countries has its own educational tradition, and the
richness which results from the confrontation of these different cultures is an enormous benefit," he said. "At the same time, it is not
easy to develop this group into a homogeneous working team."

IPN's first class will not graduate until June 1964, and even when
it reaches its "full production" of about one hundred graduates a
year, it will not come anywhere near filling the needs of the Congo's
secondary schools. Many other institutions will have to be built on
the same lines.

IPN's graduates, however, are certainly destined to become leaders
of their nation in every sense of the word. Their ideal, spelled out by
one speaker at the inauguration, is "a rather new type of man, knowing and loving his country, deeply rooted in his own society and at
the same time open to the world, capable of understanding men and
ideas from elsewhere, a man to whom nothing human will be
strange, in short: the ideal Congolese."

One rainy morning in April 1963, three young French citizens set
out from Bukavu to cross the parallel ranges of mountains which separate the East African lakes from the Congo River basin.

Three days and over four hundred miles later they reached their
destination, the steamy river port of Kindu. Their heavily loaded
jeep station wagon had averaged twelve miles an hour over roads that
were little more than jungle paths, across slippery pontoon bridges
rocked by churning flood waters, through swamps where mud choked
the axles and water reached the floorboards.

Exhausted, they arrived on the east bank of the Lualaba only to
find that the ferry to Kindu had broken down. In a daze they trans-
ferred cases of supplies and equipment from the station wagon to a
motorboat and crossed the river, returning the next day with the dis-
abled ferry and a tug to recover the vehicle.

While journeys such as this are not exactly everyday events for the
members of UNESCO's mobile teams in the Congo, they illustrate
the kind of difficulty these modern-day pioneers can expect to face.

The mobile teams, created by UNESCO at the request of the Congolese government, travel about in an area the size of Western Europe, giving four-week refresher courses to selected primary school teachers, principals, and inspectors. Each team consists of three UNESCO experts plus a UNICEF specialist in home economics, hygiene, and nutrition.

"Captain" of the Kindu team, whose base of operations is Bukavu, is Georges Vouillon, a good-humored, pipe-smoking Frenchman who teaches general education principles and child psychology. Like many other team members, he has spent a number of years in Africa as an education adviser. His colleagues include Claude Valot and Miss Annette Taburet, both French, and Jules Francisque, a Haitian.

Miss Taburet, of course, is the hygiene and nutrition expert. Mr. Valot teaches French and arithmetic, and Mr. Francisque teaches education methods in history, geography, science, and manual training.

It is a moving experience to watch the team in action in one of the refresher courses. Behind the easygoing informality of the instructors lies a desperate urge to communicate as much of their specialized knowledge as possible in the short time available. This is matched by an intense eagerness on the part of the participants bent on extracting the maximum benefit from an opportunity which is all too rare.

Instructors and participants alike face staggering odds in their efforts to improve the new nation's primary education. In 1960 only 3,500 of the 16,000 schools provided teaching beyond the second grade.

While some schools in the larger cities are fairly well equipped, the usual school in the bush consists of four poles and a thatched roof. Very often there are no tables, chairs, desks, or benches; no blackboards, chalk, notebooks, or pencils; few textbooks and no visual aids of any kind.

One man who moves around even more than the mobile teams is Eugene Palumbo, for whom architecture is anything but a sitting-down occupation. During a five-month period early in 1963, he traveled more than 24,000 miles in every part of the Congo, supervising the young nation's ambitious school building program.

To accomplish these journeys he used almost every conceivable means of transportation, from giant military aircraft to tiny, single-engine planes, and from school buses to rugged jeeps and Land Rovers for cross-country travel in the bush.

Like many other UNESCO experts in various fields, he is no stranger to Africa or the Congo. Educated in Milan and Lausanne, where he received degrees in topography as well as architecture, he first came to the Congo in 1952, following nine years' building experience in Italy. His first jobs in the tropics were designing service cities for the great dam building projects at Zongo on the Inkisi River and Bendera on the Kiymbi.

Asked why he chose to work in Africa, he answered with a shrug. "Mostly, it's freedom to work," he said. "Architects in Europe are handicapped by the old traditions, at least until they become pretty successful. If you want to do something new and different, you have to go to the new countries. I came here because I wanted to build, and I'm having the time of my life doing it."

The architect admits frankly, however, that he did not expect the work to be quite as overwhelming as it has turned out. With only two draftsmen to aid him, Mr. Palumbo prepares preliminary sketches, final designs, and complete work plans for each of the projects. He draws up specifications and cost estimates, helps to select contractors and helps the contractors find the materials they need. Finally, he supervises the construction from start to finish, and all of this in a program expected to cost 619 million Congolese francs (nearly $10 million) and covering an area of 900,000 square miles.

Mr. Palumbo waved his hand impatiently when a visitor calculated that if he received the normal architect's commissions he would make something like fifty times as much as his UNESCO salary.

"I could retire after a year's work," he said, "but one doesn't live for money; one lives for the pleasure of living. Architecture is like music. You take a program and make something beautiful out of it."

Most of Palumbo's major creations so far are still in the course of construction. They include complexes of classroom buildings and residences at the National Institute of Education and the National Institute of Building and Public Works, both at Léopoldville, the National Institute of Mines at Bukavu, and the *athenée* at Kenge.

The remainder of the program includes classroom additions and teachers' homes at secondary schools throughout the Congo. Mr. Palumbo has tried to work out standard designs for these which make the maximum use both of prefabricated elements and materials available locally. The task is complicated, however, by the fact that construction costs vary as much as 200 per cent from one part of the Congo to another. The principal factor is the cost and length of time for transporting materials, but risks of theft are also greater in some areas and this means a greater outlay for insurance.

Since no funds are available for such luxuries as air conditioning, Palumbo does his best to keep his buildings cool by using heat-resistant materials, providing sun breaks and plenty of ventilation, and orienting them on the site to take advantage of available shade and breezes.

The budget also leaves nothing for decoration, but Palumbo does not mind this. It is part of the challenge, and it fits in nicely with his philosophy of architecture.

"It is the function of the building which makes it beautiful and provides the decoration," he said. "You can do all sorts of interesting things with the play of light and shadow and the pattern of filled spaces and empty spaces in a building."

The National Institute of Education is a beautiful example of Palumbo's skill in tying building to site in a harmonious ensemble. Located on a tall hill in the residential suburb of Bimza, the buildings command an impressive view on all sides, particularly the campus of Lovanium University to the east, and downtown Léopoldville, Stanley Pool, and Brazzaville to the west and north.

Completed so far are a classroom building, laboratories, and refectory. Another classroom building and a residence hall are being added this year, with still more classrooms, an auditorium and a gymnasium to follow in 1964.

Gustave Nsubayi's father, like most of the Congolese of his generation, could neither read nor write, but he saw to it that his children got a good education.

From the family farm at Gandajika in southern Kasai, young Gustave walked daily to the mission school three miles away. Bright in class, he won a scholarship for four years of secondary school, later added a year of technical training. Today, at twenty-one, he is one of the most promising students at the new National Institute of Building and Public Works.

Across the Congo in Bukavu, students at the Institute of Mines follow a course of study just as rigorous as their colleagues at the Institute of Building and Public Works. But their director, an affable

Swiss geological engineer, Dr. Robert Kern, also insists on strenuous field trips as a means of toughening them for the rugged conditions they will encounter in the mining industry.

One day, for example, he got them out of bed at 4 A.M. to climb the steep slopes of Niragongo volcano, whose ominous shape dominates the northern end of Lake Kivu. During the trip, which lasted until well after sundown, the students also absorbed more geology than they normally learn in a week of classwork.

"You know, it wasn't easy," Dr. Kern said later. "Some of these lads from Léopoldville or the Kasai have never seen a mountain before in their lives. But I was proud of them. Out of nearly fifty boys, only one didn't make it."

At the rate of forty graduates a year, it will be many years before the institute can fill the many vacancies in the mining industry, for it occupies by far the most important place in the Congo's economy. Katanga alone produces 7 per cent of the world's copper and two-thirds of its cobalt. Its uranium mines, which furnished the raw material for the first atomic bombs, are no longer profitable commercially, but there are sizeable deposits of zinc, radium, germanium, cadmium, and silver in the province. North Katanga and Kivu are important producers of tin, while Kasai contains the world's largest industrial diamond mines.

Even to maintain present levels of production, many Congolese must be trained to fill the places of European engineers and technicians who have left the country since independence. But beyond that, the future development of the industry depends upon systematic exploration of new sources of minerals, and this is another important task of the mining school.

Stanislas Kotynski, who has been director of the Institute of Building and Public Works since November 1962, calls the students' living conditions his number-one problem.

"Things will be much better when we get the new dormitory finished," he told me, "but until then, we just have to do the best we can."

"The best we can" includes an amazing amount of voluntary after hours work by Mr. Kotynski and other faculty members to make life easier and pleasanter for their students.

Every Sunday, for example, physics professor Raymond Doret,

presents a cinema program for students and their families, using films which he begs or borrows from the Ministry of Education and some of the embassies in Léopoldville.

Twice a week there are homemaking classes for student's wives. These are conducted by Mrs. François Spirlet, wife of the young superintendent of the institute.

The two technical institutes stand at the peak of the Congo's fast-growing pyramid of technical and vocational education.

Unfortunately, there is at present very little standardization in the Congo's technical education, and these schools vary tremendously both in what they teach and in the quality of the instruction.

Therefore, the Congolese government, with the assistance of UNESCO, has developed a plan to recast the entire system of technical education, bringing it more into line with the country's manpower needs in agriculture, business, and industry.

Neither the personnel nor the funds exist to put the whole of this ambitious system into effect immediately, but the Congolese authorities are optimistic about the future. They recognize the truth in the words which Gustave Nsubayi heard the day he began classes at his new school: "It is not we who are going to profit from the independence we have won; it is our children. And the young people must understand this: that they are not working for their own personal happiness, but for the happiness of their children."

From UNESCO *in the* Congo, *by* Garry Fullerton, *United Nations Educational, Scientific, and Cultural Organization, 1964.*

Rural Animation

BY DAVID HAPGOOD

David Hapgood is an American who has made several trips to Africa, traveling up and down the west coast and into the interior during the early sixties. His prime interests are social change and agricultural development,—which meet in "Rural Animation." He knows Senegal best but is interested in studying the economy of all the newly-independent nations and the various ways in which they are attempting to make the transition from colonialism to independence.

Mr. Hapgood lived in Africa from 1961 to 1963 on a fellowship from the Institute of Current World Affairs and has returned five times as an evaluator for the United States Peace Corps. He is the author of a school text on Africa and co-author of a report on agriculture in the developing nations.

The article which follows is a chapter from his book, *Africa: from Independence to Tomorrow.*

In Sedhiou, a remote region in the south of Senegal, a group of young peasants convinced the people of six villages to build small first-aid posts for which the government agreed to supply drugs. The government did not keep its promise; the drugs never appeared. But the project was not abandoned by the young peasants. They convinced the villagers to plant an extra collective field, and with the proceeds from its crop they bought the drugs to supply the first-aid posts.

One part of this story, the failure of the government to keep its promise, is all too familiar in Africa. But other aspects of the Sedhiou story are original. The action of the young peasants in convincing the villagers to build the posts, in order to introduce the idea of

Western medicine, is rare in traditional society. Even more rare is the decision of the communities to continue the project, with their own resources, after the government failed to keep its end of the bargain.

The young peasants who set the project in motion are men like their neighbors in Sedhiou: illiterate, they belong to traditional African society, not to the educated elite; they are not government employees; they expect to live and die in the community in which they were born. All that is different about these young men is that they have undergone a brief experience known as *animation rurale*. The results obtained by "rural animation" in Senegal, in Sedhiou and other villages, make it worth examining in detail.

Mainly because of the support of Mamadou Dia, then prime minister, Senegal adopted rural animation in 1959. After a period of experimentation, the program got under way on a fairly large scale in 1961. Although the idea is foreign, the real work of animation is carried out entirely by Senegalese, under the leadership of Ben Mady Cisse, the austere and thoughtful Directeur d'Animation.

The process of animation begins with the choice of a small area, a group of villages, which are similar in culture and language and resources, and in which there seems to be the possibility of quick though modest economic progress. The local Directeur d'Animation must know the workings of politics and village society in the area, which is not always easy in a nation whose varied peoples live in twelve thousand villages, many of them almost totally unknown to the outside world. Once the director, who is usually an ex-schoolteacher, has a grasp of the area, he sets out on a tour to explain animation. From then on, animation is essentially a dialogue, very much in the African village tradition of palaver, an attempt to establish two-way communication between peasants and elite.

In village after village, the director tells the assembled population that he would like them to choose several young men to learn things that will be good for the village. The young men should be between fifteen and forty years old, experience has shown: if they are younger, they will not command respect in a society where age determines status, and if they are over forty their minds are likely to be forever closed to new ideas. They must also be members of the tightly knit village society, not outsiders who happen to live in the village but not within its culture. This means that they will be men who live by working the land and they will be, almost invariably, illiterate; for if they had gone to school they would have fled the village. They will be linked by kinship to the other villagers and ultimately to the community's mythical First Ancestor. They are men who see the world through the eyes of the village.

The young men must be chosen by the village itself, in the absence of any representatives of the administration, for it is essential they be trusted by their fellow villagers. Only in extreme cases is the director encouraged to veto a village choice. The director explains that he will come back—in the dry season, when there is little work to be done—and pick up the men chosen in his absence by the people of the village.

The director takes the group of young men—two or three each from half a dozen villages—to the Centre d'Animation. The Center is a dormitory-style building, deliberately rudimentary so that the peasants will not feel out of place. The director has no desk, by Cisse's orders. The sanitary facilities are, to a Westerner, primitive, but they are simple enough, and easy enough to build, so that the peasants may be motivated to introduce some simple sanitation in villages that have none at all. The group stays at the Center about three weeks. The director lives with them, and except for daytime visits by technicians, he is the only government man present. A deliberate effort is made to keep animation separate from the other agencies of the administration, which the peasants view with both fear and suspicion.

The program of studies begins with elementary explanations of the nature of the nation and its government, its past and present, its relation to the village—ideas that are foreign to the young peasants. This is followed by a study of the economic problems of their own area and an examination of what can be done to overcome them. Possible new techniques are discussed. In a typical day, a government official may lecture and answer questions, and in the evening, after he has left, the peasants discuss what he said with the Directeur d'Animation. Near the end of their stay, the young men are taken to a nearby village—not one of their own—and asked to spend the day making an inventory of its resources: wells, crops, animals. That evening in the Center, the director asks them: "What would you do if you lived in that village?"

On the last evening, the night before they go home, the young peasants recapitulate their experience. This is an important and fascinating event, for the peasants tell their story in the natural art form of their culture. In a play, in song, in dance, or in a combination of the three, the young men tell what they have learned, sometimes with a remarkable caricature of the director; a sympathetic outsider is easily moved to both tears and laughter. For the director, the theatrical representation of his teaching is an opportunity to see how much the young men have learned. It is also an occasion for him to see the workings of the society in which they live, and, from their caricature, how they see him.

During these three weeks, the methods used are far more important than what is taught, for animation is an attempt to penetrate the intimate web of village society and establish a dialogue with peasants who greet the outsider with "hospitality, passivity and distrust." The pace of teaching is adapted to the slow pace of village life; the evening discussion, the most important part of the daily routine, comes at the time of relaxation when the villagers would be palavering under the tree in the center of the village. Lectures must be understandable in the terms of reference of the peasants. Since the aim of animation is to give the village a voice in its affairs, discussion must be substituted for dictation. And since only what the village will accept can be adopted, the director often is forced to compromise with conservative traditions of which he may disapprove.

Then the peasants return to their villages. On the day they come home, the village will turn out for a celebration under the tree at which they will again tell what they learned at the Center—this time without outsiders present. In the next few weeks or months, the "animators" will be encouraged by the director to develop, in cooperation with government technicians, a project for their village. Once the project is decided on, the animators will be brought back to the Center for a maximum of two or three days of training in such techniques as harnessing cattle to the plow, simple irrigation systems, well construction, starting cooperatives, building a road.

These two brief stays at the Center are the only times the animators will be taken away from their village. They never receive a salary or an opportunity at formal education, and they are discouraged from seeking government jobs. The essence of animation is that the peasant must not be alienated from his traditional culture, and his village must not come to consider him an outsider. If he were to stay

away longer, or be paid by the government, or have formal schooling, he might want to flee the village, as so many young men do; and
even if he didn't flee, the village would consider him one of "them,"
an agent of the government. The animator ideally represents the village to the government, not the government to the village. If he
stayed away longer he would learn more, but his learning would be
meaningless, for he could not introduce new ideas into a society of
which he no longer was a trusted member. The villagers are only
likely to follow his lead if they consider him one of them. Obviously
he cannot absorb much technical knowledge in his time at the Center; but since the technical level of the village is extremely low, there
is a great deal that could be done without extensive training, once
the village accepts the idea of change. And that decision, to accept
change, must be made by the village, according to its rules, not by an
outside agency. No innovation is going to be welcomed for its own
sake, which is why animation is restricted to areas where quick economic progress is possible: where change can be shown to be of
value. Animation tries to find the leadership for innovation within
traditional society, not among aliens. Ideally, the animators are natural village leaders, an elite chosen by the community. As we have
seen, the agents of change usually have failed because they came from
outside rural society. If they spoke to the peasant at all, they dictated;
the alienated educated African official had little stomach for discussion with "primitive" members of a culture he himself had escaped.
And the schools built by the colonial rulers served to take the brightest children out of the village to lop off its potential leadership.

In practice, animation in Senegal is largely the creation of Ben
Mady Cisse, its director. Any such movement, particularly in Africa,
depends on the men who operate it. Austere and incorruptible in an
easygoing atmosphere, Cisse is an exceptional figure in the educated
elite. In Cisse's mind, animation and the innovations it seeks to introduce are not in contradiction with the values of traditional Africa: "We must make it clear that change is true fidelity to our ancestors. Their way of life was in tune with their own environment, but
today the environment is different. To be faithful to our ancestors
means to adjust to our environment as they did to theirs, not simply
to cling to old ways for no reason."

Animation has the advantage that it is cheap and that it aims at
mobilizing the form of capital that most African countries have in

abundance: underemployed men and animals. It does not require extensive foreign aid, machinery, or technicians. Since it is spread out rather than concentrated, there is little danger that it will create islands of privilege, like the settlers at the Office du Niger in Mali.

It also has its pitfalls. Frequently the animator drops back into the anonymity of peasant society and is lost. Sometimes, also, he may become simply another local exploiter. Suspicious villages have been known to send young men of slave descent on the assumption that the government was practicing forced labor under another name; because of their low status, these men had no influence in the community when they returned. In at least one of these cases the village sent high-caste youths the following year, after they saw that a nearby village had been successful with their animators. A blunder at the beginning by the director can close a whole village to animation, and such blunders have been all too common.

In Senegal, animation has made its greatest efforts in the fields of organizing human investment and cooperatives. Human investment —the contribution of free labor to projects of public interest—is viewed as a contract freely arrived at between the people and the state. The building of first-aid posts at Sedhiou was a form of human investment. In this contract the people provide labor (free capital) and the state provides technical assistance and, when necessary, machinery. The Senegalese see voluntary investment as the logical way to mobilize their available labor, for it draws on the African tradition of community effort; collective cleaning of villages, for example, is still common.

In other ways, also, animation has had results. Along the Senegal River, among the conservative caste-bound Toukouleurs, animation was begun in 1959. Nowadays one finds high-caste Toukouleurs working alongside the descendants of slaves—inconceivable a few years ago. In the Casamance, the non-Muslim region in the south of Senegal, animation has helped introduce ox-drawn equipment and vegetable farming on a wide scale. Animation among women, which is more recent, produced radical change in a village in the Serer country. Like many African women, the Serer wives spend several hours a day gathering firewood, far from their homes, and carrying it on their heads to their homes, a distance of several miles. After their stay at a center for animation feminine, a group of Serer women worked out an agreement under which the state would do the heavy mechanical work of preparing rice paddies, which the women would then cultivate and harvest collectively. With the proceeds of the harvest, the women bought a donkey and a cart, which they used to haul the firewood; since the cart carries much more than a woman can, not every wife has to go gather wood every day. By this seemingly simple change, each woman has saved one or two hours in a day of heavy toil. If only this one innovation, the use of a donkey and cart (or one or the other), were introduced throughout Africa, a great burden would be lifted from the shoulders of the overworked African women.

The reaction of the administration, of the educated elite, is decisive in determining whether animation succeeds or fails. When the animated peasants look around with newly opened eyes, they soon see the abuses of the present system; at this point the administration can either crush them or encourage them. In an effort to "animate" the elite itself, Cisse organized a series of "seminars" around the nation in 1961 and 1962. The seminars were palavers between the animation leaders and the administrators and technicians in the bush.

In their speeches to these seminars, Cisse and his associates were pleading for the "decolonization" of the elite, for casting off ways of thought and behavior learned under colonial rule. Here is Cisse's assistant, Ibrahima Sow, in a self-criticism that is rare in its bluntness:

"We who call ourselves an elite may have professional qualifications, but we do not have the spirit and drive that our country needs. . . . We must rid ourselves of the city-intellectual's mentality that looks at the peasant with contempt. Our first battle is with ourselves. If we do not change ourselves, we shall fail, and we shall have to lower our eyes when our children insult us. . . . But once we have a group ethic we cannot be defeated."

From Africa, *by David Hapgood, Atheneum, 1965.*

"Foyers Feminins"

BY NANCY SCOTT

All around the world the education and training of women is increasingly recognized as a necessary corollary to the education of men. In the French-speaking Ivory Coast, the Peace Corps has organized a series of "Foyers Feminins" or Women's Institutes, where the wives of local officials can learn how to take their place in the developing middle-class society their husbands inhabit. The volunteer in charge of this program in its initial stage was Mrs. Nancy Scott, a sixty-three-year-old teacher and grandmother from Pennsylvania. Assisted by six other female volunteers, Mrs. Scott organized a friendly, informal approach to the pressing problem of adult education.

Now that this program has proved practical, Mrs. Scott is training a larger corps of women who will expand Peace Corps participation in the Women's Institutes. The report which follows describes the first phase of the project.

The African sun is fierce when you have to pull yourself together after the two-hour noontime break to return to work. All the rest of the world is still sleeping. You can almost hear the buzz of sleep as you walk by the still courtyards and the houses with their shuttered windows looking like closed eyes. The midday meal has left faint odors of wood fires, fish, and fried plantain in the air. Chickens and guinea hens have hidden under bushes and the dogs are too drowsy even to scratch their fleas. Perhaps the fleas are having their siesta, too. You pass by the market, where remnants of the morning's activities are strewn about: squashed bananas, spilled tomato sauce, peanut shells. The Foyer Feminin is shaded and cool; the big classroom on the second floor usually catches whatever breeze there is.

About 2:30 my women begin to drift in, though latecomers will turn up during the ensuing hour. Most look very fresh. Many have babies on their backs or toddlers tagging after them. There is an air of gaiety as we greet one another like a bevy of college girls reassembling after a holiday. Some of the students are very young, in their early teens. A few are oldsters, but most are in their twenties. Of course, judging their ages is sheer guesswork on my part and on theirs, too, in most cases.

So classes begin. In the large room are the debutantes, in the charge of the directrice and her helper, both young African women. I have the *avancées* [advanced students] in a little room adjoining. Most of the time we keep the door between the two rooms open— until the din becomes too distracting: "*b* plus *a* equals *ba, b* plus *i* equals *bi,*" and so on, the pitch rising, the volume increasing.

There are only the essentials in the classrooms: a large blackboard, box of chalk, slates, pencils, notebooks, and a primer apiece. But I realize more and more in teaching here the truth of the observation that the best school need be nothing more than a good teacher on one end of a log and a pupil on the other. Moreover, if you need visual aids you have only to get some bottle caps for counters, some carbon sheets and stenopads for duplicator work, and so on as far as your imagination can push.

The Ivory Coast government set up these foyers to meet the urgent need for education of women. The men have had a head start in education and have left the women far behind. This has created a real problem: households consisting of a literate father and children and an illiterate mother. Many of the husbands have positions in government, in education, or in business. They are associated with men of similar education. An illiterate wife is incapable of entering into this aspect of her husband's life; thus a chasm exists in the family structure. To bridge this gap, the Foyers Feminins have been created. There are at present thirty foyers in the cities and towns of Ivory Coast and more are being planned. Enrollments range into the hundreds in the cities and down to a dozen or so in the villages.

The schoolroom language is, of course, French. My students speak it well, but when they grow excited, they switch to Baoulé, the dialect in my village of Yamoussoukro. When they switch to Baoulé, I say, *Très bien. Si vous parlez en baoulé, je parlerai en anglais,* and then where will we be?" They roar with delight at the sound of the English and immediately change back to French.

Foyer classrooms are not peaceful and orderly. Babies cry and are nursed, toddlers upset everything possible and wander out of the room so that in the midst of reciting, mothers shout and run off in pursuit.

What progress have we made in the foyer?

First of all, the women, having stepped out of their domestic routines into a disciplined environment in search of something new, have taken a monumental step.

As for academic progress, the beginners have mastered the vowels and several consonants, the simplest formation of letters, and simple addition. They have read, if mostly by rote, about a half-dozen pages of a primer. In sewing they have made layettes, stitching both by machine and by hand. Also they have learned to mend and to knit. Knitting in the tropics? Yes, indeed. Ivoiriens feel the slightest chill in the air (and we often have it, glory be!) and immediately bundle up their babies in woolen caps and booties until that old sun takes over again.

The women are delighted by handicrafts and master them with remarkable speed. We plan to enlarge this field next year. At Christmastime we made rag dolls for the children. I doubt if the children ever received them because the women themselves loved them so. Since then I have had to make dozens of them for little children who run up to me and say, "Madame Scotch, *donnez-moi un bébé!*"

The advanced students are about two-thirds of the way through the primer, can read more or less phonetically, can write fairly well, and in arithmetic are on about a level with a second-grader in the States.

There is the question we all ask ourselves from time to time: What, if anything, can I really accomplish here?

I tell myself, You can at least be a warm, understanding woman among your fellow women, sharing and understanding basic, human things with them. And since you happen to know how to read and write, you can make every effort to give them these magic keys.

Nothing spectacular—but there you are.

From the Third Annual Peace Corps Report, *The United States Peace Corps.*

One-Party Government

Julius Nyerere is president of Tanzania, the country created in 1964 by the union of Tanganyika and the island of Zanzibar. One observant British journalist, James Cameron, said of him in 1961: "Among emergent African politicians . . . Nyerere stands out for his skill, his reticence, his moderation, his humor, his realism, and his absence of bitterness and hate."

Born in the northern province of Tanganyika, Julius Nyerere graduated in 1945 from Makerere University College in Kampala, Uganda, with a teacher's diploma. After several years of teaching at a Catholic Mission school, he went to the University of Edinburgh for further study, the first Tanganyikan student to go to a university in Great Britain. When he returned, he divided his time between teaching and politics. In 1954 he founded the Tanganyika African National Union (TANU) which has become the most important political organization in the country.

Like many other African leaders, President Nyerere believes that one-party government is the best way to fight colonialism, poverty, ignorance, and disease. However, in the spring of 1966, he approved a plan to offer more than one candidate for a party office—provided both were loyal members of Tanu.

The African concept of democracy is similar to that of the ancient Greeks from whose language the word "democracy" originated. To the Greeks, democracy meant simply "government by discussion among equals." The people discussed, and when they reached agreement, the result was a "people's decision."

Mr. Guy Clutton Brock, writing about Nyasaland, describes traditional African democracy; "The elders sit under the big tree and talk until they agree." This "talking until you agree" is the essential of the traditional African concept of democracy.

To minds molded by Western parliamentary tradition and Western concepts of democratic institutions, the idea of an organized opposition group has become so familiar that its absence immediately raises the cry of "dictatorship." It is no good telling them that when a group of one hundred equals have sat and talked together until they agreed where to dig a well (and "until they agreed" implies that they will have produced many conflicting arguments before they did eventually agree), they have practiced democracy. Proponents of Western parliamentary traditions will consider whether the opposition was organized and therefore automatic, or whether it was spontaneous and therefore free. Only if it was automatic will they concede that here was democracy!

Basically, democracy is government by discussion as opposed to government by force, and by discussion between the people or their chosen representatives as opposed to a hereditary clique. Under the tribal system whether there was a chief or not, African society was a society of equals, and it conducted its business by discussion.

It is true that this "pure democracy"—the totally unorganized "talking until you agree"—can no longer be adequate; it is too clumsy a way of conducting the affairs of a large modern state. But the need to organize the "government by discussion" does not necessarily imply the need to organize an opposition group as part of the system.

I am not arguing that the two-party system is not democratic. I am only saying it is only one form which democracy happens to have taken in certain countries, and that it is by no means essential. I am sure that even my friends in the Labour party or the Conservative party in Britain would admit that if their party could succeed in winning all the seats, they would be perfectly happy to form a one-party government. They, the winning party that is, would not be likely to suspect themselves of having suddenly turned Britain into a dictatorship!

Some of us have been over-ready to swallow unquestioningly the proposition that you cannot have democracy unless you have a second party to oppose the party in power. But, however difficult our friends in Britain and America may find it to accept what to them is a new idea—that democracy can exist where there is no formal opposition—I think we in Africa should think very carefully before we abandon our traditional attitude.

It is often overlooked that the Anglo-Saxon tradition of a two-party system is a reflection of the society in which it evolved. Within that society there was a struggle between the "haves" and the "have-nots"—each of whom organized themselves into political parties, one party associated with wealth and the status quo and the other with the masses of the people and change. Thus the existence of distinct classes in a society and the struggle between them resulted in the growth of the two-party system. But need this be accepted as the essential and only pattern of democracy?

With rare exceptions, the idea of class is something entirely foreign to Africa. Here, in this continent, the nationalist movements are fighting a battle for freedom from *foreign* domination, not from domination by any ruling class of our own. To us "the other party" is the colonial power. In many parts of Africa this struggle has been won; in others it is still going on. But everywhere the people who fight the battle are not former overlords wanting to re-establish a lost authority; they are not a rich mercantile class whose freedom to exploit the masses is being limited by the colonial powers; they are the common people of Africa.

Thus once the foreign power—the other party—has been expelled, there is no ready-made division, and it is by no means certain that democracy will adopt the same machinery and symbols as the Anglo-Saxon. Nor indeed is it necessarily desirable that it should be so.

New nations like Tanzania are emerging into independence as a result of a struggle for freedom from colonialism. It is a patriotic struggle which leaves no room for differences, and which unites all elements in the country; and the nationalist movements—having united the people and led them to freedom—must inevitably form the first government of the new states. Once the first free government is formed, its supreme task lies ahead—the building up of the country's economy so as to raise the living standards of the people, the eradication of disease, and the banishment of ignorance and superstition. This, no less than the struggle against colonialism, calls for the maximum united effort by the whole country if it is to succeed. *There can be no room for differences or division.*

In Western democracies it is an accepted practice that in times of emergency opposition parties sink their differences and join together in forming a national government. This is our time of emergency, and until our war against poverty, ignorance, and disease has been won—we should not let our unity be destroyed by a desire to follow somebody else's book of rules.

If these then are the forms of democracy, what are the essentials?

First, the freedom and the well-being of the individual. Freedom alone is not enough; there can be a freedom which is merely the freedom to starve. True freedom must be freedom not only from bondage, from discrimination and from indignity, but also freedom from all those things that hamper a people's progress. It is the responsibility of the government in a democratic country to lead the fight against all these enemies of freedom. To do this the government, once freely elected, must also be free to govern in the best interests of the people, and without fear of sabotage. It is, therefore, also the duty of the government to safeguard the unity of the country from irresponsible or vicious attempts to divide and weaken it, for without unity the fight against the enemies of freedom cannot be won.

When, then, you have the freedom and well-being of the individual—who has the right freely and regularly to join with his fellows in choosing the government of his country; and where the affairs of the country are conducted by free discussion, you have democracy.

True democracy depends far more on the attitude of mind which respects and defends the individual than on the forms it takes. The form is useless without the attitude of the mind of which the form is an external expression. As with individuals, so with organized groups, this question of attitude is all-important. It is not enough to ask what attitude an African government will adopt towards an opposition without also asking what attitude an opposition will adopt towards a popularly elected government.

In the past all that was required of government was merely to maintain law and order within the country, and to protect it from external aggression. Today the responsibilities of governments, whether communist or free, are infinitely wide. However nearly its requirements of money and men may be met, no government today finds it easy to fulfill all its responsibilities to the people.

These common problems of a modern state are no less formidable in young and underdeveloped countries. The very success of the nationalist movements in raising the expectations of the people, the modern means of communications which put the American and the British worker in almost daily contact with the African worker, the twentieth-century upsurge of the ordinary man and woman—all these deprive the new African governments of those advantages of time and ignorance which alleviated the growing pains of modern society for the governments of older countries.

To the demands of the common man in Africa, intensified as they are by the vivid contrast between his own lot and that of others in more developed countries, add the lack of means at the disposal of the African governments to meet these demands. The lack of men, the lack of money, above all the lack of time. To all this add the very nature of the new countries themselves. They are usually countries without natural unity. Their boundaries enclose those artificial units carved out of Africa by grabbing colonial powers without any consideration of ethnic groups or geographical realities, so that these countries now include within their borders tribal groups which, until the coming of the European powers, have never been under one government. To those, in the case of East and Central Africa, you must add the new tribes from Asia, the Middle East, and Europe. Here are divisions enough to pose a truly formidable task in nation-building.

As if the natural challenge was not enough, with the raising of each new flag come the intrigues of the international diplomacy of rivalry and all that goes with it; the cynical and the criminal attempts by powerful foreign governments to weaken the unity of any country whose government pursues policies which they do not like. Who does not know that foreign nations have again and again poured in money to back up any stooge who will dance to their political tune? As their sole purpose is to confuse the people and weaken the legal government for their own ends, they are quite indifferent to the fact that their chosen puppets have no following at all in the country itself.

It should be obvious, then, why the governments of these new countries must treat the situation as one of national emergency, comparable almost to that of a country at war. In the early days of nation-building as in time of war, the opposition, if any, must act even more responsibly than an opposition in a more developed and more stable, a more unified and a better equipped, country in times of peace. Given such a responsible opposition, I would be the first person to defend its right. But where is it? Too often the only voices to be heard in opposition are those of a few irresponsible individuals who exploit the very privileges of democracy—freedom of the press, freedom of association, freedom to criticize—in order to deflect the government from its responsibilities to the people by creating problems of law and order.

The admitted function of any political opposition is to try and persuade the electorate to reject the existing government at the next election. This is reasonable in the case of a responsible opposition with a definite alternative policy in which its members sincerely believe; but that sort of mature opposition is rare indeed in a newly independent state. Usually the irresponsible individuals I have mentioned have neither sincerity, conviction, nor any policy at all save that of self-aggrandisement. They merely employ the catch phrases copied from the political language of older, stable countries in order to engage the sympathy of the unthinking for their destructive tactics. Nor are the tactics they use those of a responsible democratic opposition. In such circumstances the government must deal firmly and promptly with the troublemakers. The country cannot afford, during these vital early years of its life, to treat such people with the same degree of tolerance which may be safely allowed in a long-established democracy.

To those who wonder if democracy can survive in Africa my own answer, then, would be that, far from its being an alien idea, democracy has long been familiar to the African. There is nothing in our traditional attitude to discussion, and current dedication to human rights, to justify the claim that democracy is in danger in Africa. I see exactly the opposite; the principles of our nationalist struggles for human dignity, augmented as it were, by our traditional attitude to discussion, should auger well for democracy in Africa.

"One-Party Government," by Julius Nyerere, Transition, December, 1961.

The Prize Winner

BY MARY BENSON

When the Nobel Peace Prize was awarded in 1961 to Chief Albert Lutuli of South Africa, it singled out a man who had become a leader by force of circumstances rather than by ambition. He was brought up at the Groutville Mission in Natal, where he absorbed both Zulu traditions and Christian teaching. For a few years he lived in the household of his uncle, Chief Martin Lutuli. He studied at a Methodist institution and began teaching at nineteen in a one-room school, also in Natal.

After further study, he became a member of the staff of the Teacher Training College at Adams, specializing in the Zulu language, music, and school organization.

Fifteen years later Albert Lutuli was asked to take over his uncle's chieftainship at Umvoti. A dedicated teacher, he found it a hard decision to make and he refused several times over a period of two years before he finally accepted. It proved to be the turning point in his life. He became a leader in the African National Congress and was instrumental in developing their insistence on nonviolence in combatting the government policy of white supremacy and apartheid.

Chief Lutuli, now in his sixties, lives in exile on his farm in Groutville, in Natal, forbidden by the Government of South Africa to travel or engage in any political action. What he misses most of all in exile is the constant contact with people, which enables a leader to know what his people are thinking and feeling. Besides, he says, such contact "keeps your spirits up."

Mary Benson is a specialist in African Affairs who lectured in American universities in 1963. Born and educated in South Africa, she is the author of a collection of biographical sketches, *The Afri-*

can Patriots, numerous articles on Africa for British and American periodicals, and a biography of Chief Lutuli, from which the following is taken.

One day in October 1961 as Albert Lutuli trudged home from the fields his friend, E. V. Mahomed, drove up in his car and said, trying to control his excitement, "I have a most important message for you, Albert." He opened the car door as he added, "Come, let me drive you home so that I can give it to you in the presence of your wife."

As soon as they reached the small, red-roofed house and had found Mrs. Lutuli, Mahomed, almost overcome with emotion, announced, "Albert, you have been awarded the most important prize in the world—the Nobel Peace Prize."

Lutuli was unbelieving: "You are confusing it with the Gell award," he said (an award in memory of Christopher Gell, a great South African, that had been awarded him only a week or two earlier).

"No, no—" Mahomed eventually persuaded him that he really had been awarded the Nobel Prize. Lutuli said only, "I thank God who has answered the call of the oppressed people of South Africa."

And as the news swept South Africa there was great rejoicing among the vast majority of the people—Africans proud of their leader, sensible Europeans, delighted Indians and Colored People whose leaders expressed their excitement. As Alan Paton said, over the years Dr. Verwoerd had lowered the prestige of South Africa throughout the world but "Lutuli has raised it again." While Dr. Naicker, the Indian leader, said, "We are all so thrilled by this great honor bestowed on a great son of South Africa, a prince among men."

To the crossroads town of Stanger came journalists and photographers from all over the world, some interviewing Lutuli in Mahomed's busy bookkeeper's office, some going out to the little farmhouse in the sugar fields, photographing Lutuli and his wife, his eldest daughter (now a doctor), and his grandchild, Msomi, an engaging small boy probably rather like the child Albert who had come to Groutville from Rhodesia fifty-three years before.

To each of the dozens of interviews that he gave at this time he came freshly, listening to each question attentively and giving to each an answer that had a singular appropriateness. Often he would disarmingly turn the table and begin to question the interviewer with genuine interest. Through the interviews ran the theme: "I think they gave me the Nobel Peace Prize because they quite correctly believe I was leader of a liberation movement that pursued nonviolence. I think so. The credit is not mine at all; my regime of the former African National Congress inherited policies that go back fifty years which I have been happy to carry out. You take the policy of being nonracial. If Congress had followed a racialist line, I would just not have been a member. No, oh, no."

During one interview he was interrupted by a phone call from London. He was enchanted by this—"As clear as anything, as clear as anything, gee!" he exclaimed with a gust of laughter. His sense of humor is always near the surface. When the Minister of Justice refused him permission to attend a local celebration of the award, he did not, as he understandably could have done, deplore the minister's meanness, he simply remarked: "It's making history to get the minister to reply within two days. Something he has never done, honestly." And when someone pointed out that the minister's telegram expressed "regret," Lutuli let out another gust of laughter: "*And* with regret; that is something. That *is* something!"

The local celebration in Stanger was marred only by his absence and by the refusal of the transport authorities in Durban to allow buses to transport the crowds of people who wanted to go to the gathering. The packed audience trilled and shouted with pleasure when Mrs. Lutuli received a scroll for her husband and when Alan Paton read his praise song "You there, Lutuli." But perhaps the greatest delight followed Yengwa's Zulu praise song. He spoke of the great bull that enemies had tried to fence around in a kraal; the bull, he said, had broken the strong fence and wandered far, as far as Oslo! "*Nkosi yase* Groutville! *Nkosi yase* Afrika! *Nkosi yase* world!" (Chief of Groutville! Chief of Africa! Chief of the world!)

As the air filled with their laughter and ululations, women waved their umbrellas high. Perhaps most moving were the words of Fatima Meer, a beautiful and militant Indian woman, as she spoke of the small victory which the prize meant for all those who shared Lutuli's vision of the future South Africa. The vision which had taught people to demand freedom with love and tranquillity, which had led to the martyrdom of many, to imprisonment and banishment, even to death as at Sharpeville. The vision that the world was heralding. The Lutulian vision.

On December 5, 1956, Lutuli had boarded a plane in Durban—to be flown to jail in Johannesburg and to be tried for high treason.

On December 5, 1961, he and his wife boarded a plane in Durban —to be flown via London to Oslo, to receive the Nobel Peace Prize for 1960. Soon after his arrival he received a warm message from President Kennedy. Though the South African Government might not recognize him, the President of the United States addressed him simply as "Chief John Albert Lutuli, Oslo, Norway" and said: "I have been moved by the award to you of the 1960 Nobel Peace Prize and I join with many others from all parts of the world in extending sincere congratulations to you. This high recognition of your past and continuing efforts in the cause of justice and the advancement through peaceful means of the brotherhood of man is applauded by free men everywhere. Please accept my best wishes for your continued health and well-being."

On December 10, in the presence of King Olaf of Norway, of the prime minister, of many diplomats and other distinguished people, Lutuli received the prize. Wearing a chief's ceremonial garb, he was given a standing ovation. Gunnar Jahn, the chairman of the Nobel Peace Prize Committee, described Lutuli's work and said that his efforts to seek equality by nonviolent means while being confined to his own country had a much wider perspective. It concerned the struggle for human rights not only in South Africa but also in other countries. "If the nonwhite population in South Africa manages to raise itself from its humiliation without the use of terror and violence, it will be first and foremost Lutuli's work." But, he added, if violence came in South Africa and the country drowned in blood "let us remember him then, and never forget that his policy was unshakeable and clear. He did not want it that way."

Lutuli was clearly overwhelmed by feeling. His few words of thanks were barely audible: "I regard this as a tribute to Mother Africa, to all peoples, whatever their race, color or creed," he said. "But I also regard it as an added responsibility laid upon us. We have been made answerable for our part in the future development of the world." And as before, when he had first been told of the award, he paid tribute to his wife, Nokukhanya, without whose help he could not have done his work.

On the following day Chief Lutuli gave his Nobel Peace Prize address. Standing very upright as is characteristic of him he spoke of the three-fold significance of the award: a tribute to his humble contribution among people of all races to find a peaceful solution to the race problem; a democratic declaration of solidarity with those fighting to increase liberty in South Africa; and "a welcome recognition of the role played by the African people during the last fifty years to establish, peacefully, a society in which merit, and not race, would fix the position of the individual in the life of the nation."

He spoke of how little peace there had been in Africa in our time, from the war in Algeria to the shootings in Sharpeville in South Africa. "Ours is a continent in revolution against oppression. And peace and revolution make uneasy bedfellows. There can be no peace until the forces of oppression are overthrown . . .

"How great is the paradox," he went on, "and how much greater the honor that an award in support of the peace and the brotherhood of man should come to one who is a citizen of a country where the brotherhood of man is an illegal doctrine, outlawed, banned, censured, proscribed and prohibited, where the work, talk of campaign for the realization in fact and deed of the brotherhood of man is hazardous, punished with banishment or confinement without trial, or imprisonment, where effective democratic channels to peaceful settlement of the race problem have existed these three hundred years, and where white minority power rests on the most heavily armed and equipped military machine in Africa.

"This is South Africa."

But it was not necessary, he said, to speak at length about South Africa, for it had forced itself on the attention of the world. "It is a museum piece in our time, a hangover from the dark past of mankind, a relic of an age which everywhere else is dead or dying." He analyzed the mythology of white supremacy, of apartheid, and paid tribute to such opponents of it as Livingstone and John Philip, who had stood for social justice in the face of overwhelming odds, men whose names were still anathema to some South Africans.

"I, as a Christian," he said, "have always felt that there is one thing above all about apartheid or separate development that is unforgivable. It seems utterly indifferent to the suffering of individual persons, who lose their land, their homes, their jobs, in the pursuit of what is surely the most terrible dream in the world." A dream which is the deliberate policy of a government, supported actively by a large part of the white population and tolerated passively by an overwhelming part but "fortunately rejected by an encouraging white minority who have thrown in their lot with nonwhites."

Generally the passing of time has seen barriers to freedom going down in most parts of the world, Lutuli went on. "Not so South Africa. Here the barriers do not go down. Each step we take forward, every achievement we chalk up, is canceled out by the raising of new and higher barriers to our advance. . . . All too often the protests and demonstrations of our people have been beaten back by force, but they have never been silenced." In this modern struggle, in spite of cruel treatment in the name of law and order, the freedom fighters had remained nonviolent.

"If today this peace award is given to South Africa through a black man, it is not because we in South Africa have won our right for peace and human brotherhood.

"Far from it. Perhaps we stand farther from victory than any other people in Africa. But nothing we have suffered at the hands of the government has turned us from our chosen path of disciplined resistance. It is for this, I believe, that this award is given."

When he came to speak of the things that had sustained the spirit of freedom-loving people in South Africa in their fight for lasting values, he paid high tribute to "the magnificent support of the progressive people and governments throughout the world, amongst whom number the people and government of the country of which I am today a guest, our brothers in Africa, especially in the independent African states, organizations who share the outlook we embrace in countries scattered right across the face of the globe, the United Nations Organization jointly and some of its member nations singly."

In expressing heartfelt appreciation for all this support, however, "we South Africans," he said, "equally understand that much as others might do for us, our freedom cannot come to us as a gift from abroad. Our freedom we must make for ourselves."

When Lutuli ended he did something never before heard of at a Nobel ceremony: he sang—"Nkosi Sikelel' i Afrika"—and soon all the assembly joined in, singing or humming the great anthem.

A Norwegian newspaper, *Arbeiderbladet,* describes the effect of his visit: "We have suddenly begun to feel Africa's nearness and greatness. In the millions of huts of corrugated iron, mud, and straw lives a force which can make the world richer. . . .

"Lutuli, the Zulu chieftain and schoolteacher, is an exceptional man. But in his words, his voice, his smile, his strength, his spontaneity, a whole continent speaks.

"Africa's laughter and tears are now breaking against our own shores. . . .

"Albert Lutuli must now return to his people in chains, to his guards in exile. We have never seen a freer man."

The Nobel Prize, as the Johannesburg *Star* remarked, was "a measure of the gulf that divides South Africa morally from the rest of the civilized world"; it did indeed show up the contrast in values between the South African Government and the outside world, and it is interesting to think that the reasons for which the Nobel Prize Committee conferred this high honor on Lutuli are the very reasons for which the government bans, confines, and imprisons him.

From Chief Albert Lutuli of South Africa *by Mary Benson, Oxford University Press, 1963.*

Dangers of Leadership

BY DUNDUZU K. CHISIZA

Dunduzu Kalui Chisiza was born in 1930 in Northern Nyasaland. He was educated at a mission school and attended college in Uganda and in Birmingham, England. He worked as a clerk in the Government of Tanganyika and in the office of the Indian High Commissioner in Southern Rhodesia. He also traveled in the Congo.

In Salisbury, Mr. Chisiza helped found the African Youth League and was deported to Nyasaland, where he continued his political activities. In March 1959 he was arrested and imprisoned along with other leaders of the Nyasaland African Congress. During his eighteen months in prison he studied economics and spent his time planning for the future of his country.

After his release from prison, Mr. Chisiza served as Parliamentary secretary in the Ministry of Finance, of the Government of Nyasaland which became the independent state of Malawi on July 6, 1964. He had traveled in the United States and India and was one of the most brilliant young political economists in Africa when he was killed in an automobile accident in September 1962.

Mr. Chisiza was the spokesman for a rational approach to independence. In a pamphlet entitled *Africa: What Lies Ahead,* he described the pitfalls that the leaders of Africa's newly independent nations must avoid.

In January 1960 Mr. Dag Hammarskjöld, secretary-general of the United Nations, toured twenty-four countries in Africa and met "most of the national African leaders." Of these leaders he had this to say when he returned to New York: "I found the present generation of African leaders to be of high seriousness, devotion, and intelligence. I am sure in their hands those countries will go to a happy future."

The cause to which these leaders are consecrating themselves is noble, their trust is sacred, their problems manifold, their tasks immense. Accordingly, they must be on the lookout against pitfalls which might sabotage their work and plunge their countries into chaos. There are seven main dangers against which they have to guard.

The first of these refers to the policy of "rewarding friends and punishing foes." When independence has been won, leaders of governing parties are understandably anxious to prove to their followers that steadfastness in the national struggle does pay, by bestowing favors in the shape of jobs on those of their followers who were loyal to "the cause of freedom." No realist would quarrel with such gestures. In countries where the government is also the main employer, it would be inhuman for the leaders to leave in the lurch those who toiled and sacrificed all they had for national liberation. What is deplorable is for leaders to go to the extreme of leapfrogging suitably qualified non-party people in favor of unqualified party supporters to fill posts which require technical skill. To pursue such a policy would be not only to drive countries into disastrous bogs of inefficiency, but also to set dangerous precedents which might culminate in the corrupt system of "spoils." Let unemployed "ex-soldiers of freedom" get a fair proportion of the available jobs, by all means. But where skill is called for, proper qualifications rather than loyalty should be the criterion.

As for "punishing foes," there are two aspects of it: revenge against past "enemies," and victimization of present "foes." Revenge against preindependence "enemies" is ignoble and unworthy of the leadership of a governing party. The freedom which the ruling leaders fought for was not meant only for their immediate followers but for all—including thieves, prostitutes, murderers, and "those misguided quislings who do not know what is in their interest." Victimization of present foes raises moral issues which can have very disturbing effects. A distinction must be very clearly drawn between enemies of the state and enemies of one's party. Confirmed enemies of the state, all would agree, must be dealt with in accordance with the law of the land. But dealing with rival parties is a tricky business which, if mishandled, can occasion for political leaders (on both sides) much unnecessary suffering. Vindictiveness directed at the opposition parties has its nemesis when tables are turned—not to mention the adverse effects of resultant strife on economic development. The verdict seems inescapable that, all things considered, a policy of "rewarding friends and punishing foes" will do far more harm than good.

An allied danger to the foregoing is that of nepotism. Here again we are confronted with favoritism, but this time the emphasis of the leaders is on their relatives rather than on their party supporters. In this case, uncles, brothers, nephews, cousins, and in-laws are preferred above others in the allocation of offices, not because they are better qualified than other candidates but because they happen to be the relatives of the leaders. This kind of discrimination is just as offensive and iniquitous as color discrimination. It results in the waste and misallocation of a scarce resource—trained manpower; it stifles the emergence of efficient business as well as administrative executives, it encourages people not to seek knowledge or training but to brace up their relationship with the leaders, and above all it may lead some hard-hit men into the tragic belief that they can remedy the situation only by assassinating and replacing current leaders with their own kith and kin.

Fortunately, the chances of nepotism laying its hold on the present generation of African leaders seems remote. Still, in view of the fact that when nepotism comes, it does not do so with fanfare, African leaders must be constantly on their guard against it.

The third danger assumes the form of blurred vision. It has been said that "where there is no vision people perish." This holds true for almost every country, but it is even more so for underdeveloped countries. Blurred vision of what things should be results from the failure of nationalist leaders after the attainment of independence to switch from their role of freedom-fighters to that of economic modernizers. But it is an understandable failure. It is not very easy to change from the former role to the latter any more than it is easy to change from carpentry to agriculture. A man who has spent years fighting for the freedom of his country acquires techniques and develops a fighting complex which are of little use in the task of modernization. Those leaders who succeed in adjusting themselves to their new tasks are the ones who never lost sight of the fact that freedom is merely a means to the end of social and economic reorganization and who consequently punctuated their fight for freedom with reflections on the measures that would be required to effect the reorganization.

The main symptom of blurred vision is the tendency of the leaders concerned to busy themselves in routine work to which colonial administrators of preindependence days had lashed themselves. Such a tendency turns the group of leaders into a mere "dominant minority" lacking creativeness, initiative, and drive. But leaders of underdeveloped countries cannot afford to wallow in routine work. They must initiate development schemes which will raise the levels of living of their peoples, thereby exhibiting the blessings of freedom. People must see new things happening and feel that there is a change; otherwise disillusionment will set in. To do these things, leaders must have clear vision, a clear picture of the new state of affairs that must be brought about.

There are two ways of acquiring such a vision: delving into literature which deals with development problems, and consulting economic and social experts as to what should be done. Both are essential. It is not enough for leaders to have experts around to advise them on technical details; they themselves must have a fairly good idea of (a) the problems involved, (b) the possible solutions, (c) the economic potential and limitations of their countries, and (d) what other leaders in similar situations have done, are doing, and propose to do. Only when they have such an overall picture will they take interest in development work, be in a position to accept or reject intelligently the advice of experts, and disentangle themselves from the shackles of routine work.

The fourth danger stems directly from the danger just considered. It relates to two closely linked things: (a) dwelling in the past and (b) petty jealousies. Leaders who get lost in the details of routine operations have little to show in the way of concrete achievements and so the temptation to rake up and extol the past glories of their countries becomes irresistible. But past glory is no substitute for contemporary glory. Leaders of new countries can ill afford to dwell in the past. Their concern is with the future. Some inspiration can be drawn from past achievements, of course, but the main inspiration for the leaders as well as the masses will have to be drawn from current achievements.

When leaders are apparently doing and achieving nothing remarkable, people tend to regard leadership as merely a means to personal enrichment and prestige. This view leads to the bedevilment of intrigue, petty jealousies and personality clashes among leaders of the same party or the same country. It is significant that where leaders are bent double on the task of development, petty jealousies among them are almost nonexistent.

The fifth danger lies in the competition of African leaders for preeminence. There are two facets of this competition: (a) several leaders may each try to be a cut above the others by posing as the "big brother" of other African nations, and (b) several leaders may each try to impress the outside world more than the others. As more and more territories in Africa become free, there will be some leaders who will try to bring some of the countries under the economic wings of their own countries. Some may do so because they sincerely believe that their countries are economically better off than the countries of their brethren and that it is therefore their moral duty to help them. Others may do so because they secretly hope that in so doing they will eclipse other leaders and be looked upon as leaders not only of their own countries but also of the countries they help. Yet others may do so with the intention of boosting the prestige of their countries.

Help which is given in the true African spirit of "mutual aid" will unmistakably be known for what it is and will not be resented by the people of the receiving country. But aid motivated by personal ambition and untempered nationalism will succeed only in sowing the seeds of mistrust, hatred, and strife. No self-respecting leader with enough guts and stamina to have wrested his country from the horrors of colonialism will want to play second fiddle to an African power maniac or to see his country dance to the tune of another. It is to be sincerely hoped that those leaders who believe in cooperating on an equal footing and helping one another without ulterior motives will not hesitate to spurn and ostracize leaders who show signs of being motivated by mean ambitions, thereby avoiding getting involved in wrangles which might make nonsense of all that Africa has suffered and struggled for for so long.

Those leaders who vie with each other in an endeavor to impress and convince the outside world that they are the greatest, the "real," force among African leaders indulge in a game which has a built-in tendency to degenerate into a vulgar competition, to deteriorate into personality clashes, and eventually to burst into open hostility. This kind of competition provides effective ammunition to those people who would like to set African leaders against one another and see the solidarity of the new Africa broken up. It is an unnecessary competition which deserves the condemnation of those people who want to foster African unity and to promote harmonious cooperation. It is unnecessary because if there is any leader who is an undiscovered genius, he can be quite certain that the world will spot him in good time even if he does not advertise himself. If he does not happen to be a genius, no amount of self-advertisement to the contrary will dupe the world into believing that he is one. Indeed, a man who finds it necessary to proclaim his greatness is the one who knows he is not great, otherwise he would not even think of the idea. Really great people are far too busy performing great deeds to think of strutting around impressing people with their greatness.

The sixth danger relates to the policy of aligning with power blocks. It has been argued by some African leaders that it is mean to sit on the fence and enjoy the best of both worlds. According to these leaders, Africans must take sides somehow. A good many Western nations would endorse this view wholeheartedly. Some of the nations seem to hold the view that "those who are not for us are against us," and are therefore anxious to separate friends from foes. But in this case a policy of alignment defeats its own purpose—that of keeping communism out of the emerging states.

It is almost a universal tendency in the less developed regions of the world that if the ruling party is pro-West, the opposition will be pro-East. It is true that the pro-East outlook is also to be found in countries where a policy of nonalignment has been adopted. But the nonalignment policy of ruling parties, in these countries, takes so much wind out of the sails of their opponents that for all practical purposes the would-be Communists are nothing more than impotent minorities. Some people believe that a policy of alignment with the West can also keep out communism, provided the leaders make up their minds to be tough with people who have communist leanings. Maybe it can; but communism has a reputation for thriving on persecution. The policy of aligning with the West creates a burning issue for communists, and so long as they have a legitimate issue to fight, "firmness," persecution, only add fuel to the flame. Paradoxical as it may sound, the safest way of aligning with the West is not to align with the West.

The seventh danger is that of dictatorship. Three things will bring about a dictatorship in Africa: (1) too much trust, (2) too little trust, and (3) neurotic ambition. Of the three causes, the third presents the least problem. A man who makes up his mind to be another Napoleon, Hitler, or Mussolini in these changed times can be certain that resurgent Africa will deal with him the way Europe dealt with the European misanthropes. People cannot heave off the yoke of colonialism and then fail to pulverize under their feet a demented individual who wants to sit on their necks.

The real problem is posed by those leaders who will lapse into dictatorial tendencies either because their countrymen trust them too much or because they trust them too little. When too much trust is reposed in a leader, (sometimes) the thing goes to his head and makes him believe that he is infallible. Such a man is not likely to brook criticism or to welcome alternative suggestions. It is his idea or nothing. On the other hand, when a brilliant, self-assured, well-meaning leader is begrudged trust or is dealing with an illiterate populace, he too will tend to force his measures through in a dictatorial manner, believing that the masses will appreciate what he is doing later.

Both of these leaders need a dose of humility. They need to remind themselves that getting to the top of the political tree does not necessarily mean that they are more intelligent than other people. Indeed, politics the world over has the uncanny knack of attracting the most mediocre of brains. There are people in the population of each country who, intellectually, are by far the superior of political leaders. In framing policies and designing measures, therefore, leaders must rely more on public opinion and the opinions of colleagues than on their imagined superior intellects. The task of leadership involves following as well as leading.

From Africa: What Lies Ahead? *by Dunduzu K. Chisiza, African-American Institute, 1962.*

Suggestions for Further Reading

AUTOBIOGRAPHIES AND OTHER FIRST-PERSON ACCOUNTS

ABRAHAMS, PETER. *Tell Freedom*. New York: Alfred A. Knopf, Inc., 1954.

AWOLOWO, OBAFEMI. *Awo*. London: Cambridge University Press, 1960.

COWLES, RAYMOND. *Zulu Journal: Field Notes of a Naturalist in South Africa*. Los Angeles: University of California Press, 1959.

GATHERU, R. MUGO. *Child of Two Worlds: A Kikuyu's Story*. New York: Frederick A. Praeger Inc., 1964.

GICARU, MUGA. *Land of Sunshine: Scenes of Life in Kenya before Mau-Mau*. London: Lawrence and Wishart, Ltd., 1958.

JABAVU, NONI. *The Ochre People*. New York: St. Martin's Press, 1963.

KANE, CHEIKH HAMIDOU. *Ambiguous Adventure*. New York: Walker & Co., 1963.

LUTULI, ALBERT JOHN. *Let My People Go*. New York: McGraw-Hill, 1962.

MPHAHLELE, EZEKIAL. *Down Second Avenue*. London: Faber & Faber, Ltd., 1959.

SAMPSON, ANTHONY. *Drum: the Story of a Newspaper that Won the Heart of Africa*. Boston: Houghton Mifflin Company, 1957.

THOMAS, ELIZABETH MARSHALL. *The Harmless People*. New York: Alfred A. Knopf, Inc., 1959.

THOMAS, ELIZABETH MARSHALL. *Warrior Herdsmen*. New York: Alfred A. Knopf, Inc., 1965.

TURNBULL, COLIN. *The Lonely African*. New York: Simon and Schuster, Inc., 1962.

USEFUL BOOKS FOR BACKGROUND READING

BOHANNON, PAUL. *Africa and Africans*. New York: Doubleday & Company, Inc., 1964.

BOWEN, ELENORE. *Return to Laughter*. New York: Doubleday & Company, Inc., 1964.

CAMERON, JAMES. *The African Revolution*. New York: Random House, Inc., 1961.

CARTER, GWENDOLYN (ed.). *African One-Party States*. Ithaca: Cornell University Press, 1962.

DAVIDSON, BASIL. *The African Past: Chronicles from Antiquity to Modern Times*. Boston: Little, Brown and Company, 1964.

DAVIS, JOHN A. (ed.). *Africa, Seen by American Negro Scholars.* Paris: Presence Africaine, 1958.

GLEASON, JUDITH I. *This Africa: Novels by West Africans in English and French.* Evanston, Illinois: Northwestern University Press, 1965.

HERSKOVITS, MELVILLE J. *The Human Factor in Changing Africa.* New York: Alfred A. Knopf, Inc., 1962.

HUGHES, LANGSTON (ed.). *An African Treasury: Stories, Poems, Articles, and Essays by Black Africans.* New York: Crown Publishers, Inc., 1960.

KIMBLE, GEORGE H. T. *Tropical Africa.* 2 Vols. New York: The Twentieth Century Fund, 1960.

KITCHEN, HELEN (ed.). *A Handbook of African Affairs.* New York: Frederick A. Praeger, 1964.

LEUZINGER, ELSY. *Africa: The Art of the Negro Peoples.* New York: McGraw-Hill, 1960.

MPHAHLELE, EZEKIAL. *The African Image.* New York: Frederick A. Praeger, 1962.

PAULME, DENISE (ed.). *Women of Tropical Africa.* Berkeley: University of California Press, 1963.

RADIN, PAUL AND J. J. SWEENEY. *African Folktales and Sculpture.* New York: Pantheon, 1964.

RUTHERFORD, PEGGY (ed.). *African Voices: An Anthology of Native African Writing.* New York: Vanguard Press, Inc., 1959.

SENGHOR, LÉOPOLD SEDAR. *On African Socialism.* New York: Frederick A. Praeger, 1964.

USEFUL MAGAZINES ON CONTEMPORARY AFRICAN AFFAIRS

African Forum: A Quarterly Journal of Contemporary Affairs. Edited by John A. Davis. Published by the American Society of African Culture, New York.

Africa Report. Edited by Helen Kitchen. Published by the African American Institute, Washington, D. C.

Black Orpheus. Edited by Ezekial Mphahlele, Wole Soyinka, and Ulli Beier. Ibadan, Nigeria.

Journal of Modern African Studies: A Quarterly Survey of Politics, Economics and Related Topics. Edited by David and Helen Kimble. University College, Dar es Salaam, Tanzania.

Nigeria Magazine. Edited by Onuoua Nzekwu. Lagos, Nigeria.

Présence Africaine: A Cultural Review of the Negro World. Edited by Alioune Diop. Society of African Culture, Paris, France.